Text © 1987 Charles Neal (except where indicated).

Published by SAF (Publishing) Ltd.
PO Box 151,
Harrow,
Middx. HA3 0DH
England.

Tel: (01) 904 6263

First Printing 1987
Edition: 5000

ISBN 0 946719 02 0

Printed in England by Redwood Burn, Trowbridge, Wiltshire.

Typeset by Wordsmiths Typesetting Ltd., 55 East Road, London. N1 6AH

Interviews: Charles Neal
Design: Jon Wozencroft

Matt Johnson, Dave Ball, Coil, Clint Ruin, Cabaret Voltaire interviews by Charles Neal/Mark Williams. New Order interview by Jon Wozencroft/Charles Neal.

Cover Photograph: Panni Charrington.
Publisher's logo by Cornel Windlin.
With thanks to Jon Savage for additional material.

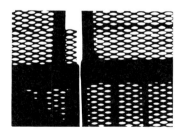

CONTENTS

FOREWORD

Compilations and collections of any kind usually reflect the comfort of familiarity and a hunger for certainties. The musicians, groups and artists who have contributed to this book will to some be well-known and to others unheard of — either way, we ask that you suspend any predetermined conclusions. The purpose of *Tape Delay* is to provide a more concentrated focus for ideas that, in spite of or even because of their plunder, essentially fall outside the reactive marketing games centred within a few square miles of London, New York and Tokyo. Many included here witness such exploits at first hand, and to what extent the contributors work can 'liberate' this environment as opposed to being sucked into it in the future, is one of the book's main contentions. However, *Tape Delay* is not about independent music by 'indie' groups, a scene that supports the hegemony of CBS, EMI or WEA as much as it competes with it; nor is the book a full expression of work done in the field of sound and image experimentation, whose first lesson is that nothing is ever so complete.

In 1977, the contrast between 'the underground' and the entertainment industry was fairly clear. Today, making room for any profitable diversion, the scope of the arts and media is wider than ever. The problems of non-multinational distribution ensure that many groups and their labels present a freeze-frame facility for the majors, whose promise of upward mobility inhibits a self-sufficient challenge to their guarded diversity. It is, of course, A&R on the cheap for those too sheltered in their office blocks to catch anything but publicity shots on the way up. So much for the "Age of Chance".

Values based on catchy retrospection, marketability and media exposure go hand in hand; obvious coverage is a

prerequisite of good sales, and if it has happened before, it is
easier to knock off some quick copy. Distribution, however, is
equally determinant of what the public gets to hear, involving a
different sort of censorship. Here, media constraints do not
necessarily force the choice of what can be successfully
distributed. Scandals, in any case, can translate any
intervention into the most conservative of outcomes; the
record company and group make a fortune, while the threat
goes out of fashion. Frankie's *Relax*, previously banned by the
BBC, is now being used for suncream commercials for
example. The real problem comes from a commercialism that
pretends to accommodate so much, leading to the release of
more and more records, books, magazines in every sector of
the market, and yet only manages to support a pluralism that
projects itself as varied while selling countless versions of the
same thing.

Safety has always come first, matched with a now insatiable
thirst for novelty that should not be confused with an equal
opportunity for those, who in the process, might actually
transform the way we look and listen. Their impact can be
diffused in several ways, of which categorisation is the most
taken for granted. By constantly testing the present against
past achievements (the ubiquitous Dada and Velvet
Underground spring to mind), those who seek to dismantle
illusions of yesterday's lost purity are denied the possibility of
creating something truly of the moment. To belong to a
category, then, is to obstruct singularity, like making a cover
version of something before it has happened.

In spite of this ward against change, centralisation is not as
closed off as sales might suggest. Chart return shops are,
after all, as trustworthy as loaded dice. The public buys what
there is to choose from, but this does not mean that
consumerism is synonymous with desire. Falling record sales,
on the other hand, are hardly an accurate barometer of a
declining interest in recordings; not for sometime has the
music business held its monopoly. It is because music is now
everywhere — in restaurants, shops, and railway stations, that
silence becomes increasingly desirable. All this might suggest

that *Tape Delay* is an implicit rejection of everything and anything that appears on a major label, but it has actually got little to do with the music. The example of Cabaret Voltaire, The Jesus and Mary Chain or The Smiths shows that independence is ultimately reliant on mass manufacturing. The choices seem to be increasingly limited.

New technology is however becoming more accessible, inviting new possiblities in sound projection. With the advent of new equipment into any business area, its early days act as a kind of insurance policy, as a buffer zone for those who have the money to seal off its advantages, helped by manufacturers who need to convert the in-built obsolescence of their inventions into the fastest and most lucrative adoption. For the music industry, this has meant investment in technology, rather than in new groups that will make the product. The result has been playback culture, and, contrary to the business's fear of Digital Audio Tape, there's really very little that's been worth recording. Sampling, as it is currently practiced, is a circle that will choke itself.

The assimilation of earlier experiments with tape, with film, and with performance of every kind is only skin deep. Impervious to the long term distractional effects of the cut-up as blind technique, the fragment becomes an end in itself. The purveyors of pop video fail to grasp that something based almost entirely on form rather than content will only be successful for as long as creativity is isolated from the systems of recording, manufacture, marketing and distribution that surround it. These connections can be made to work more effectively. Editing is an artform that has a far greater application than to connect two adjacent sounds or images into a slick presentation. Fast thinking and short attention spans can hardly be said to be a 'chicken and egg' situation, for as Greil Marcus has pointed out, the archetypal MTV is a medium that was born dead. If editing is usually a means of 'trimming back' material in the name of improvement, just the opposite can apply, and a simple edit can resonate in the mind for hours afterwards — more common so far, in films than sound recordings. Small wonder that TV people cling to their control of it, for everything runs on time when everything has already been seen.

The early days of digital recording and manufacture have so far entirely suited the laziness of the retro-music industry, though compact discs are only a pointer to a larger information system that includes cable TV, desk-top publishing and facsimile machines. The real work of the individuals and organisations in this book is also in its infancy; *Tape Delay* is concerned with the ideas and provocations that cannot adequately translate to the record market when the medium itself is founded wholly upon entertainment. As fragments become increasingly opaque, so does the real become visible once more. The echo returns to its origin.

There's 70 billion people on Earth (Where are they hiding?)

BACILLUS CULTURE

by Biba Kopf

I

The song upholds pop as a celebration of the night. In reality pop rarely ventures beyond the limits of evening. Jukebox Britain shuts down at 11 p.m. and the neon is quick to follow. Plunged in darkness the city is encouraged to sleep. Those clubs permitted to stay open simply extend the evening to the early hours. The very vocabulary of licensing shuns the word 'late'.

Prohibition (in Britain) appears reasonable: the evening is for play, for winding down after work, the night is for sleeping. The makers of pop who want to get ahead abide with this reasonable formula. TV pop is an early evening activity and, at midnight, state controlled radio switches over to a heavily sedated ambrosia that will not disturb the heavenly sleeping.

Those who want to journey through the dark to the end of the night must go it alone. Perhaps this is only right and proper. The night traveller shouldn't expect anyone to light his way from passive voy(ag)er to dormant antibody and on to active abject.

Night-time desires, when fully realised, are by definition anti-social, for they leave their pursuer in no fit state for work the following morning. Wherever the work ethic governs so rigidly, the Body of State is only interested in the state of the citizen's body in so far as it is fit for work. The night traveller by day, then, runs the risk of censure, of being condemned by those on their way to work. Inculcated with a sense of social responsibility, they cannot mind their own business. Focussing their reproving gaze through mediated ideals of decency and beauty, they see in the state of a body worn out by desires pursuits a threat to the general well-being. The stink of raw love rubbed into their nostrils alerts them to the traveller's disregard for hygiene, self-abuse marking him as anti the body — an antibody within the State Body.

Finding no allies on the Left or Right, the night travelling antibody is an object of disgust. He is forced outside — abjected from the society of the everyday. This wouldn't be so bad. But he is not left alone even after abjection. He is now caught in the trap between his own desires and their prohibitions. The pull of these two polarities is irresistibly downward, tugging him deeper into a paralysing depression. And when he can't get any lower, the abjection others confer on him tightens, making it difficult to breathe. Feverish, he is lit up by an illumination: down here at least I feel something. Anything, even pain, Lydia Lunch has said, is better than feeling nothing at all. It might not be much of an escape, but the hole abjection opened up constitutes home, a state in and of itself, within which the antibody is the sole subject — that is, the fully fledged Abject. At base at last, all the frustrations accrued from imposed silences and prohibitions finally explode into expression, blowing away the rock with which others block the Abject's hole and splattering anyone peering curiously down at him with searing purples and cold black splotches of night. The stain is indelible.

II

Abjection's first flowering in British contemporary music was seeded in its industrial culture (1974 — 1980). Throbbing Gristle (defunct) and Cabaret Voltaire (extant) were it's parameters. They did not, as sometimes supposed, celebrate industrialism. Britain's industrial age was over well before TG and CV began operations. In effect, the pair bridged the gap between its end and the beginning of the coming computer age. Though it was already dead, TG sniffed a potential energy source in the gases given off in the chemical reactions within the decay of the corpse.

Its fumes set off their cold rattling laugh in the face of industrialists struggling to maintain their power base. Elsewhere they transformed the imagery of its decline into a mixed media assault, into which they folded the horror of the Nazi collapse into barbarism. They paralleled so well the latter's multi-national arms-entertainment manufacturers of today, relating both to the destructive impact on the spirit of porno-mass entertainment empires, that their presentations rapidly became a blueprint for an entire subculture cliche. In the mean time, they concentrated activities on an 'information war', choosing pop as the arena inside which they could most effectively conduct an escalating media guerilla campaign. Veering from extreme ugliness to moments of astonishing beauty, their music at once satirised and exposed the drift of pop and its attendant media baggage from relaying real and felt experiences to received and heavily synthetic spectacle.

TG always brought real cruelty to their staged representations of inhumanity. They piled horror on horror, matched brutal noise with brutal image. No filters here to reduce them. For their trouble they were rewarded with accusations of grossly exploiting abject situations. Their grim disinterment / reportages occasionally leavened by a death's head cackle earned them the everlasting stigmata of the true Abject.

III

The other major British post-industrial practitioners Cabaret Voltaire always sustained a more distant approach than that of TG. From William Burroughs and James Brown they forged the idea of meshing taped reality fragments and savagely stripped down funk. They isolated poisonous phrases picked up from slot TV preachers and politicians, two-bit carney entertainers and vagrant conmen, lonely phone-in subscribers and their smug grinning hosts, and lopped and looped this flotsam and jetsam of the airwaves with manic disregard for their original contexts. Crushed between taut rhythm slabs and electronic stabs of noise, familiar phrases pressured and cracked, allowing the listener glimpses of their hidden meanings. Perhaps. Even if no new truth was revealed, CV's applications of Burroughs' cut-up theories were stimulating in themselves. At minimum they introduced the tape recorder and the camera as weapons in an information war to a different audience.

But, paradoxically for experiments in repetition, the very repetition of their experiments through every level of the media has undermined the group's impact. Techniques they perfected proliferate promiscuously. You can hear electro-fusion, rap, talkover, stutterfunk in Malcolm McLaren scams, bad movies, TV advertising, everywhere. Just as its profusion attests to the perfection of the CV techniques, it also defuses it, leaving the group standing desolate like a dismantled time bomb, slightly embarrassed to be discovered unexploded.

IV

The Abject imagination cannot be readily transcribed in 4/4 time and regular orchestration often proves inadequate of mapping its contours. To realise completely the music struggling to escape their abject minds, its practitioners look beyond instruments for suitable tones and noises. The South

London group Test Department eschew all proper instruments in favour of percussion sculptures constructed from junkyard debris. Over the years the highly influential Berlin group Einsturzende Neubauten have amassed a vocabulary of unusual metal decay times. Sounds beaten, drawn out or scraped from different materials are bled into electronic screeches and shards of bizarrely tuned guitar noise, catching the listener up in their delirious abstraction. Einsturzende Neubauten's music is the most perfect expression of the Abject imagination there is. It's the result of steeled wills forcing their bodies to the point where they locate the searing pitches that mirror the agony of their physical efforts. Here, body, language and noise become inseparable.

The Californian noise-maker Boyd Rice, known as NON, has gone furthest to blanking all external signals coming his way. Any light shining down on him he transmutes into a seething ball of negative energy, the aural equivalent of a black hole, from which no light returns. Its dark pulsing vitality exerts a magnetic pull on the curious. Many find his noise an extension of the possibilities suggested in rock feedback. Where the latter rarely means more than the odd curlicue of aggression added to otherwise ordinary songs, NON's is a totally realised noise without end or beginning. For once a listener can really get lost in its night sky. NON's liquefaction of forms could be the indispensable warp through which the music can be started up again.

V

The Abject speaks with an authoritative voice, even as he is expressing the most debilitating of doubts. For the Abject speaks for and about himself — after all, the one subject he knows best. The outside is only broached when it encroaches on the self. Objective commentaries or pointless railing against the superpowers do not interest the Abject. (Test Department's recent interrogations of what it is to live with the decline of the British empire is a notable exception.) He has realised that such opposition confirms his own powerlessness while at once affirming the might of others.

So the Abject is committed to trawling the self for truths denied him elsewhere. If the resulting expression contains fragments of outside realities it is because the Abject is as prone to the everyday as anyone else. Specially during the process of being abjected, the descent into the hole of the self, during which time every barb, every hurt is absorbed.

The events of the descent imbue the Abject with a deeply felt horror, the purest horror in fact, a horror not of death — after all, a final escape — but a horror of being, that life sentence in the hole with no chance of parole. The hole, the New York group Swans make only too clear, is essential to the Abject's self-reservation.

"This is mine." sings Mike Gira, "I own this thing / I hate everything I don't own / I own this / I own this hole / Get out of my hole." (From *Raping A Slave* EP).

His hole is defended by the barrage of noise erected by the group. They realise his seemingly gimlet concentration on disgust for the body as a form of musical inertia. It is utterly and frighteningly unique. Swans have completely redefined ideas of musical dynamism as a matter of intensification of difficult emotions.

So this is how the Abject copes with a life sentence in the hole: he discovers it to be far more flexible than the outside hedging it in. It expands and contracts according to the dictate of the Abject imagination.

VI

The Abject imagination is as rich and as varied as there are Abjects exercising it. For at bottom they have nothing in common other than the sense of abjection. It touches them all differently: to each Abject his own abomination. Their condition being the result of their inability to accept society's norms, they find themselves in the realms of the taboo — that is, the unspeakable. They must invent their own language to name the state that so disturbs them.

There is, of course, a massive literature of prohibition going right back to the Old Testament. But sensorious tones are inadequate for describing the desires they bring into play. The Abject cannot live by censure alone.

It is said that in the beginning was The Word. So it is with The Word the battle to wrest the individual's voice from the tangle of laws and traditions begins. The Abject must disinter a language that accurately summons his desires without leaving the usual aftertaste of guilt.

It is not an easy ambition. For one, he has to negotiate a prohibited zone clogged with pulp and porn writers, who rarely go beyond impoverished descriptions of mechanical couplings, before arriving back at his own voice. The great achievement of New York raconteuse Lydia Lunch is to reclaim the territory as her own, infiltrating the normally male dominated domain of S&M literature and flipping it on its back, using its meccano structures as a grid for the working out of her own emotional drives. She projects herself into the vortex of her own suffering, into which others are sucked to mete out whatever it is she desires from them.

The look in the victim's eye suggests the damage done to her. In this way she assumes control. She decides on the terms, draws the limits, defying boys to cross them. Their worst is never good enough. In the film script for *The Right Side Of My Brain* she tantalizingly outlines how the submissive twists herself into a dominant position:

"My irritation was swelling... My impatience and desires were sweeping me overboard. Just like I liked it. Just like I wanted it. Out of control. Rocked from horror to horror. But it wasn't the agony... it was the ecstasy. That delicious reckoning. That true and final moment. Feeling like it's really up to you, because you allow them to go as far as they want... But they still go only half the way..."

Needless to say Lydia Lunch's position is none too popular with lovers of cautionary tales.

VII

"You want to know what this putrefaction is? You want me to tell you? It's all the shit we have to put up with". (Celine)

In *Powers Of Horror — An Essay On Abjection* — to which this piece gratefully owes its shape — Julia Kristeve cites Celine as the ultimate Abject. What with his loathing of Jews and women and his Nazi sympathies there is certainly something in Celine to offend everyone at least once. His very existence was a transgression of what many hold dear. No-one else separated himself so totally from his fellow man, no-one else so consistently tested most every commonly held virtue. None of this is noteworthy in itself. Indeed he would not have been remembered as more than a cranky pamphleteer if he had not completed his transgressions in a loud and clear singing language that never betrayed or played down his disgusting self. On the contrary, his writing crackled with malicious wit and sheer nastiness. Like a sea of foaming vileness, his novels bubble over with bile, soiling the shores of reason with wave upon wave of petty wickedness.

Without suggesting they have anything in common in the way of shared prejudices, I'd say Clint Ruin, the man behind the Foetus / Wiseblood projects, is a modern musical equivalent. Like Celine, Ruin chains himself to towering pillars of respectability and then pulls the temple in on himself. Emerging from the ruins with a rattling laugh, he invokes the apocalypse as a carnival peopled with miscreants and freaks.

The carnival impression is wrought in immense musics culled from the rubble of rock 'hysterie'. Each song is a tremendously loud belch compounded of part remembered TV themes, poptunes and fat slabs of melancholy dragged behind breakneck rhythms. His lyrics pun and spin big, bloated and grimly hilarious metaphors describing abject states so horrifyingly terminal it's a miracle he ever raised himself from the pit to report them. They explode as great gashed grudges against the dull realities that stifle his need to feel life to the full. Fired off at tangents from his bewildering mobiles of musical styles and terror-go-round of words are lines so devastatingly lonely they seer the soul.

The British duo Coil, which arose out of Throbbing Gristle and Psychic TV, share something of Ruin's carnival glee. However, theirs' translates more directly into deviant sexual practices. They locate the source of their celebration of filth back in the cradle, where a child meets his first prohibition, his earliest denial of base pleasure: toilet training. From this early act of defilement they press inward and onward. Their debut LP *Scatology* is a catalogue of abject defiance, running the gauntlet of possible transgressions, abominations and outright assaults on the cathedral of heaven. The measure of their success is their broad church of music, which follows every twist and turn in their abject imaginations, alternately creating queasy moods with emulated noises and working various source sounds into blasting Jericho fanfares heralding the dawn of a new pagan age.

VIII

The abject state manifests itself Einsturzende Neubauten's Blixa Bargeld as a monstrous all consuming ego. On the group's LP *Halber Mensch* he records its euphoric states and the occasional terror of being trapped in a body turned inside out by a speed racked nervous system.

Long ago a member of a Berlin communist cell, Blixa has undergone gradual withdrawal through a series of ever tightening cycles into the tiny human cell that is himself. He has accepted a life sentence locked in his body. Having completed the psychological leap inwards, nothing can harm him now. He is his own state. He is impervious to any threats from the state.

Maybe this is why he is identified as a symbol of resilience in Eastern Europe, where the physical movement of marginals is more likely to be restricted. Bargeld's withdrawal into his own human cell, where no amount of bullying or cajoling can penetrate his hole-ness, might constitute a possible gameplan for the East European A-social.

The East European group Laibach, from non-aligned Yugoslavia, take the opposite path to Blixa Bargeld's. They wholly embrace the State. Laibach is a Gesamtkunstwerk as a microcosm of the totalitarian State. But the totalitarian State itself is nothing less than a Gesamtkunstwerk already, the vision of a single dictator looking to realise it on the grandest of all scales, involving every level of his captive country, its means of production and its citizens. Such a figure is hardly likely to tolerate the existence of a microcosmic model under his jurisdiction. But Yugoslavia is not a totalitarian state and Laibach is, at base, an art project, albeit a highly charged and provocative one. The group's apparent embodiment and endorsement of such a State has teased ugly tendencies from a once liberal socialist country rapidly sliding into economic chaos. Ironically the group are the ones who suffer most for the potency of their art. They have been subjected to bans and public harassment in certain provinces. Are they simply accelerating tendencies dormant in Yugoslavia from before the decay set in? Or is totalitarianism really their ideal for living? Whatever the answer, Laibach doggedly keep their motives bravely hidden while playing a cat and mouse game with once and future cultural dogsbodies. The ultimate Abject adventure: Here the risks are genuine. Not only must a life of the mind be undertaken with a degree of silent caution. There is a very real threat to the Abject's liberty.

IX

As the earth shrinks the sense of abjection arising out physical restrictions will inevitably spread beyond a loose community of musicians, writers and artists. No place left to go and no money to take you there, abjection itself will become the last accessible frontier. But the wherewithal to undertake this exploration has been severely blunted by the media's aestheticising the hell out of horror. Thus the Abjects. They explode the aesthetic filters slapped on horror, restoring it to the capacity to affect again.

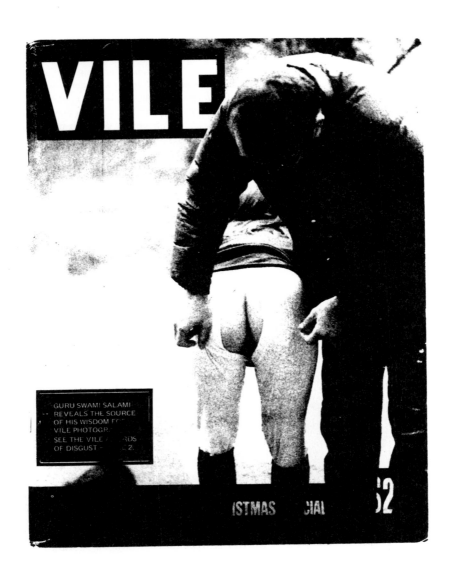

VILE Vol 3 No 7, Dec 1975
Mail Art Compendium pub. San Francisco

GENESIS P-ORRIDGE

In 1981, Industrial Records released its final album, *Nothing Here Now But The Recordings*, documenting the tape experiments of William S. Burroughs. The album materialised after Genesis P-Orridge and Peter Christopherson persuaded Burroughs to give them the tapes which had been in a shoe box for over twenty years. The record finds Burroughs recording himself, television and radio while randomly stopping the tape machine — a demonstration of the cut-up technique invented by Brion Gysin and demonstrated repeatedly in Burroughs' books. Genesis P-Orridge first met William Burroughs in 1973 after the two had exchanged a few letters. A friendship developed which led to an exchange of ideas. During this period, P-Orridge edited *Contemporary Artists* with Colin Naylor, a huge encyclopedia describing various people working within the arts. At Gen's insistence, a section devoted to Brion Gysin was included.

At that time, P-Orridge was also involved with COUM Transmissions, along with Cosey Fanni Tutti and Peter Christopherson, a unit which would later, together with Chris Carter, transform into Throbbing Gristle. COUM Transmissions, an art group in general, was mostly involved with communications, and realised this through mail art, performance art and touring around Europe's cramped art centres, culminating in the infamous *Prostitution* exhibition at London's Institute of Contemporary Arts in 1976.

Records and live performances, however, seemed a much better form of communication. Forming Industrial Records to maintain total control over their output, Throbbing Gristle released *2nd Annual Report* in 1977. Subsequent releases included 3 further studio LPs as well as three seven inch singles. Always interested in personal, collectable merchandise, TG made variations on subsequent pressings of the records on Fetish and Mute. *2nd Annual Report* was re-cut backwards with chamber music mixed in throughout Side Two. Sleeves and scratchings were changed on other recordings. Industrial was the first independent label to release music on cassettes only, and in addition to releasing material by The Leather Nun, Richard H. Kirk, Thomas Leer and Robert Rental, SPK and Clock DVA, they also released a limited edition of twenty four cassettes packaged in a suitcase of their last 24 live performances. The group became notorious for the public display of their varied interests with photographs and record covers often containing subject matter including Nazi death camps, skulls and unclothed bodies. Branching into other areas, TG composed and performed the soundtrack to Derek Jarman's film *In The Shadow Of The Sun*, shown at the Berlin Film Festival and cinemas worldwide.

When Throbbing Gristle terminated in June of 1981, P-Orridge and Christopherson joined with Alex Fergusson (of Alternative TV) to form Psychic TV, the propaganda side of the Temple Ov Psychic Youth. It was, "Not intended to be a replacement for conventional programming, but rather the first step towards deprogramming". Combining many 'magickal' elements with an interest in subversion, Psychic TV do not accept the pre-occupations of institutionalised TV with its assumptions about entertainment and value. Psychic TV allow raw material to be used and manipulated by the viewer. Live, they incorporate a visual backdrop through the use of television and video screens, often showing their own films of rituals, genital piercing and montage, along with films of others with whom they work and respect.

The group released two albums after they signed with Some Bizzare in 1982. The first through WEA, *Force The Hand Of Chance*, contained a limited edition record including the use of holophonics, a 3D recording technique. The second album, through CBS, titled *Dreams Less Sweet*, combined holophonics with recordings of Charles Manson, Jim Jones, telephone calls and wolves amongst other things.

In 1984 Sleazy and John Balance left to concentrate on their own project, Coil. Psychic TV also left Some Bizzare and formed the label, Temple Records. While PTV remains a flexible unit, incorporating different individuals as they are needed. The Temple Ov Psychic Youth works to become, "A worldwide network to help encourage and support the development of multi-dimensional individuals". Psychic TV have worked in many diverse areas. They have recorded soundtrack music for several of Derek Jarman's films, including *Imagining October*, *Home Movies*, *Pirates* (a film about W.S. Burroughs), and *Mirrors*. During 1984, PTV were commissioned to produce a one and a half hour programme on their ideas for TVE (Spanish National Television). Parts of this show, *La edad D'oro*, were filmed in location in Barcelona and Cadaques, and directed by Derek Jarman, utilising Gaudi's Parque Guell and the beach by Salvador Dali's house (where Bunuel filmed *L'age d'Or*) as settings.

In 1986, the group had their first chart success with the single, *Godstar*, a song about the late Brian Jones, bringing their records to an entirely new audience. In 1987, the group began a long series of releases, a month-by-month documentation of their live performances.

YES COUM ARE

FAB AND KINKY

tim

spydeee

cosey

john

tom

gen

COUM

What is the Temple Ov Psychic Youth?

P-Orridge: Well, for us it's a lifetime project, and the people who are really involved in the concept of The Temple are people who are committed to trying to stay awake 24 hours a day — not necessarily physically, although sometimes we try and do that as well. It's difficult to know what part of it to describe because it infiltrates everything that we do and all the people that we know. There is an actual occult side to it, if you like the magickal side to it, there's the propaganda side of it — of which Psychic TV is a part, and then there's the concept of the world-wide network of people collaborating to get projects done. For me, privately, The Temple means everything that's important to do, think and feel, and the system that I use to remind myself that I'm less important than the sum total of what is done. And the people who are really involved with it are people who are committed to that and are prepared to work for the greater good of the idea, rather than their own private ego. And the people who are expelled are usually the people who start to confuse the idea of their own ego gratification and the product as a thing in itself, which it's not. The product is just spewed out as propaganda, or as documentation of the research, it is ephemera. It is not the thing, the thing is intangible. And the thing has to do with the neurology of our brains and also with trying to find a solution to being alive.

The British people are the most sleep-ridden and lazy, undisciplined and banal culture in Europe at the moment. Everyone's taking easy options and looking after themselves to survive on the easiest path, accepting a downward spiral of more and more innocuous and meaningless popular culture as well as real culture. I mean there hasn't been any real culture for God knows how long here. How many famous or even radical painters can you think of, English painters?

Maybe one… Well in the past thirty years.

P-Orridge: Thirty? In the past ten?… There's nobody. And the only place where there is any kind of radical movement is on the musical side. Interconnected with that, you could argue clothes a bit, but clothes and fashion are basically just tricks to seduce people into thinking change is happening when it's not. But I think most groups are now opting for easy pathways as well.

So, would the purpose of Psychic TV be to express their views through the most popular medium?

P-Orridge: Well, we make use of any medium. We'll make use of the concept of a cult, or a religion, just the same way as we'll make use of a music paper, or a flyposter or a cassette tape. As far as we're concerned, no medium of communication is sacred, we try to investigate how they work.

Basically The Temple is the sum total of all the people that we've come to know, the ones that haven't given in and succumbed to something else. They are basically outlaws and are the only people that we've learned are completely and utterly honest with themselves and with us, whether financially or morally, or even by saying when they think we're shit. And it's just the sum total of everything that they've learned and acquired, information, ideas about social control, ideas about anthropology, ideas about human psychology, and a conclusion that there is some sort of need for initiation and ritual; a very jaded cynicism with human behaviour in general — politics, religion, television and the mass media as well. A feeling of being disappointed overall, with the neglect of opportunity that most people demonstrate, that life could be far more exciting even if you don't like half of what is going on. Almost any aspect of life could be more varied and much more crisis ridden, but also much more exciting.

Many articles or programmes that appear about Psychic TV often concentrate on the way that you look, the contents of your flat or your lifestyle. Are you annoyed with these reports or do you abide by the adage of any publicity being good publicity?

P-Orridge: No, I'm fed up with people taking easy options. I'm sick to death of everyone using us as a scapegoat or an easy way out of them having to think. Then we have to spend six months talking to people and explaining that it was all bullshit that was written.

Our basic policy now is that we're just going to do what we do, and if the world doesn't like it, tough shit. And if they don't want to come, they won't come, and if they don't want to write to us, they won't write to us. And if they do want to know, we want them to trust us because we've gone totally out on a limb, even if it means we end up in prison. But we're going to say what we want to say, do what we want to do, and show the videos that we want to show. And we'll give good reasons why we're doing it. I think Britain, and in a sense most places, is crying out for someone to take the risk. No-one else is doing it, they're all just making little noises as if they're being radical or dangerous. All I know is that we had Customs and Excise around here again yesterday saying that they've seized videos in Germany and, "Are we sending out subversive and obscene videos?" And then today they seized another video that was being sent to me from France.

How can they do that?

P-Orridge: They just open our mail. It's illegal to open it, but they open it to see what's in it, and of course they just defend that by saying, "Well, suppose it was a gun, or it was heroin?" But they can use that power to harass or intrude upon anybody. A month or so ago, Scotland Yard were around here saying, "We've been receiving letters saying that you're an organisation dedicated to subverting and corrupting the youth of this country".

So how do you handle that?

P-Orridge: I just said, "Do I look like the kind of man who would want to subvert and corrupt young people? And they went, "Well, uh huh...". (laughs) The irony being, in a sense, they're right. Yes, we do want to subvert and corrupt young people, but not in the sense that they mean. They mean according to a Christian, moral scale imposed by people who exist to make everyone else feel guilty. It's the same people who imposed the video law. Everyone knows on one level that people in privileged positions are the most corrupt, the most decadent, the most dishonest, and the most vicious in any society. And yet people allow those people to subject them to completely repressive, guilt-ridden, violent laws that state that you are not allowed to say what you want, you cannot write what you want and you cannot watch or make videos of anything that you want. You can only do what you are allowed to do. And I personally have always found that an intolerable and insulting situation.

Should there be any laws?

P-Orridge: I don't think there should be any laws about information at all — videos, films, books, magazines, political pamphlets, religious pamphlets, no matter how obnoxious or ridiculous. And I don't subscribe to the view that this lets in people like Adolf Hitler, because Adolf Hitler was not let in just because he had access to the media — he had access to the funds of big business and a million and one other things. And those sort of steamrollers do not exist without an awful lot of collusion with everybody. I think the alternative is intolerable, which is a world of complete zombies. I would rather have a world of danger than a world of zombies to be quite honest.

Would you say that's what the world is now?

P-Orridge: I think that's what most societies are trying to achieve, because they set things up in one way which goes back thousands of years through human social history. The scale of society has changed, there are now too many people, so it doesn't quite work. It's crumbling, they're patching it up all the time, but for them the alternative is too frightening — which is the unknown and the abyss of complete radical change, splintering and chaos for a period of time. The irony is that there is probably another route, another alternative, which is based on the fact that the majority of people do actually want to be left alone and have a quiet life, therefore there's probably a road of tolerance and reorganisation which could be gradually achieved. But that has to come from people's attitudes being re-educated.

At the moment, the big problem with the popular culture is that it is educating people's attitudes to become more stupid. Nobody's encouraging you to think, it's as simple as that. Thinking is considered a sin, even by the left wing, even by your so-called Time Out, City Limits crew. The only crime which anyone could possibly pin on us, is firstly having opinions, and secondly telling people what we think, and actually living out what we say we think should happen. And I personally think if that's a crime, it's a pretty sad society and an incredibly sad youth culture. And I get most angry with people like NME, Sounds, Time Out, City Limits, the journalists and the mass media who are talking directly to the least tainted generation who are unconsciously begging to be treated as intelligent instead of being patronised.

Why do people get drunk and take acid? A lot of people do both now at the same time around here, just soul boys, 'cause they just want to be confused. And that is a shame, that basic expression of need for stimulation or risk — to feel something is happening, is just thrown away and insulted all the time by the groups which they go and listen to. And they usually go away from a gig feeling anti-climactic because it was exactly as they expected and because there's very little passion, very little aggression, and very little intelligence involved. This is a big mistake everyone makes — they're all pandering to what they think people like, it has got to be liked or their group has failed. We've inherited this system, but the people who have the best chance to break it are the media by championing the idea of collaboration and a network of people just trying to make things happen that otherwise wouldn't. Even if some of what happens is just presenting you with ideas, films, people speaking, or sounds which you might find obnoxious, or suspect, or unpleasant, or drab, or boring. But, nevertheless, you go away better informed as to what different possibilities there are, or why you actually do like Duran Duran; that you've made a real choice all the time rather than accepting what you've inherited. Our society and most societies now have been trained to accept pre-recorded types of behaviour and expectation.

You use the concept of the temple, which historically implies religion…

P-Orridge: It implies a lot of things, because temples go way back. In The Bible they talk about the body being the temple of the soul. And in Japan, they have the Buddhist temple, and there are Roman, Greek and Aztec temples. It's just basically a word for a gathering of people which often involves sounds, concepts, attitudes and a desire to demonstrate some kind of solidarity — even fleeting.

What we do is take the structure, but we don't inject it with dogma and a manifesto. Therefore we leave the structure itself. But also, it can be used symbolically as an example or a word or a name that people can feel is a representative body without them having to belong to it. It stands for people who don't fit in. You know, the rest of the world has clubs of different kinds, organisations of different kinds — why can't we have one and make it work for us? Let's throw it back at them, instead of just moaning and saying, "Yeah, this is a bad system", let's take it and mutate it and twist it until it's almost unrecognisable. Also it's a camouflage, let's see what happens if it starts to grow big enough as an edifice for them to get worried by it. Because it's something that they accept as one of their models used for control, so if they have people they know are completely anarchic and nihilistic with the same role model, the same structure, which has all the trappings but they know is instinctively bad and is their enemy, it completely confuses them because they're getting a double message. Whereas if we were just running around, "Stop the city", and all that, then they know what that is. "That's those scum, that's the young scum and we can deal with that, we know what to do with them".

But couldn't they just pass it aside as being a cult?

P-Orridge: Well, they passed aside other cults like Charles Manson and Jim Jones and they paid the price, didn't they? So they're more paranoid than they used to be about anything they think is a cult. And they'll be even more paranoid about a cult which has no definition.

Do you enjoy that confusion on their part?

P-Orridge: Yeah, of course! I'm more interested in confusing the people in power than the man on the street. We don't care whether anyone on the street is interested or not in the Temple Ov Psychic Youth, it makes no difference. It can work as a concept with five people, because it is a means of organising things, a means of disseminating information, of giving it an identity, a style and structure. We like to have everything the way we want it, very precise, very organised and mischievous at the same time.

Much of your work seems to incorporate the spontaneity of the moment. Do you feel that this is a good way to operate?

P-Orridge: Well, the cut-ups were started by accident, and lots of the best stuff begins through accidents. And yet, accidents are always treated with great scepticism officially. When you're at school, you're not taught history in terms of random chance or mistakes that were made that turned out to be fruitful, and you're not taught history in terms of the occult. In fact, all history is riddled with freemasonry, occult and alchemy. When I was taught about Queen Elizabeth I, I wasn't told about John Dee, and about Enochian magick, and scrying and stuff like that — nor the fact that so few could be so powerful and could effect the destiny of Great Britain. And at the same time there were people in the courts of Rome, Germany and elsewhere, who were also wandering alchemist magickians and doctors — who were advising the royal families, the aristocrats and the bankers. Even the American Revolution was founded by people, many of whom were in secret societies. But you're not told that. You're told secret societies, the occult, and alchemy are all bullshit.

The people at the top have a vested interest in presenting something which reinforces their position. And once they've started to lie, the longer the lie goes on, in this case hundreds of years, then the less they're going to say, "Actually, we've been lying to you for the last six hundred years and we're actually a bunch of hypocritical bastards", because the public might say, "Oh, we don't want you anymore".

It just so happens that we've inherited enough obscure morality to still feel responsible once we've realised something seems wrong and try to do something about it. That's probably a leftover of Christianity too, but I'm lumbered with it. See, all the questions you've got, they're really all the same one. Everything that we do now is so integrated and basically has to do with motives and intentions. That is the only way of measuring ourselves. We are to such an extent outsiders, even now, which is quite an achievement really, to remain dangerous outsiders after twelve years of doing things. So although it's a bore in that it means that you're presented wrong to the public, it's a compliment because it must suggest that you are still, in some way, thinking a bit, and accidentally touching nerves.

There are so many games you can play and so many things you can do, I just don't know why people sit and say that there's nothing else to get on with. It's ridiculous. Most people have been trained to be bored, they've been told that everything is supplied. It's true when you talk about a consumer society. But a lot of people just don't recognise to what extent they are consumers and most of the time are trying to fill time rather than use it. I'm in no way an exception, nor are the rest of the people that I work with. And yet we actually find our only problem is getting enough time. There are people working with us who used to be heavily into heroin, and as you probably know, we're very, very anti-heroin because it's the ultimate submissive, time killing drug, as well as playing totally into the hands of the people who are the enemy. On every level, it's just really the worst — symbolically, practically, financially, and physically. And they've said that they've stopped using it because they haven't got time anymore, they've got so much to do that they couldn't possibly get anything done and maintain a habit. They're now out there getting fit and working their bums off. And it's not because anyone has said stop, it's because it became irrelevant. But I think that addiction is just a basic problem, people are addicted to everything, from sitting around to going to clubs, from listening to records to watching TV. And all of us fall, nobody's immune, we all fall into these traps, everyone, we all find ourselves moping around, distracting ourselves. It's impossible to be completely separate from it, but it's also possible to fight it much more.

Why is some information protected?

P-Orridge: Because that's where the real power lies, and the armies and police forces, in reality, are there to protect the bank of information that each country has. Espionage is the real war that goes on all the time, and that's about information. Or, in the British Museum, what you can and can't read. The Vatican has huge vaults of books which nobody is allowed to read. They say they're too dangerous to allow people to read them. Now what on earth could be in a book which is so dangerous that we're not allowed to see it?

Something that might topple their religion and power...

P-Orridge: Precisely! Therefore information is an equal power source to any other source. You can also include technology with information. When I was in Poland, before Solidarity, each town had one photocopy machine that the public could get access to. But there was somebody working it for you, you had to show them what you wanted copied before they did it, and they wrote your name and address and how many copies you had done. The more totalitarian any government, the more rigidly they control all sources of information because they know revolutions are based on propaganda or scandal. Governments fall on information. Look at Watergate. The American government fell on one piece of information. The police forces are often used to stop espionage of any form, whether it be radical, political groups, underground newspapers — journalists are told that they're not allowed to print it. We are never told the truth, the whole truth and nothing but the truth, yet it is demanded of us.

What does the symbol of the wolf, which recurs with Psychic TV imagery, mean to you?

P-Orridge: It keeps changing and growing, and we keep finding out more and more about wolves. Initially, on the most simple level, we thought of them as being an outcast group. Illogically, most people don't know why they've been told that wolves are bad or why to be frightened of them. They are loners but can also be in packs, and when threatened, turn and fight. They're basically animals of survival, and they're also the ones, ironically, which were claimed to have set up civilisation with Romulus and Remus. And in Viking legend, at the very end of history, the wolf devours the earth. And on 'Dreams Less Sweet' we had wolves as part of evolving our own symbolic language. We also had orchids, and then we heard that there was a legend that orchids only grew where wolf sperm landed. I can't remember them all off-hand, but lots of little anecdotes like that, all of which appealed to us. American Indians had great respect for wolves too. I just think they're fascinating creatures, and I think the way they're kept now, mainly in zoos, is symbolic of the way that a lot of us are treated. So they're just symbolic of Psychic TV as a potential wolfpack that could turn, and let's hope that it does and devours the world that it dislikes.

Most of our designs, symbols, even lyrics, are actually more appropriate after we've done them. That's why we often talk about intuitive magick, because it's like falling back on your intuitions and then discovering later that those were more accurate than mechanical thought. And it's more exciting — letting in the subconscious and letting it have a fair role to play in what you're doing. Instructing you and teaching you even more about the true nature of things than you ever would have guessed from a straight analysis.

We're not in the business of one answer, we never were — that's the thing we're fighting. We're in the business that the possibilities are endless, and that is the only positive bit of life. We don't personally inherit and subscribe to there being Gods, demons, outside forces or anything else. We subscribe to those feelings as being manifestations of brain activity, and that's why we go back on that. And the reason we have an interest in magick is because it is an exploration of the brain and its abilities. It's very possible, as anyone with common sense knows, that the brain can do far more than we've been told or learned to do with it yet. If we'd been doing the equivalent of weight training on the brain, then a lot of amazing things would happen. And I'm always in favour of new and amazing things happening.

With the 23 numerology, what are its origins and what does it entail?

P-Orridge: With me personally, it was Burroughs that told me about it. He just thought, "I'll keep a scrapbook about 23's". And then he noticed that the more he did, the more they seemed to crop up, beyond the laws of statistics. Obviously, there's a degree to which, because you are looking, you notice it — whereas before you didn't. That's true if you learn a new word, suddenly you find you hear everyone saying this word you never knew, and you think, "That's odd". But we've checked ourselves, even with computers, and it's way beyond statistical average.

Why is that?

P-Orridge: Well, we don't have any explanation. We're not into saying, "This is why." I don't come to any conclusion. I simply think it's interesting.

I'm not saying personally with you, but with Burroughs...

P-Orridge: Burroughs is the same basically. He just says that it seems to occur a lot in both good and bad situations. It acts like it has a personality or a consciousness, that's all you can say, and that it has a mischievous side to it. I told Cabaret Voltaire about it when I first got interested, and they went, "Oh yeah, that's fun, but you know...", and then I got a phone call about two days later from them and they said, "You bastard!", and I said, "What?". They said, "We've come to Holland to do three gigs and in every hotel we've had room 23, and the gig on the 23rd was a complete disaster. And everywhere we turn, there are 23s. What have you done?" And I said, "Well, I did say you'd start noticing it". (laughs)

Nobody's totally sure why. Then again, why 23? It's a funny number in that you can't divide it by anything. Some mathematician in an Eastern block country apparently did a huge book about the number 23. It started to obsess him because, even with his advanced mathematics, it was playing games with him. It got to the author and he decided to try to find out about it. And at the end of it he just said, "I don't know what's going on, but something is." And there are quite a few statistics to do with the human body which are 23, like the blood going round the body in 23 seconds and 23 chromosomes. And there are 22 Tarot cards. But I was reading just recently a couple of books on magick and they all mentioned that several people going right back had put forward the theory that there should be 23.

Even in my own life, I met Paula, and she was born on the 23rd of February and I think, out of say ten close friends, something like seven were born on the 23rd. Almost everyone I ended up working with in 1983 was born on the 23rd. It started to irritate me. If you start cutting things out of the newspapers and collecting them, you'd be amazed at how many murderers are 23. What was that recent case, that guy that was cutting everybody up, a civil servant? He was living at number 23. I bet he killed 23 people, they don't know how many he'd killed, but I wouldn't be at all surprised.

It's also useful if you're in doubt as to how long to make a side of an album last, it's as good as any number to work around! So you can make it even more self-perpetuating if you want. On a basic level, it's just saying to people, "Nothing is what it seems, look out — watch everything. Here's one game you can play, if that works, then presumably that could work with a lot of other things too". Therefore these strange synchronisities are happening the whole time, and they can be applied — either in terms of being another way of making life more exiting or more entertaining or as a structure. If you have to make arbitrary decisions, they're as good a reason or way as any, and when you get bored, change them, just out of spite.

What was it that first interested you in William Burroughs?

P-Orridge: I read two or three books at school, and I wasn't completely sure of what it was to be honest. I knew they had some very potent effect on me, but I was actually quite naive. I didn't understand all the drug and homosexual references completely, basically a lot of the slang and scenarios were totally outside my experience, but I just felt this incredible potency. And the things I picked up on quickest were the ideas of control and the ideas of cut-up, the theories behind them, rather than them as literary novels, you know? I don't read Burroughs' novels anymore. I certainly wouldn't read them for fun, whereas I would always read his essays, short theories and lectures. Or listen to him talking about ideas of what is possible. Because that is where I think he is absolutely brilliant, and that is where I think, in a sense, he's a modern alchemist. He puts together elements that shouldn't go together and turns up something uncannily accurate.

What exactly is an alchemist?

P-Orridge: It's somebody who uses self-discipline to develop and maximise what they want to achieve. They take into account what they don't know as well as what they do know. Part of the idea is that a random factor that you have no knowledge of completes the formula, and that's how we try and work. We think that including and integrating random chance and intuition is actually the most precise way of working at anything. It was through Burroughs that we started using tape, and we still do.

How do you apply Burroughs' work into that of Psychic TV?

P-Orridge: At the moment, what we're using a lot of is climaxes. We're taking climaxes from sound — mainly ritual sound, whether it be Tibetan rituals, New Guinea rituals, Catholic masses, opera, Beethoven, sport, or the crowd cheering at a goal. We use tapes of orgasms too. You have all these different climaxes which are normally very transient peaks, you take the exact moment of peak and loop it so it becomes flat and continuous, and you get confusion. Therefore, when the brain is being told there's a climax going on, and on, and on, the brain and body are confused because you can't respond over and over again, so something goes wrong, something gets twisted up, and short circuited. If you then start to layer climaxes which are sexual ones, intellectual ones, control ones, religious ones — entertainment ones, then you are really fucking up the brain because you're giving it all these different realities at once and you're giving them a different reality that it can't compute. And then you see what happens. When we played in Boston and Chicago it just polarized people to the point of hysteria, and a week later they were still having fist-fights over it. Some people fainted and some people vomited on the spot. Some people said that they felt like they wanted to masturbate and ejaculate. Just extreme confusion expressed physically. My theory, and obviously people could argue with me about it, is that we're deliberately treading in dangerous water and we're playing with people's brains and responses. But we argue, "That's exactly what is going on with that stuff anyway... but it's camouflaged. We want to get to the nitty gritty, none of this arty-farty stuff. Let's just take this three seconds and see what happens — and get it over with quick".

I don't think many people are going to come to see us by sticking a pin in a magazine, I think they come to see us 'cause they know they'll get almost the equivalent of a physical, drug experience rather than a musical experience. And also to be treated with and shown a mixture of respect and information that they can't get anywhere else.

Is there a car starting right at the beginning of the album 'Dreams Less Sweet'?

P-Orridge: Yeah, that's the journey you see, every man's journey. There are several journeys I think. That's why I think 'Dreams Less Sweet' is the most complicated thing we've ever done. It is actually about a lot of things. It's just one huge, mythological web. A lot of people thought that album was pretty pretty, but I thought it was pretty dark. It's just that it was presented in a slightly less than obvious way. I thought it was actually the most degenerate record that we've ever made. (laughs) I thought it was quite amusing that people thought it was really pretty because they didn't bother to check what it was. And it's the ones they think are the nicest that are the sickest. Like having Charlie Manson sung by a choir boy. Or 'The Orchids', which is actually all about castration as well as love — two songs in one really. You get an optimistic and a mutilation side combined. The whole LP is interlinked, and 'The Orchids', in a sense, is setting up the language of the rest. In a way, it's the most complicated one of them all, and yet it sounds really simple. It has that optimistic chorus, "In the morning, after the night, I fall in love with the light". So it's saying that the idea is hopeful, but you go through the darkness in order to have an experience to make sense out of it. And that is not valuable until you've seen every aspect. We're optimistic but dangerous. We're emotionally, spiritually and morally damaged by what society and societies' history over a thousand years has done to us. Genetically damaged probably. We're just damaged in every way. Damaged by the education we've had, by the parents we've had, by the friends who have let us down, and by lovers. And anybody that tries to pretend that they're in any way balanced, perfect and pure, is bullshitting. We're damaged people trying to find some way to remain vaguely stable in an unstable situation. And we try, by a survival technique, to stop going under into either mental or physical depression or the catatonic stage of just giving up and being passive.

You said before that you wanted people to get a feeling of strength or optimism, but some of the videos seem very... nasty.

P-Orridge: Nah, they're not nasty. I disagree, I think they're very compassionate.

I'll say dark then, darkly compassionate.

P-Orridge: As long as you include compassionate, because if you look at them closely, the only ones that actually are dark and nasty are the anti-religious ones, the ones that actually are attacking something. Anything that has to do with us and our visions, even the rituals, are quite obviously voluntary. And if you look, you'll notice everything is done in a very gentle, concerned way, and nobody is suffering at all in any way. All those rituals were dedicated purely to pleasure, and from my own experience, were very pleasurable — and are still. But by the same token, initiation is not initiation without a feeling of the unknown and a feeling of slight fear. Initiations have always involved the giving up of oneself to the unknown and trusting other people with your physical well-being. Casting off normal preconceptions and normal concerns, and therefore opening up the brain to allow in sensations, thoughts, or empty spaces which otherwise are not there. We initiate ourselves because we want to find our own thresholds. We don't have to say at the end of it, "I believe this, I believe that." We do a physical initiation, but each one is designed for the person. And if people write in and say, "I want to be initiated", we don't say, "OK". We don't initiate people that we don't know, because we don't know what's appropriate. With people who are close to us, lovers and close friends, we do rituals to find out our own mental thresholds and to discover new things about what happens to our brains and perceptions. And it might be one day something very sexual, another day it might be whether it hurts or not to get cut on the arm, and on another day it might be sitting in a box for two hours, just to see if you can handle that.

In a live performance however, you're using people who might not be close friends.

P-Orridge: Oh yeah, in a live performance we impose a certain form of initiation on the audience deliberately. In Boston, I was really pleased with it because it was an initiation, and people responded the same way that initiates do individually — but more collectively. And that's what we're aiming for; to find a means of collective initiation minus dogma, and at the same time reveal to them the true nature of television. We're trying to hype it up to the pitch where it's very obvious that television is the most recent form of magickal attack, and that it attacks the brain, and possibly even attacks the body and causes cancer — nobody knows yet. There was research done on that in America and it was suppressed. They discovered for sure that it caused hyperactivity and mental instability. I know because I met one of the doctors that worked on it. They began to do research into it causing cancers, actually causing psychopathic tendencies, but the report was suppressed and they were all sworn to the Official Secrets Act or whatever they call it in America. It was just stuck in a vault in Washington and scrapped, the whole project. One has to assume that they were at least aware that there was a high danger quality. With our live shows, there is a subliminal effect but not subliminal manipulation, because there is no pre-planned message, except be careful of TV — it's a beast, it's like getting in a cage with the wolf. And if you use the language of magick, you can just make it clearer to people what's going on. They are being subjected to subtle spells. They are being manipulated, their subconscious is being emasculated all the time, more and more deliberately. There is a vested financial, political, and moral interest in television. Television is used like an opiate, it is programmed to make people go to work and rest when they get home. Even more so in England, it goes off when you're meant to go to bed. They more or less say it,

October 19th-26th 1976

SEXUAL TRANSGRESSIONS NO. 5

PROSTITUTION

COUM Transmissions:- Founded 1969. Members (active) Oct 76 - P. Christopherson,
                    Cosey Fanni Tutti,Genesis P-Orridge.Studio in London.Had a
kind of manifesto in July/August Studio International 1976. Performed their works
in Palais des Beaux Arts,Brussels; Musee d'Art Moderne, Paris; Galleria Borgogna,
Milan; A.I.R. Gallery, London; and took part in Arte Inglese Oggi, Milan survey of
British Art in 1976. November/December 1976 they perform in Los Angeles Institute
of Contemporary Art;Deson Gallery,Chicago;N.A.M.E. Gallery,Chicago and in Canada.
This exhibition was prompted as a comment on survival in Britain,and themselves.

2 years have passed since the above photo of Cosey in a magazine inspired this
exhibition.Cosey has appeared in 40 magazines now as a deliberate policy.All of
these framed form the core of this exhibition.Different ways of seeing and using
Cosey with her consent,produced by people unaware of her reasons,as a woman and an
artist, for participating.In that sense,pure views.In line with this all the photo
documentation shown was taken,unbidden by COUM by people who decided on their own
to photograph our actions.How other people saw and recorded us as information.Then
there are xeroxes of our press cuttings,media write ups.COUM as raw material.All of
them,who are they about and for? The only things here made by COUM are our objects.
Things used in actions,intimate (previously private) assemblages made just for us.
Everything in the show is for sale at a price,even the people.   For us the party
on the opening night is the key to our stance,the most important performance.We
shall also do a few actions as counterpoint later in the week.

            PERFORMANCES: Wed 20th 1pm - Fri 22nd 7pm

                           Sat 23rd 1pm - Sun 24th 7pm

INSTITUTE OF CONTEMPORARY ARTS LIMITED

"Now it's time to go to bed, bye bye, good boy, good girl". But they do that with muzak too. They do spectrum analysis, and they work out the optimum frequencies and the optimum pulse patterns and just rewrite any music to fit within the spectrum. They use it in slaughterhouses because they've got one which makes the cows carry on bleeding and not clot, which they now use in hospitals for patients who have had heart disease. They even had it in the first moonshot to keep the astronauts content. And it's in the silos with nuclear weapons in Nevada as well to keep them awake and not go crazy! (laughs)

You've been working on various projects with the writer Kathy Acker. Is she in London for long?

P-Orridge: She's been living in London for a little while but getting a bit fed up with the stupidity of the British. She's decided that the society here is completely S&M orientated. She's a lot more clear about it than I am, but it made a lot of sense, especially when you remember that the public schoolboys still run the show here and they are renowned for being into deviancy — whether it be gay or S&M. It actually is true; the most perverted people in Britain are in the government, or rich businessmen.

So Kathy likes to take a sexual view of society and she also likes to take an extreme view. Like the way the public let television sadistically manipulate them. If you just start changing the language, if you start using the words sadism or masochism instead of advertising or whatever, you get a whole new way of perceiving what is going on. And recently, through talking to Kathy and through working on films for Spanish TV and so on, I have become re-obsessed with the idea of language. Not language that you write down, but the language of symbols, invisible languages — the ones of power.

For instance?

P-Orridge: I think the most powerful language on the planet at the moment is the way that television is edited, and the way it is actually editing itself.

Are the TV programmers aware of what they are doing?

P-Orridge: Some of them pretend to be, like advertising executives. But I don't think anyone has actually conceived how dangerous it is. It's like tampering with the atom. They don't know, and yet the medium of television is pervading everywhere all the time.

I have this theory about brainwashing where you get the brain into this state of emptiness, and then you fill it with something dogmatic, which is, "Go and kill somebody when you get back to America", or, "Communism is great". And television, I think, accidentally creates the same hypnotic vacuum, but fills it with nothing or random garbage. In a sense it's far more dangerous than straight brainwashing because it's leaving people dissatisfied and confused. We're trying to deal with television in the way you edit it, so that what we're creating is the first surrealist television in the true sense of the word. Now you see adverts which pretend to be surrealistic by using surrealist influenced images, but what surrealism is actually about is trying to find a path for the subconscious through the conscious — to express the true nature of our imagination. And that's what television should also be trying to do.

Can people use television to their advantage?

P-Orridge: Yes, I'm sure. They can use it like a crystal ball. Burroughs says, "If you do cut-ups, then the future leaks through". He was talking about words, and later about tape, but the same principles apply to video and film. Eventually even to floppy discs and computer programmes. We believe that you can try to achieve the crystal ball parallel as follows: turn the television to a channel without a programme and the screen will be filled with 'snow', as it's called. Turn the brightness and contrast up full. The best time to do this is between 1 a.m. and 6 a.m., as we are trained through social conditioning to be most neutral at this time — therefore the most receptive. Now get close to the screen, switch off all other light sources and stare at the screen. First try and focus on the tiny dots that will be careering about the screen like micro-organisms. You'll find it very hard to focus — just keep on trying. Suddenly time will alter along with your perceptions and you will hit a period of trance where the conscious and subconscious mind are triggered in unison by the mantric vibrations of the myriad dots. It's quite possible that the frequency and pulse rates of the TV 'snow' are similar to certain ones generated by other rituals in other societies (e.g. Dervish dances, Tibetan Magick etc.). What we have here is a contemporary magickal ritual using the medium, in all senses of the word, of television. A very basic form of Psychic Television. You can also get similar effects for instance by staring for long periods at mirrors and dream machines (see 'Planet R101 — Here To Go' by Terry Wilson and Brion Gysin). And you may also get cancer, I don't know. (laughs)

What we're doing now is trying to integrate the music with what we call, 'New Television'. We also call it 'Psychic Television', but if you can't handle the word "psychic", it's 'New Television'. It's television revealed as what it is, a system of manipulation and a very sophisticated one. It's also revealed as a very brutal form of contemporary magick — one which we hope can be turned in our favour. If you like, we're into the de-programming of television, and the music is part of that. But there will be odd records which will be made as self-contained in themselves as they can be. And if that means they sound incredibly attractive and listenable — fine, because there's going to be some element within the way they were recorded or the lyric which is not as it seems. They might even appeal to some major label and they might release them, and they might end up in the top ten, but we will still be running Temple Records and releasing completely uncompromising tapes for other reasons. At the end of the day, people either trust us or they don't trust us.

I'm 34 and I've been doing this for 15 years, and I'm living in a legalised squat with an outside toilet and an overdraft, and I'm still frightening to people like Time Out, so I don't think there's any evidence anyone could possibly produce to suggest that we're trying to get loads of zombie people to do what we want. Far from it, we immediately eject people who mimic us, we're just not interested. I personally don't have the time, the energy, or the inclination to pander to emotional cripples who want to be told what to do. That is completely the antithesis of what I'm trying to do — which is fight anyone who tells me what to do. All we can fall back on is, "Produce the evidence. When did we do that? When did we say that? Where's the proof of what you say we are?" And there is none. We are not monsters, we are not Nazis and we are not trying to bleed people dry to set up a pseudo-religion. It may well be that in America we decide that it's a good tactic, out of curiosity, to register as a religion, because in America that's what people do. And to investigate the phenomenon, and become tax exempt. It seems the obvious thing to do. Why not? Everyone else does — if they're going to have one, let's have one too. Ironically, if they get pissed off with us, they might have to fuck up everyone else's religion to get us, right? If they have to change the law, it applies to all the Moonies as well. Will they want to do that? It's going to really put them in a quandary. Do they want to start cracking down on all those privileges that they give religions? Because then they're being anti-religious and American governments do not want to be seen as being anti-religious. Because there's a lot of votes there.

So it's the old story. They set up this edifice to protect themselves and maybe there would be enough loopholes for us to go down and partly protect ourselves and exploit them. To take the piss, and attack them, and just generally cause a lot of mischief — and have a lot of fun doing it. It quite appeals to me. Why not? Go and visit our brothers in California — who are Mark Pauline and Monte Cazazza, the same so-called troublemakers — but now they're ministers. And I'm on the plane and I'm listed on the flight as just the Reverend Genesis P. Orridge. (laughs) I think we have to do it — just to see what happens. And I think more people should be sarcastic to those powers. You could say that we're obsessed with being sarcastic to the powers that be.

Do you find that the musical output of Psychic TV is approached in similar ways with most other bands?

P-Orridge: The way we do the music, the fact that it has so many layers, is because we approach it more from the literary or fine arts basis, whereas most people approach it from wanting to be musicians. Originally, when I was young, I wanted to be a sort of art-world, art-history type of artist. But when I got mixed up in that world, I was just so disillusioned and saddened and disgusted by what I saw. And the people that I met who were supposed to be artists just didn't have the dedication, the vision, or the determination to change the world or change human perception. When I was younger I romantically thought that art was a state of total being, a thing you couldn't escape. It was a traumatic drive; you didn't want to be an artist but you had no choice. And I just ended up feeling that the word "art" itself was an embarrassment because it just reminded me of the disgust I felt for those people. And it made me aware of why, even for the wrong reasons, the majority of the public think that art is a joke and have no respect for it. And I was really upset.

I think that everything since then has been a response to that disillusionment, and trying to find another language in another medium to be able to be an artist without being called one. Occasionally, in a weak moment, I will say to people that I would like to think that if there's such a thing as an artist still, then I'm probably an artist. And I want to be remembered as an artist and a thinker, or a writer and a thinker — not as a musician. Because I'm not a musician, and we've said many times, "We are not a music group, we just happen to use music or tape because that's what we can get access to and that is what's worked better than anything else so far". But at the end of the day, it is a neurosis, I can't do anything else.

Monte started as a fine artist, and then a performance artist, an then just became totally disillusioned and anarchic. Even Burroughs and Gysin are rebel artists and literary figures, they're all people who I think were damaged by the hypocrisy of the world that they originally believed in. They had a traditional image of the literary or art world, and I think none of us have ever recovered from that childhood shock of what it is really like. The music business is equally as bad — but you've always been told that, so it's not quite such a surprise, you're expecting it. But it's there, the feeling of being tainted and soiled can get so strong — and that's the primary emotional reason that we left CBS and Some Bizzare. We just felt that we were being infected with something insidious and filthy and that we weren't in control. And we felt that our public were getting worried that it was happening too.

With Psychic TV USA and Psychic TV Iceland now beginning operations, do you feel that takes a lot of pressure off your back — since some people might look at you alone as being Psychic TV?

P-Orridge: We're trying to educate people into the idea that we're not a normal group, that we're a network of collaborators who trust each other. Which is what we are. There is no other group that I know of like that. We are trying to prove that the options are far more than anyone says and that I don't have to be on a record for it to be Psychic TV. Eventually, I could retire and never make a record again, and Psychic TV could still release things in

Japan. There could be a Japanese Psychic TV, for example. We're trying to set up examples, models and new ways of operating so everyone else can make use of the bits that are applicable to them. And it has worked to a degree already. TG had a world-wide influence, we didn't sit there and know it would, but we took note. We were just intuitive enough and lucky enough to execute what was inevitable in our eyes. And enough other people agreed that it was inevitable to relate to it.

We can do what we want and get across to people. The question is, "How many before you've compromised?" I don't think anybody really knows where the border is. Did Jim Morrison get across something intelligent to a lot of people with his music, or did he just become popular? It's a fine line. I think The Doors are one of the few examples of popular music which did retain intelligence most of the time.

But how much of the intelligence was acknowledged in their day, and how much of it was established in retrospect, with the release of the books and general Doors revival?

P-Orridge: I don't know because I didn't really follow their progress at the time. I thought they were a bit boring when they first came out. (laughs) I did get more interested after reading about Jim Morrison. Then the records became more interesting. So it could be that it's retrospective to a degree. Nevertheless, that is the aim, to try and create intelligent music. I'm not concerned with being popular, but I've got no fear of something getting accidentally popular either. At the end of the day music has to remain functional, and if that function is purely propaganda or tactics, that's still a function.

But the music I find most interesting is the music which affects the body. I really want to be able to make the live things that we do as sexual as possible in their effect. I want to make people feel very sexually aroused and find the frequencies and pulses that arouse people sexually. There are very few live events now where there is any sexuality. That's one thing that apparently The Doors did generate, obviously more deliberately — Jim Morrison rolling around in his leather trousers and stuff. (laughs) But I think it is lacking in music at the moment. Although there's all this dance music and body music and bands sing about coming, in reality, there's no sex music.

Most ritual music is either for an ecstatic state, for visions, or it's a form of fucking. In fact, most of the best rhythms are fuck rhythms. People tend to hint at it but, in fact, they are very puritan about it. I think it's time to get back to fucking again. (laughs) Let's have everyone going home and having a good fuck. Let's throw in sex, blatant sex, because there should be an enjoyment quota. We always said we were interested in sexual magick and the idea of focussed sexuality. I think that with the idea of focussed sexuality. I think that with the drumming, we're beginning to get back to that primitive root of pure sex, and I think that having realised it, that's what has been missing for so long. Even now, the only sex music is gay disco music, and that's only because it accompanies what happens anyway. It doesn't make gay people feel sexy, they play it whilst they're cruising anyway, and that's fair enough. Take Jim Morrison, he used to whip up sexual feelings, as did the early Rolling Stones — Brian Jones and Mick Jagger, both of them. And that sensuality side of it seems to have diminished greatly. That's probably a reason why people are dissatisfied. I really think that in a symbolic way, going to a live gig is going to be fucked. You're fucking the audience and on a good night, they're fucking you. That's why I think that music has to be loud and physical. And there are certain really simplistic functions of live music which people have forgotten. They're into demonstrating their own prowess, it's masturbatory at the moment. People should look much more closely at the sexual parallel of what they do live — and do it consciously.

Don't people like Wham! and A-Ha act as sex objects?

P-Orridge: Yeah, but they're the unobtainable. They're the playboy perfection of it. They're a cosmetic version which is very sterile, they're the sex that you, if you actually got it, wouldn't want because they'd smell of scent rather than sex. They'd be looking in the mirror to see how they looked as they were doing it. And they'd wear their make up in bed. I'm talking about real sex where you like the smells and the sweat and you forget yourself in it. And at the end of it you feel changed. You've been in another mental state which is the state of the conscious and unconscious combined, which is what happens at orgasm. And a lot of people have this misconception that if you're lost in sex, that you're promiscuous — which isn't true. You can have a completely enclosed relationship with one person and still have incredibly ecstatic, invigorating sex. But in this society people are so terrified of the freedom, mental and spiritual, that sex can give that they try to dismiss it or alienate people from it.

Especially now with the huge sexual backlash.

P-Orridge: Yeah. That's where we get back to what Kathy Acker was saying about the S&M situation. What we need is a healthy interest and animalistic freedom within sex. Sex can actually be focussed to bring to bear all your best energies to improve everything about your character and direction. That's the second stage, where you realise that the power of sex can be channelled to enhance your individual freedom and give you back to yourself. S&M grows from guilt and fear. That's why, when we first mentioned it, it sounded crazy, but now we've talked some more and what Kathy's saying is actually accurate in many ways.

I think that's another reason why we are important and why people are so scared of us. It's the sex that scares them because they've been trained and conditioned to be scared of it. We've all been made to feel embarrassed and there's a residue of that in all of us. In reality, I think it's about time we said, "No, we're not embarrassed". It's time for us to take that risk. But 'rock and roll' is dying, if you like. I used to hate the idea of 'rock and roll', but I'm beginning to think maybe it's not such a bad idea. Give people sex and all the power back and the music could take off again. Wildness, you know, let's have a bit of wildness again.

SOME WEAKNESSES

You've got soft skin. I like the insides of your thighs, running my hand slowly up to the lips of your cunt. Your cunt was dry a second ago. Now it's faintly wet, not quite soaked, just beginning to lubricate. That's supposed to suck me in, supposed to make the blood rush to my prick, so it'll get hard and want to go up inside you, so you can steal my come. I refuse to accept that ploy. I'm only tender with you in order to watch you respond, to watch you thinking that I'm something that I'm not. You're moaning like a stupid animal. You think I'm a very passionate dildo. The truth is, I could murder you right now. But I won't. Then you'd be useless and I need you. I have to pretend that I'm caught up in this, that I'm "abandoned", so that you in turn will respond exactly how I want you to. I'm standing above us watching our imbecilic bodies press and grind, each of us thinking we've fooled the other. I'd like to throw gasoline over the sweating heap and light it, watch us scream dumb pain as we burn. I make myself sick.

The idiot cop is telling me to move. I'm standing there like meat. He's prodding me with his club. He knows I'm pliable meat. He's meat. His head is solid muscle. I'm also meat. My mind tries to convince itself that it's not meat, but the physical fact of being prodded, pressed, locked in dead concrete, dulls each thought, each hate, making them meat. This makes me want to cut meat. I've been thinking; "I'll never leave here. I don't want to leave. When I stare long enough without thinking time stops. I move dead. It doesn't feel. I don't have to think. There's no reason to think. I'll stop thinking". I continue to think. I cannibalize my thoughts until nothing remains but hate. Hate makes me strong. I'm willing to kill him because I'm meat. It's the last thing to think about before I become permanent meat. Meat that eats and shits, moved when pushed, sleeps when tired, nothing else. He pushes me again. I pull out a knife and slide it into his stomach. I cut his throat. His face lights up. He's surprised. For a second he's not meat. My mind begins to work. One thought after another, against my will.

© **Michael Gira**

CBGB's
SAT
Skull
Sonic Youth

Within the cramped confines of downtown New York live Sonic Youth. Formed in 1981, guitarists Thurston Moore and Lee Renaldo were once a part of Glenn Branca's Guitar Army, a massive collection of traditional 'rock' instruments on stage creating a wall of noise. Keeping the fullness of Branca's sound, Sonic Youth began to manipulate 'rock'. The group's 1985 LP *Bad Moon Rising*, featured a collaboration with Lydia Lunch entitled *Death Valley 69*, continuing the group's fascination with that period of wrongs in America — the Vietnam War, Charles Manson, and the apparent greater concern with happenings on the moon than those at home.

Live, the group creates a cacophonous noise intercepted by harmonious melodies. Moore, Renaldo and bassist Kim Gordon vary the tension on their strings, by occasionally placing objects underneath them or by hitting them with sticks and mallets. In this way, Sonic Youth mesh structure with experimentalism, while refusing to be classified within either area alone.

In 1986 Sonic Youth released their second full length album *Evol*, playing dates on Brighton Beach, part of which was documented on the semi-official bootleg *Walls Have Ears*. They also joined with Mike Watt as Ciccone Youth to cover a Madonna song, their version titled *Into The Groovey*. In the summer of 1987 they topped the independent charts with their most accessible album *Sister*.

What makes Sonic Youth different from other bands that were operating around 1976 and 1977?

Thurston: Bands in '76-'77 were in a unique position of rebellion. Bands like the Sex Pistols, Wire, Eater, etc. were in their late teens. The only popular music on the market was supergroup innocuous pop, with the exception of such things as The Stooges and the New

York Dolls. With the help of crazed businessmen like Malcolm McLaren they were able to exploit, for the most part, underground and teen-angst rock into a household item and 'turn on' a whole new generation. An extremely radical slap in the face of the rock music world-wide scene. It has been a decade since and anything goes, especially in the light of the constantly rising international conservatism. Being a part of that / this generation, we've evolved with it and what you hear from us is just our side of the effect. The freedom the '77-'78 groups espoused is a major inspiration (Wire, Swell Maps, TG, Pistols..) as is music from past eras (Stones, Creedence, Seeds, Grateful Dead, Doors...)

How do you like to feel after a performance?

Thurston: That the ego surrounding our creative impulses is satisfied without being ultimately stupid. A re-affirmation of faith in the extreme emotion of our hearts, minds and souls. Seriously, that probably sounds pretentious, but it's where the inspiration lies and how we'd love the audience to feel — inspired.

Do you feel that music is the best way for you to express yourself?

Thurston: For me personally, music is what I've responded culturally to the most and it is the form which follows strongest from whatever thoughts and feelings go on inside. It seems the best communicant with the spirit, or at least the most successful, and that communication is a full time effort and pleasure.

Do you find that New York is a good place to work out of?

Thurston: I'm not sure if it's the best, not having the chance or finance to work anywhere else at any length of time. It certainly proves to be a very conducive element for working as materials are always readily at hand.

Would you say that there is an overall message behind Sonic Youth?

Thurston: Maybe just that divinity can be peeked through honest display.

How closely are Swans and Sonic Youth related?

Thurston: On a working and careerist way, maybe we are working on the same levels. Musically we differ, but there's a respect, liking and appreciation of each other that both bands have with no other. It's funny.

Is your aggression aimed at anyone specific during a performance?

Thurston: No-one specifically. It's aimed at anybody who is at least partly human.

Why aren't Sonic Youth heard on commercial radio?

Thurston: Most of the people listening to commercial radio aren't that seriously involved in music and would rather have a palatable formula than the more sinister abandon of freak-out bands like us. At least that's what the programmers seem to think.

How important is it for a mass audience to hear your music?

Thurston: It's not important so much to the music as it is to the welfare of the band.

How important do you think your lyrics are?

Thurston: They're as important as the music. They're written separate and stand alone.

Why should the music of Sonic Youth be heard?

Thurston: Because it answers prayers.

LYDIA LUNCH

Lydia Lunch began her musical career in New York City with Teenage Jesus And The Jerks, a band which arose in 1977 along with Mars, DNA and The Contortions. This cluster became known collectively as 'No Wave', whose aims were to destroy rock and its emotional, artistic, musical and intellectual trappings. Subsequent bands included the abrasive Beirut Slump, while Eight Eyed Spy saw Lunch return to a more established rock form. Through *In Limbo*, Lunch explored more lyrically complex material of her own with varied musicians including Thurston Moore and Richard Edson, while *The Drowning of Lucy Hamilton* saw Lunch collaborate with former Mars person Lucy Hamilton to create an instrumental landscape.

In 1985, the female Immaculate Consumptive released her second spoken tape entitled *The Uncensored Lydia Lunch*. She had previously shared the *Hard Rock* tape with Michael Gira — Lunch's piece being *Wet Me On A Dead Night* — but rather than the predecessor's inward directed sexuality, *The Uncensored Lydia Lunch* focuses on more fully realised characters. Lunch has also had a book of observations published by Grove Press entitled *Adulterers Anonymous*, which she compiled with Exene Cervenka of the Los Angeles group X.

In addition to Lunch's spoken and musical projects, she has had several film appearances within the New York underground, including Beth and Scott B's *The Offenders* and *The Black Box*, and Vivienne Dick's *She Had A Gun All Ready, Beauty Become The Beast*. Lunch also co-wrote and starred in Richard Kern's *The Right Side Of My Brain*. In 1987 a collection of some of her previous work was released entitled *Hysterie*.

Is the switch from your musical activity to your work with short stories a permanent change?

Lydia: None of my changes are permanent. I mean I don't predict the future, I'm basically a stream of consciousness woman. I would prefer just to be a writer, to sit in a fucking hole and rot, and write the story of my life, but I'm too busy creating it. I wish more people would do the same.

What do you see as the benefits of a spoken short story as opposed to a short story one comes across in a book?

Lydia: That way people don't read it in their own tone of voice. You dictate it to them and it's more emotional in the way that you're portraying it. That's why I felt kind of weird after 'Adulterers Anonymous' came out because I realised those very personal thoughts, (and I don't call it poetry) were going to be read in people's own voices which really disgusted me.

I have a lot of material compiled now, but I have no urge to put it out yet because it's not enough to my liking, it's not full or fat enough. I started telling stories because the point was always what interested me. I mean that's why I began in music in the first place, it was the easiest format to prostitute, to get the point across with. Although I had been writing since I was twelve, you just don't think you can get a book published. I mean no-one reads books, there's no information about books, no-one finds out about them, and it's just like a different reality. But in New York City, all that was going on was conducive to creating a musical format. Especially because I didn't necessarily agree with everything that was going on. I mean that's why I had Teenage Jesus and the Jerks, basically it was just me screaming, "AHHHHH NOOOOO", in the face of the public, as loudly as possible, and as hideously and brutally as possible. Just a baby screaming, that's all it was, hence the title, hence the music.

Is that attraction for New York still there?

Lydia: It's a different attraction. At first it was a change from living in Rochester, New York, an industrial shithole with lots of boys with fast cars who are in gangs. I mean fun, fun, fun, but they're only so much fun and there are only so many of them. Different things interest me about it now. I'm a creature of incredible convenience and New York City is the most convenient city in the world. I mean I'm lazy and I like to luxuriate in that, and it's very difficult to do that in London unless you have slaves which I don't enjoy keeping — contrary to popular belief. I like New York's immediacy, it's necessary, but it's a very difficult place to stay for a long period of time which is why I tend to travel a lot. I haven't lived there for about five years, apart from last summer. I'm going back when I'm through with this place. But it's just too much, it's sensory bombardment, it's overkill, and that's why I want to move to Harlem. That to me is like moving to the country.

I mean I spend most of my time between travelling and huge periods of hibernation, which I really need desperately. I'm not very social, so the times when I'm travelling or being away from my home, which I haven't had for about eight months, can really get on my nerves — but they're necessary. I basically feel like a snail without a shell, and I really need that shell.

Do you feel there is any place in the world which seems to act as a progressive centre, in terms of culture?

Lydia: People always think in terms of L.A., London, New York and Berlin possibly, but those are such crude examples of the modern world. Except for New York which is just convenience and immediacy and a few friends, these cities are pretty redundant. One place is as good or bad, or as dead or alive as the next. It's all just what you make it. I do seek out new territory, but as yet, I haven't found that exact Utopia where you just go to rot.

How would you describe 'Adulterers Anonymous?'

Lydia: It's just a book of some shit. It's a book of thoughts, it's not poetry. It's just girl talk, Exene and I kept two notebooks, we'd write in them, we'd comment on each other's and then we'd put it in a book.

Were you pleased with the outcome of it?

Lydia: I was pleased with doing it. The outcome of it, I guess so, yeah. But it wouldn't be enough for me to do something like that now because basically it was a very selfish thing. I do a lot of things that are very selfish, that's a term that is often misinterpreted and misused by many people. I think that someone who is truly selfish is usually the most generous person because they want everything to be as good as possible for themselves, therefore being as good as possible for everyone else. People misuse selfish and greedy, I mean greedy is one thing. I'm not greedy at all, I want for very little and have even less actually. I do want the best for myself and I want to be the best I can be. But that book was very selfish in the sense that it's almost like only giving the punchlines without any of the other meat, so that people are just going, — "What?" It just eliminates all the fodder and bullshit.

Was your direction in literature changed at all after the publication of 'Adulterers Anonymous'?

Lydia: Well, I learned that I wanted to tell stories rather than write them basically. But I think there are some voices that are universal. For instance, if you read Bukowski, you start reading it in his tone of voice. Henry Miller, you read it in his tone of voice. The next thing that I write is going to be in a particular tone of voice. And that is the most important thing in writing, finding your own voice, because people will naturally, if it's rhythmical and dictatorial enough, have to assume it when they read it.

Do you feel that you are no longer able to get across your ideas or feelings if there is 'rock music' behind you, for instance during a gig?

Lydia: Well, I have never dealt in 'rock music' except for one time. For me, it's just because my music is so sentimental or of a particular sentiment that it's much better on record than in the live format.

With storytelling, I can interpret whatever mood I'm in into the story and it's more a variety of inflections and moods. My music is so specifically conceptual of one mood or the other mood that it is limited in the way that it is for — a specific day of the week shall we say. Basically, I'm a conceptualist and not a musician, and not a singer, not a songwriter. I work in concepts, I say, "OK, delve into this, now that".

If your lyrics are to mean something, do you think that singing them with a group backing you is beginning to become slightly archaic?

Lydia: Definitely, because it's too easy for people to either grasp onto the music or not grasp onto it. It's easy for them to ignore it, reject it or embrace it. When I'm up there spouting verbally, first of all, I'm totally in control. If anyone has anything to say to me one to one, fine — say it. I'll give them their time and they will hence hear me out. Since the point is always the main thing with me, now I don't have to embellish it or disguise it behind the music. For me, it's a more direct means of communication.

My music is sometimes unlistenable to some people, it's unpleasant, it's disturbing, it's depressing, or whatever you want to call it. But when there are just words, you can bait people in by tone of voice the same way as you can with music. But the concept of my music is not particularly seductive in the format, with words it's different. You can approach it because you're only concentrating on that one specific thing, not, "Is the bass too loud?" You can concentrate better on me. It's more direct.

Why do you think some of your material is disturbing to some people?

Lydia: Well, some of it is unpleasant to some people's aesthetic of what music should sound like. Some is just depressing, some is just melancholic. I mean, why is it disturbing? I don't know. Because it's honest, because it's the bare ugly truth and real sentiment. Quite often people don't look to music for that. They look at it for entertainment and I'm not here to entertain anyone, not even myself quite often. Therefore, I tell it like it is and most people don't like to hear it like it is, they just don't. They want to dance, they want to be amused, they want to see someone throw themselves around on stage, all of which I have no interest in doing whatsoever.

Do you ever indulge yourself in listening to music for entertainment?

Lydia: I'm not a big fan of music, but in general I'd say that I don't like music just because there are so many bad connotations and hideous things connected with it — so much lousy fucking music. However, there are moods that some music does express that I feel very akin to, that I do like to listen to — basically instrumentals. I much prefer instrumentals, classical music or soundtrack music. Occasionally there is a band in existence that I might care to peek at for a moment. I mean I know what I like. For instance, I do like to see a certain breed of male performance. Basically I'd see a nice strip show if one existed, but they don't. When I feel the urge to go and entertain myself, I would be quite pleased if I could find the ultimate sexual, dynamic, violent, typical crotch throb. I mean it exists occasionally, there have been three or four people in the history of music who have done it successfully, but they either stop, get old or croak.

Basically it is the typical; Jim Morrison, Iggy Pop, Nick Cave, Foetus Flesh. I mean it

exists for a small period of time, these throbaphiles, but it's voyeuristic. Like I say we could boil it down to a strip show or something, but it's rare. I've seen it done, so I don't feel the urge to reiterate the format because I know it has existed, I know it's out there. I have dined deliciously on the aforementioned individuals and I don't see the need for anyone to repeat them or take it further. "Go ahead, surprise me, make me wet my pants... please".

Operating in a field that is so dominated by males, do you feel at times that you are viewed sexually and not for your actual work?

Lydia: I would say that perhaps I haven't received the respect I would have received if I was male — and if I was English. I think, unless it's in the eyes of some of the audience who may view me in a sexual fashion, that most of my work has avoided that. A lot of it has been, not anti-sexual but, anti-recognisable in a sexual format. Like Teenage Jesus was very cold, very hard and very ugly. Most people don't find those attributes sexy.

I mean it's a matter of what your aesthetics of sexuality are. Except for one brief stint in Eight Eyed Spy, which I look at as my humorous 'Rock Mama' period — "OK, the girl you love to hate most is now going to be your little purring (cough) sex kitten" — which I wasn't, just a snarling fucking tom cat. I don't think I've ever performed in a way that would make people think, "Oh isn't that sexy", because it's too hard, too nasty, and too real. And most people think sex is something... so much nicer.

However, some women performers have been worshipped for their hardness, and many sexual acts are both hard and violent.

Lydia: I think I'm an intellectual basically, that's how I would like to be viewed. I mean my ardent sexuality is kept out of the public eye if possible. My stories are much more sexual because they're real life and there's a lot of sex involved there, but they're not related in a fashion to make someone necessarily go, "Ooh, I'd really fucking like to take her home". I think that most people hearing them would probably go, "Yikes, no... please... anything, but don't torture me with her!" I don't think I've ever been built up by the media as being a sex object and most people probably think that I'm quite a hideous, horrifying, ugly creature... You, of course, can testify otherwise if you like.

Do you ever think of writing anything longer than a short story, for instance a novel?

Lydia: No, because I don't read them basically, so why should I write them. When I do write a 'novel', it will just be an accumulation of short stories strung together. I won't sit down and plot it out from front to back because the format bores me.

Why does the short story format interest you?

Lydia: It's more immediate. It's quick. You get to the point, you get the punchline and the punchlines are important. And I don't like to pad the point.

Do you feel poetry gets to the point even quicker?

Lydia: I don't know anything about poetry and I don't care to. The word disgusts me, I call it 'poohetry'. It has a bad reputation in my mind's eye and most other people's minds too. And that's because the lowest common denominator of writing is poetry, which it always wasn't, but now seems to be.

How would you describe the describe the feeling behind 'Wet Me On A Dead Night'?

Lydia: It's observatory. I mean that's what my stories are. I'm just an observer. I'm just passing through this life and taking notes, making notes on your death, "It's not as late as it seems, it never is, it's always later, so much later". I just observe, I write the facts, I call it as I see it — that's it. I don't think that I assume too much of an opinion one way or another, I try to express both sides of an argument. It's factual, that's all.

Do you sometimes view yourself as being too much of a realist?

Lydia: Definitely, reality being so much more interesting than fiction. I mean that's why I deal with a real format, there's nothing as gristly as reality and there's such an extreme range of realities. It's so vivid that I don't see why anyone would have to fictionalise. I mean it's just too colourful. Sobriety is an ugly place to sit, let me tell you.

With a piece like 'Wet Me On A Dead Night', would you want a listener to feel or think deeply about it, or strictly be entertained?

Lydia: Of course I want them to think if they're listening to what I do, I would hope that they're a thinker and not a drinker. I wrote that four years ago, it was the first short story that I'd ever written and I'm trying to recollect it... That was a piece of entertainment more so than most of my other stories, and I just want them to feel drained. I mean, like the story, it just dribbles away.

Who are some of the other story tellers that you respect?

Lydia: Mike Gira. Henry Rollins tells good stories. Exene Cervenka, the people I work with, I mean that's why I work with them. I respect them and I like their stories. Nick Cave. Henry Miller, he's dead so I guess he doesn't count, and Bukowski... American greats.

What are your thoughts on the relationship between contentment and complacency?

Lydia: A lot of people, especially my friends, which number under five — and I don't mean years of age, tend to confuse contentment with complacency, which is totally incorrect because they're two separate things. I'm very content, but it's only because I've sorted out the correct priority system which is very important. I've gotten rid of a lot of my traumas and all the horror of living for twenty five years and have come out of a bed of shit stinking of roses basically. In my opinion, only because I'm realistic, nothing is horrible. People seem to confuse the words comfort and complacency. They think that if you're happy or content, then you're complacent. That you have to suffer to be a great artist — bullshit! I mean you have to suffer, but there is a point when you no longer have to because you know. You've toed your fucking line, you've broken enough rocks, the ball and chain grows so big that you can finally sever it. I would not trade one iota, one breath of torture that I had to go through, one iota of misery and torment for torment for an easy life.

But the fact is that there comes a point when you should be able to realise that enough is enough. I mean it just gets boring. You just go through the same agony over and over again. And there comes a point when it's just too miserable and you have to either sink or swim, and I decided, "Hey, I know the backstroke daddy", did it and took to the water like a fish. And I'm fine. I just wish more people would understand that they don't have to torture themselves endlessly to create. Life can be easier, it's not a horrible thing. It's not so bad to not have everything in the most excruciating agony. I mean I've had enough for one girl.

What is success to you?

Lydia: I guess that I've achieved success in that I've gotten over all my for catastrophes. I have reached my conclusion because I'm ever striving for an open mind, not perfection because I'm not unrealistic. I want to be realistic, not to fall into the same traps that everyone else around me seems to fall into repeatedly, not to make the same mistakes, to learn and to

I started out trying to write the story of my life, but it was so full of shit I just thought I'd wait until tomorrow or the next day. Or never. Just to save the bullshitting to the twilight of my years. You know, cut the crap jack. Shit or git off the pot, right. Well in that case, you better move it on over. Re-evaluate the whole value of nothing and see what you get. Start at scratch and work your way back. Know what I mean?? I know you don't, but that's okay, I wasn't talking to you anyway. Not at all. Not a single grunt uttered in your direction. Not a peep. Period. Nothing. And plenty of it. This bum's fer you. Hey! Dickhead, are you listening or what?? What the hell better have you got to do anyway?? You filthy fucking jerkoff. Fer one helluva lazy no good fer nothing you sure don't have a whole helluva lot to say for yourself, now do you?? Uh-huh. Right. So just cut the fuckin' gnarl. How long can one man be expected to suck shit through a straw anyway?? Any longer and I'm gonna puke blood — preferably yours. Or the next best thing. Or the next worst thing. Or anything, anything at all. Anything you can think of, that is if you're still thinking. That is, please don't strain. You seem exceptionally constipated for a man of your great breeding. And not to berate you any more than absolutely necessary or anything, but you stink. Once again, like shit. Total shit. Is that you or just my fetid imagination?????????????

educate myself. That's what I strive for — not to have a home in the country, nor 2.3 kids, nor a car or a TV. I mean I am successful, I am satisfied — which is not complacent. I do exactly what I want to do, which a lot of people can't because they have too many hang-ups or problems or they're not allowed. I am allowed and I am totally liberated from a lot of the pettiness, bullshit, self-aggravation, self-torture and self-abuse that makes up many people's lives.

It's just a matter of sitting down and thinking for a few minutes of your rotten life. Getting things in order. I don't want anything more than I have now. I just want more of the same and not that much more. Basically I just want an easy life, which to me means not putting up with people who are full of shit, not being bothered, being able to go to the corner store without being agoraphobic, a roof over my head — and I don't care if it's a dog shed. I have very few possessions.

I just long for intellectual stimulation from others who are as emotionally stable as I am, which is rare. I have three immaculate friends scattered around the globe, that's all. Basically the only thing that I have been striving for the entirety of my life is appreciation and understanding for how and what I am — not for what I do — but for me. Who can really ask for anything more than appreciation for how you are, especially if you really work at being the best you can be — which I do. It's important, especially when there's so much misconception about the way you are, that you re-evaluate. Most people never re-evaluate, the more attention they get, the less they re-evaluate because they just start believing all the bullshit that's scooped into their corner. I'm afraid I just won't buy it, I'm afraid it means nothing to me, I am so unimpressed and I'm not looking to be impressed at all, I mean that's not what I want. I just want stimulation, satisfaction and an easy life. How much less could one ask for?

Do you think that somebody reading this could misinterpret you as being arrogant and egotistical?

Lydia: They can misinterpret it, misinterpretation runs amok constantly, but I, unfortunately, am not a door to door salesman. I cannot go to each person individually who may be reading this and tell them, "Open your fucking eyes, ears and mind for once and listen to the truth!" I'm not a breastbeater, at least not my own breasts. But egotist is another word like selfish, words that are constantly misused. I'm not here to educate the ignorant. I can only relate or preach so much without just wanting to shut up and haul myself away. Misinterpretation, as we all know, starts with the pettiest and gets more petty. I really can't be concerned with what people are going to think about what I'm saying because I'm only telling how I feel. So, if you don't like me, then I'm sorry but I don't care. I might not like you either. Think about that. You never know.

Since you do write stories, do you feel hindered in expressing yourself through the brevity of a song lyric?

Lydia: In the past I would never re-write lyrics or edit them down, they would just come out exactly how I felt, sometimes in five lines and sometimes in fifteen lines, to express a certain sentiment. Sometimes I would write them down, I wouldn't even know what I meant until months and months later. They would come to me only because they were abstractions of exactly how I felt, which I couldn't take time to decipher at that moment because they were so personal. Sometimes you can't see your nose because it's on your face, right? I write lyrics in the two minutes they come to me, and they're immediately either transmitted into a song or dispensed out. I don't have volumes of unused material because I don't need that. I'm a big fan of notebook burning because I myself should be enough. But then again, a fifty LP box set, a couple of hundred books and a couple of movies doesn't hurt.

Do you ever perform stories spontaneously?

Lydia: There's a lot of spontaneity in them, there's room for me to say whatever, but to just go up there... I've done that in musical formats where I've just had no words and would go up there and sing whatever came into my mind; but in a spoken word format, I like to be concise, I don't blabber endlessly. I do that everyday, I'm blabbering constantly. Now I have to do it on stage and get paid to boot? Thank you. Not a bad idea!

How would you describe your video, 'The Right Side of My Brain'?

Lydia: It's a psycho-sexual, emotional, nymphomaniacal drama based on one poor, unfortunate girl who just gets abused throughout, and possibly why one may want to get abused. Abuse may titillate one's imagination or emotions which could be far superior to feeling rot or nothingness. So it's just a little expose, and the possible reasons for why one girl could be led to be so distraught. It's not my life story, it's just a little film.

Because your work is so vivid and real — therefore alienating potential audiences — do you feel that you are getting through to the mainstream?

Lydia: No, because I don't expose it to the mainstream. I mean I do readings and I do it to fifty people, almost hand chosen. I'm not going to have a book out for some time to come so they can't get it into their greedy little paws and start tearing the pages out. I have no desire to expose it to the mainstream really. I just want to do what I want to do for those who want to see it done and for those who want to hear it. I have no interest in branching out, expanding my popularity or whatever. I just like to document things because I know that there are 'X' amount of people who feel exactly the same way I do.

NOTES ON THE ALIENATION

I've got a place
I've got a desert
I've got a good thing going
Don't climb down here
You put me on the outskirts of town
Now you want in?
You think you do.
I'll turn your lights out
I'll take your virginity away again
Can
you
dig
it?
I live in a hanging garden
Suspended from your world
In alienation: No Sears and Roebuck dreams
No credit is good
In alienation: I am whole
Complete
Full circle realised
In alienation
In the alienation
In the peace of 21,361 minds
It's only cold in your world
When I'm with you I'm cold
Alien
Your world is such a lonely place
When I am there
I am cold
You are a bad trip
That's why I quit you
That's why I spat you out
That's why I went up river
Into the desert
Into the jungle
Into the sun
I exist in alienation
I am not alone
I am joined by those who know that paradise lies
In her eyes.

EINSTÜRZENDE NEUBAUTEN

Berlin's Einsturzende Neubauten delight in seeing how much sense can be made out of chaos, and conversely how chaotic you can get and still make sense. A five man group consisting of Blixa Bargeld, Marc Chung, F.M. Einheit, N.U. Unruh and Alexander Von Borsig, Neubauten use cement mixers, pneumatic drills, springs, metal cutters and sundry hunks of found metal objects to make a primarily percussive music leavened with guitar, bass and vocals. This provides a sometimes destructive, abstract, sophisticated and physically devastating sound. Their treatment of sound has gained acclaim from some of the most unlikely sources.

In early 1984 Marc Chung and Alexander Von Borsig and a host of others, including Genesis P-Orridge, Stevo, and Frank Tovey performed *The Concerto For Voices And Machinery* at the Institute of Contemporary Arts in London. During the performance, a large part of the stage was destroyed — primarily by the instruments of the performers, which included electric saws, acetylene torches and generators. Even though the I.C.A. forced a quick end to the Concerto, its original intention — to incorporate sounds such as those produced by the aforementioned instruments into an orchestral arrangement, was realised. In 1987 the group released their fifth album *Five On The Open-ended Richter Scale*.

Singer, guitarist and leader of Einsturzende Neubauten, Blixa Bargeld, has been known to treat his body with absolute disregard — best exemplified during the recording of *Thirsty Animal* with Rowland Howard and Lydia Lunch. Bargeld's ribcage was miked up in an effort to record the effect of being beaten with gruelling blows by fellow Neubauten member Mufti. Some of the lingering manifestations are evident upon viewing the body of Bargeld — his Theatre of Cruelty. Self-abuse of this nature has brought about an understanding of his body, his cell, his self; while the limits to which he pushes it radically reshape his perceptions. The most powerful beast it releases, however, is captured in the output of Einsturzende Neubauten.

What are your feelings about Germany?

M Chung: Of the country, the state of consciousness, the economics? My feelings about Germany? It's home.

Are you happy with the present political situation in Germany?

M Chung: I'm a marxist, so how can I be happy with it?

Would you call Einsturzende Neubauten a band?

M Chung: That's just playing around with terms. If we call ourselves a band, we can play in clubs and do tours. If we don't, we can play in museums. And that's alright too.

What were the reasons for the band forming?

M Chung: Well, seeing it in the negative way, for me personally it's just an ability of coping with a nine-to-five job. I'm the oldest in the group so I have had a couple of years seeing what I want to do. Naturally it gets cut down to certain things that you can do and certain things where you feel you have to compromise more than you want to. And Neubauten meets my willingness to compromise so far.

So what were the actual reasons for getting together?

M Chung: That's an interesting study of coincidence and selected action. It's partly coincidence of meeting up somewhere, and it's partly that you tend to get together with people that you share ideas with. I came into the band in 1981 with a friend of mine, Mufti. I played together in Abwarts with him before, so we knew each other.

Did you want to change anything?

M Chung: I didn't expect to change very much by giving an output, not beyond any other output that you do, like knocking over a motorcycle in the street or eating a bag of fries.

What were you trying to do with music?

M Chung: Earn loads of money, get girls... what else? Big cars? No. Work, contribute to the Gross National Product.

AVB: Also to make a strong back for the whole thing. In the beginning there were just two people and to get that sort of power, you actually need more people. Twenty people would be best actually. But you cannot find twenty open minded people that can stand this sort of pressure.

Did you want to change music in any way?

M Chung: Last year's favourite quote was, "We want to expand music until there's nothing left except music".

AVB: If you make everything music, the music you usually hear is no more, I mean it's just narrow-mindedness then.

M Chung: Actually, when you read this, this might not be actual at all. What does Blixa say? "Conservative is revolutionary", is his new saying now, which of course is nonsense.

Are you trying to break down the barriers of music?

M Chung: I wouldn't say that. Expand is a nice word I think.

What are the underlying concepts of the band?

M Chung: Through the years we've been doing different projects all the time, either records or performances or this or that. Almost every record has been based on a different concept. The concert at the ICA was one example, and we did a maxi-single once where we just had concepts of working with organic materials as far as possible — another example.

What concept was behind 'Drawings of O.T.'?

M Chung: 'O.T.' was really very much concerned with broadening and widening the use of material to create sounds. At that time, it was absolutely necessary for us and I think it was an important thing for Britain as well. I think that's why things happened in England for us at that time. I mean at the moment every band, Depeche Mode or whoever, are sampling sounds. And now they're developing computers for it. We're not so much concerned with that right now since we are going on to new stuff. But at that time we were.

What are you concentrating on now?

M Chung: We've just done five days in the studio, just working differently than we did before, actually playing like a band together. Perhaps in that context, conservative is revolutionary! (laughs) Oh yeah, we've been trying to do love songs — emotionally touching.

Is that to soften up the sound at all?

M Chung: Love is not soft, is it?

In music it traditionally is.

M Chung: Well, we're not concerned with that problem. Love is not soft, that's nonsense. The toughest things happen in love. "Crimes of Passion", if I may quote. It has nothing to do with softening.

Are you disturbed that some people categorise you as a 'metal' band?

M Chung: Well, it doesn't apply anymore. It didn't even apply on the last record one and a half years ago. It applied at the time we did 'Kollaps', which was in 1982, because that was when the band got rid of the drum kit. At that time we were a metal band, playing metal instead of drums. But for 'O.T.', we hardly used any metal.

What would be your reaction to a person who might think that they could produce what's on your records by just banging things together in the street?

M. Chung: Well that's absolutely correct. Well no, they couldn't do the same thing. But they could do something on the street.

AVB: People say they can go out in the street and do what we do. Well, I would just say that I'm the person who figures something out, and that's why it's important — because I make something out of it.

Do you look at the output as being a release?

M Chung: Yeah, in some respects. But it's refreshing. Refreshment, that sounds nice, "Have a Coke, have an Einsturzende Neubauten". (laughs) Actually, there is only one category that I hate to be put in. Especially in America we were asked a couple of times whether we were in the context of post- industrialism, which is a terrible term. I hate it. Especially the word "post" because all that implies is that you're always orientating back in that sense. It's not industrialism in the western world anymore, which is objectively true, but to label something post-industrialism just means that you don't know what's going on. It's the kind of thing, "We're after this and we don't know what's really happening now and we don't know what's going to be next". So that's definitely a term I won't have anything to do with.

Why is music the best way to achieve what you want?

M Chung: Well that boils down to whether we call it music or not. It's convenient in England to call it music because the music business is very well developed there. What we're looking for, of course, is distribution. We want to be available to anybody who wants to listen or look or whatever. Actually the term music has very much to do with the fact that we produce records, and with records, you obviously do music. Whereas live performances, where we might do a song completely differently can also be called theatre, performance or whatever.

Is it important for people to know about Einsturzende Neubauten?

M Chung: Of course, what a question! (laughs) I don't know. I mean important is one of my most hated terms as well. I've just tried to form a company called The Very Important Pudding Productions, which implies in a way, "What is important?" Relevant means, in a way, the same thing but it doesn't sound as if it is the same. So it is relevant for mankind to be innovative and to push developments and to get into new terrains in general. Whether mankind can develop without Einsturzende Neubauten is beyond what I know. For instance the 'Kollaps' record was planned to be the most unlistenable record we've ever done, which it didn't quite turn out to be — apparently. For people who are interested in the development of things like music or performances, it is good to know about us, yeah.

Would you consider what you do to be music?

M Chung: We do because we put it on records. That part of what we're working with, and the idea of expanding the term "music" is a good concept basically. It was a good concept by that time in any case, so that means everything is music.

Is everything music?

M Chung: Only the things that you can't hear are music.

AVB: The gaps are the music.

M Chung: I don't think music has anything to do with how far you organise it, it's a matter of perception or definition. Like the moment I start listening to a motorcycle and listening to the rhythm and the sound, it's music obviously. And if I don't listen to it and it drives past, it might be music for somebody else. So what is it? Anything that makes a sound, especially the things that don't make sounds, are music.

What doesn't make sounds?

M Chung: A Zen Buddhist probably, at certain stages of his life. They're great musicians! But we've chosen to define what we do, and even what we don't do, as music. We've had things like 'Sweat Song' that just consists of standing somewhere and sweating, which we've called music. So if you're asking me, "Is this music or is that?", I'm bound to say yes to everything at the moment. But we might change our attitude on the next record and say only what we're doing now is music and everything before wasn't.

Do you think your music will be remembered in thirty years by a broader public?

M Chung: Yeah, I think so, because it has quality and style.

More so than something high in the charts right now?

AVB: That's not honest, that's just a repeat of something that has been done before.

M Chung: I mean there are some classical music pieces that are repeats of other things that are still remembered. But of course nobody that does pop music will say, "Pop music is a throwaway product" — even though it is essentially true. It's designed to be consumed for a certain while and it's designed to be of a certain structure the next year. I don't think we fit into that category very much because ours is so difficult to consume. It's hard to throw away as well.

AVB: I'm really into honest things, being really honest. It's like religion. Say you read The Bible and you do that stuff and then you repeat something, that's it. But if you make your own religion and you make your own mythology, you then have something really honest because it comes right out of you. I don't think Wham! really have something to say, you know?

M Chung: Wham! is a nice statement... Wham! (laughs)

"Bad Boys Stick Together..."

M Chung: True, that's mythology actually. (laughs)

A lot of people regard your music as being destructive...

M Chung: We have that attribute put towards us mainly because of live performances in which we've obtained some sounds from destroying things, which we hardly do these days. I mean if we wanted to be destructive on record, we'd have to build in a hook or something to break off the needle or whatever, which we don't do... Not at the moment anyway.

AVB: A lot of it's just a state of mind. When they put me in jail, I tried to concentrate on relaxing things, but I wasn't really able to. All my thoughts were turning in circles and I was repeating the same thoughts all the time until I had a rhythm, a rhythm between sentences. I had things in my head that were not really necessary to think about. That happens when you stare at something too. You know that you have to concentrate, but you repeat things in your head that you see.

Do you reflect that idea in your music?

AVB: I really like to amplify things that are not there actually.

Are you interested in subliminals?

M Chung: We haven't really been putting things in consciously. I think we've never really explained what we're doing, so it's obvious that things have subconscious effects. For instance on this organic record, we never wrote onto it that this track is played on dead meat. But basically we assume that if somebody listens to a sound that is recorded from inside a piece of meat, that in some way, even if a person would go through it and say, "What is this, what is that?", it will have a different effect on him subconsciously than if it was played on a drum or whatever.

Do you consider the work of Neubauten to be aggressive?

M Chung: Some tracks, it differs really. Actually I think 'O.T.', for instance, is not a very aggressive record. I think of it now and I can only remember two tracks that are really aggressive, but apart from that I think it's quite romantic actually.

Do you ever include tracks from albums when you play live?

M Chung: We do kind of, I mean when we play live we sometimes use the same backing tracks. There's a song called 'Black' which was done in the studio by just switching off all the lights completely so that you're not able to find any instruments or anything, and we play live

by imagining things like that. So it may sound completely different than the same song by name.

What made you start using instruments which were in some ways non- conventional.

AVB: They sound good. Polystyrene, for example, has got a great sound but nobody ever thinks about that.

M Chung: We've had so many explanations for that. I think we had four models in the end. Socio political model — on the dole with no money for instruments. Or the innovative development of mankind model — I mean whatever you want. (laughs) I don't know, sickness of man, trying to be special, attract attention from our mummies. (laughs) Actually, that has been the only persistent thing really, that until now we've been interested in doing things that haven't been done before, at least not in that context or that way, but it doesn't necessarily apply anymore. I don't think we will be very concerned with that with the next record.

Do you think your music is accessible to the mainstream?

M Chung: What we sometimes think is that it will become more accessible less by calculation and more by just taking a look back. Because 'Kollaps', for instance, was not accessible to hardly anyone at that time. And it was apparently accessible two years later and there were loads of people listening to it. So apparently it's accessibility grew. And that might well happen with other things.

What do you attribute that growth towards accessibility to?

M Chung: Well that comes to, "Do we expect to change anything?" The mainstream try to define a kind of taste phenomena that naturally develops, and the problem of the music industry is that they don't know what direction that is! (laughs) But obviously there are changes in what is perceived as mainstream, and that is just a matter of numbers, records sold or things like that. I think that we do have a certain influence in which direction the mainstream will develop. Naturally if we have that, we are bound to move closer to what is called "mainstream".

As the accessibility of Neubauten grows more toward the mainstream, do you feel your motives for making music are changing as well?

Blixa: No, I think that the mainstream has changed since we began. The motives are just more subtle.

Are you still trying to expand people's conceptions of the word 'music'?

Blixa: I'm working more to expand my own idea about it, not changing other people's ideas. If I wanted to say something to people, I wouldn't be a musician. I would be a preacher... or Adolf. But I don't do it strictly for myself, I see myself as public property. So my experience is maybe useful for a lot of other people.

Do you feel that people have misinterpreted some of your work?

Blixa: I don't have any interpretation for what I'm doing, so anybody else's interpretation is the only interpretation of it. I don't know if their interpretation is right, but I think it is their right to interpret what I'm saying.

When did you write 'Halber Mensch'?

Blixa: The song is something I wrote between 1984 and 1985. I first wrote it in a shower in Amsterdam. I had a fever and had to cool my head and I was sitting under a shower for a very long time — a whole night. That was the start, and the second part of it was written in Lindenstrasse last year. So I was thinking about that story for a long time. It's kind of the Marmite effect. I concentrate things more and more, I boil them up, and in the end there is this really concentrated piece of thinking. But I'm happy with every word in it, and every word in that song is as heavy as lead. We've done a couple of versions of it until I did this one. And that's the one we're all happy with.

Lyrically can you cite a change between 'Drawings of O.T.' and 'Halber Mensch'?

Blixa: Yes, it's less esoteric, in the true sense of the word. Describing the connection between the listener and the one that wrote the song.

What was the reason for releasing a cover version of Lee Hazlewood and Nancy Sinatra's 'Sand'?

Blixa: Well, the cover version is a statement. We've never done any cover versions, but I don't think that's a very big change. A lot of people wouldn't even think we would be able to play a cover version. I think it was a very Neubauten-like cover version. When I heard the original song for the first time, I just thought, "This is it, this is the thing we can cover". I think it was a statement just to do that, something to put the balance back in the right position, and to say, "We're not just a metal drumming noise band, we're talking about something completely different". We're not talking about the way to do this music and we're not talking about just using secondhand instruments. We're talking about a certain emotional attitude.

Do you still get those remarks directed towards you about being 'metal bashers'?

Blixa: I don't know. I actually gave up reading everything. We just came back from Japan, and I can't compare Japan with any other place in the world where we've played. I see these fan letters we get from Japan and I see what they write, and I just forget about all those things that I've heard over and over again from all over Europe — "Are we metal banging or not metal banging", or whatever. I can forget about all these things because the Japanese have got a totally different idea about what we are and they don't have any of those ideas in their arguments anyway. And that's fine with me. It's not as if I want to put Japan in a certain position, but I just don't think they're as narrow-minded about it.

Do you feel that is because people in the West are much more exposed to new music coming out or...

Blixa: No. They are much more exposed to music in Japan than here. The information is really fluid. They have about ten times as many music papers there, and the best record shop I've ever seen was in Japan. They have everything there. It was going from Hans Eisler to Japanese original Kodo drumming or whatever.

Do you enjoy using real drums now?

Blixa: We don't have any real drums. Did they sound like real drums?

On 'Yu Gung', yeah.

Blixa: Well, that's something else, "It sounded like real drums!" (laughs) Tell all the companies that produce musical instruments that our plastic buckets sounded like real drums and that they should stomp the factory into the ground! (laughs) We don't need a real drum set. We used a real drum set in the beginning and we've used a real drum set after that, but we definitely didn't use one for 'Halber Mensch'. I know that the plastic buckets, in particular, sounded like a real drum set. 'Seele Brennt' sounds like real drums, but it's just plastic cannisters.

What percussion did you use for 'Yu Gung'?

Blixa: It was just a metal table that we'd stolen and a bass spring — one of our favourite instruments. It was part of an elevator.

Would you say that the majority of Neubauten listeners speak English?

Blixa: I don't know. I think quite a big part speaks Japanese. Japan is the second biggest record selling market in the world. We sell most of our records in Japan because they are like old allies of Germany. And we've got quite a few listeners in German speaking countries, Switzerland, Austria and The Netherlands. (Glancing down at an empty drink glass) Can I have another one?

(Looking at small amount of change in pocket) Well you can, but I'm broke.

Blixa: Oh, so am I.

I don't even have enough to go to the gig tonight.

Blixa: Do you want a ticket?

Yeah, if you have one.

Blixa: Yeah sure... Can I get one now?

Interviewer leaves... A bus goes by the window... Interviewer returns.

Blixa: What's that for?

A new driver.

Blixa: No, he's got a big steamboat sign on the front. It doesn't look like a steamboat to me, it looks like a double-decker red London bus. But it's a steamboat in the rivers of London, the Venice of the North. (laughs)

Do you feel there's any validity in the comment that Neubauten are still rooted in the past heritage — that heritage being rock music?

Blixa: No, it changes from year to year to me. All the even years I think that rock music is something bad, and all the uneven years I think rock music, in the true meaning of the word, is something good. Mufti is the rock I built my church on.

Can you explain the statement, "Conservative is revolutionary"?

Blixa: I have to think about that for a very long time to find out what I meant by that statement. (pause) This country, Great Britain, is very hungry for new tendencies all the time, because without them, the pop music business would drown in the rivers of London — where the double decker steam boats cross. And so they need new tendencies to keep all these workers employed. So conservative is revolutionary, not in the sense to keep workers employed, but just in the sense of the new tendencies that are declared revolutionary are not revolutionary. Like if you bang on metal or you bang on a restaurant table, it doesn't make any difference. As we've got an uneven year, that means that rock music is something good. Keeping the original ideas alive is revolutionary.

Do you feel that the music of Neubauten has a distinct Berlin flavour to it?

Blixa: What is it, paprika or what flavour?

Oregano, I think.

Blixa: Oregano as well. You know the English kitchen is not very spicy. I can say that to you. (another bus passes) Wow, it's full of steamboats in here. No, I don't think it has a distinct flavour, but some people think it has. Not to mention the Japanese again, but for them it tastes like Berlin. They take one bite and they've eaten all of East and West Berlin. I'm not the right person to ask about that because I've lived all of my life in Berlin. I can't judge it by the taste.

'Armenia' from 'Drawings of O.T.' has an orchestral quality to it. Was that a found piece of music or did Neubauten compose it?

Blixa: It was a found piece of music. It is an Armenian folk song. Armenia was a country — there is a part of the USSR which is called Armenian SSR. There is a part of it in Turkey and a part of it in Greece. They've got a very old culture and they've got a very old musical culture — they have the most beautiful music in the world, as much as I can say. They are not Turkish, they don't speak Turkish — they speak Armenian. We erased all the vocals — just took over the melodies, played on top of it and did some additional vocals in between. And the main idea was to translate, not the meaning of the words, but our emotional idea of it to Western culture. It's our favourite song on the record.

Who is O.T.?

Blixa: He's a schizophrenic guy that did drawings. He's still alive, he's Czechoslovakian or East Prussian or something like that. He did drawings and was in a mental hospital. I don't know him. I just know the book that has the same name — 'Drawings of O.T.'

How would you define sanity and insanity?

Blixa: I think insanity is a good viewpoint. Friedrich Nietzsche, a philosopher — unfortunately Adolf's favourite one, wrote about it and I basically agree with what he says.

What are your views of some of the other forms of expression?

Blixa: I don't separate them much really. At the moment I'm writing because I have to think about what I say in a way that other people write.

Do you think that most people view music as a valid form of art?

Blixa: I don't know. Or should I say... I don't care.

Do you have a personal definition of music?

Blixa: Yeah, I keep it as a secret. (laughs) One final day when they open up my testament you will find out.

Should everyone keep their definition as a secret?

Blixa: They should all keep my definition as a secret, yeah. (laughs)

How has 'Yu Gung' sold?

Blixa: We've sold about three times more records of that than we've sold of any other record. I think it's a good record, so if someone thinks it is popular or not popular or commercial, or if someone thinks we're selling out our ideals or whatever, I don't care. I mean 'Der Tod Ist Ein Dandy' is just like a version of Lou Reed's 'Metal Machine Music' with vocals. So if 'Metal Machine Music' suddenly becomes something that people listen to, I can't do anything about that. It always was one of my favourite records — the only thing that gets me out of bed!

SNAKE EYES STUNK
THE CONSTANTLY WRONG ROLL OF THE DIE
I WANNA GO WHERE NO WINDS BLOW AND ALL IS DEAF AND DUMB AND
QUIET AS HELL,
BUT THERE AIN'T NO DESERT BIG ENOUGH TO STRANGLE THESE
DESIRES.
SHE SAID, "THE NOOSE FIT LIKE A GLOVE KISS MY WET THROAT WITH
YOUR WARM FINGERS
GOODBYE".
NONE OF THIS SURVIVAL OF THE SHITTIEST.
WHOEVER SAID THE GOOD DIE YOUNG BETTER RE-CHECK THE FACTS,
JACK.
CHECK IT OUT, RIGHT, AND THEN COME BACK TO ME IN FIVE YEARS
TIME AND WE'LL START
KEEPING SCORE.
1984 TO NOTHING, JUST IN CASE YOU'RE COUNTING
SURE. SURE. SURE. THINGS GOTTA GET WORSE BEFORE THEY CAN GET
BETTER, BUT THIS IS
GETTING A LITTLE RIDICULOUS.
WE MUST BE STUCK IN AN ALL-TIME LOW. EBB TIDE EBB I'M
SCREAMING
SHITTING THE SHEETS IN DESPAIR.
IF I THREW MY ARMS UP TO THE HEAVENS THEY'D BE RETURNED
STOCK FULL OF FILTHY
SOCKS, UNPAID BILLS AND COFFEE GROUNDS. GREAT.

MATT JOHNSON

Matt Johnson first became involved with the music industry after he left school and worked in a recording studio in Soho. However, making cups of tea proved intolerable for Johnson, who spent the next two years unemployed. He subsequently advertised in the music papers for people with similar affections towards The Residents, Throbbing Gristle and The Velvet Underground, eventually forming The The in 1979. After releasing two singles, *Controversial Subject* and *Cold Spell Ahead*, and supporting Wire, Scritti Politti, DAF, This Heat and Cabaret Voltaire live, Johnson liquidated The The; under his own name he released *Burning Blue Soul* in 1981 — an album on which he played all the instruments and recorded for a mere eighteen hundred pounds.

Re-adopting the name The The, the East-end native signed to Some Bizzare and released the album *Soul Mining* through CBS in 1983. Work over the next three years culminated with the release of *Infected* in 1986, in which Johnson explores addiction, affliction and attrition — his view of the Western condition. In addition to The The, Johnson has also recorded with The Gadgets and Marc Almond in Marc And The Mambas.

How do you want people to see Matt Johnson?

MJ: I don't know really. As a serious musician in that I'm strong in my beliefs and sincere in the music that I do without being po-faced, because there is a lot of humour in my stuff too. I don't really think about it that much actually — those things which are important to distinguish me from the mass of music coming out. So much of it now is just the same. To see me as being quite innovative, and if not one step ahead, then one step sideways from everybody else. Just different from everybody else, because I've always thought of myself as different. I certainly don't want to be seen as an electronic wonder or anything, like a singer-songwriter, or a modern day folk singer dealing with fairly close to the heart questions. I just want to be seen as the first Matt Johnson, not the new anybody or the second anybody. I would just like the name The The to be synonymous with high quality and passion. That's as brief an idea as I can give because I've never really thought about it that much.

What would you define as the "rock business" game?

MJ: "Music business", "music biz", or "rock biz" immediately sums up commerciality to me. I suppose it's just a gimmick, a lot of back biting and a lot of dog eat dog. Surrounding yourself with the right people and the right producer, plagiarizing the moods of the moment and the ideas of the moment, using the most successful video-maker, and going with the most successful company with the most singles in the charts at the moment. It's quite nasty, it's quite an infested business really, but I suppose no more than something like the film business or any business where there's a lot of money involved.

From an A&R person's point of view, it seems like they enjoy the music biz more than the music itself, they like the whole coke sniffing kind of thing that goes on at gigs and the whole idea of being seen at the right place. But the game is totally disgusting really — and horrible. It's quite simple to play, but you have to be fairly good to play the game well. And I'm trying to play my own games within the limits of that game obviously. I'm trying to detach myself slightly from it but I've got to work with those people, so it's a question of doing it in a way which is the least harmful, I suppose — if that makes sense.

If CBS dropped you or you left CBS, do you feel that you could still play your game without a major company behind you?

MJ: I was thinking about this the other day funnily enough. What would happen if CBS dropped me? It would shock me a great deal, because I know I'm fairly highly regarded there anyway and I do pay for myself — so that's no problem. No, I don't think I'd have any problem getting another deal actually, I'd just make it more clarified and sharpen everything else, and I'm starting to do that anyway. Like my brother does all my illustrations and we're going to start doing some video things together. He's becoming more involved and I'm developing a visual side of things anyway. I've never really done anything I didn't want to do apart from go to school. Again, it comes down to having enough confidence in yourself and self-belief, just gambling everything, and knowing in yourself that you're right in what you're doing. Doubts decay the empty mind, but they're quickly dismissed by a strong foundation of optimism which defeats any kind of negativism or any doubts. That's basically what it is.

Why do some people allow themselves to be prostituted?

MJ: Some people are weaker basically. Like at school, some people get bullied, don't they? Same thing. So all the way through life, there are comparisons to be drawn with every level or strata of life. In every area, there are always the weak personalities.

Do you feel that your product fits in with the image that a person on the street might have of Some Bizzare?

MJ: Well, to be quite honest with you, I don't know what image a person on the street has of Some Bizzare, I mean, are Some Bizzare well known on the street? Soft Cell were known, but Some Bizzare, I guess it's a real cult thing, isn't it? With the family of Some Bizzare, I'm a bit of a black sheep anyway. I've always felt to be the black sheep of the family so to speak anyway, lots of people have always said that, and I think that's good in a way, I feel good about that, I'd rather be the black sheep. Even with my own family I've felt the black sheep. I like being the black sheep. It's just a feeling, it's difficult to put into words. But I've always felt slightly detached and in my own little world. I live in a little dream world most of the time, and I feel quite detached and cocooned from things. And I've always been like that, always the one to just wander off by myself. Our family used to go out to the seaside, and I'd be the one that used to run off and hide and didn't want to go out and stuff like that. I've always felt that, I think that's good.

How do you feel that your music inspires people?

MJ: I've always felt that music is important on a personal level as a great motivator. I've got about a dozen albums at home that I've listened to for about five years, and if I put them on in a certain mood, they just make me feel really good and make me do things. I can hear a line off them which will suggest things to me, or the music will. It's like food for the soul in a way, and hopefully, my music does the same thing for other people — it implants something, so I think my music is very important. I think eating the right food is important and listening to the right music is important. What a quote for you! "Only buy The The, no artificial additives or sweeteners!"

Oh, I'm starting a magazine, 'Bugle Boy'. A The The information service magazine. What I want to do is have articles written by other people in it and stuff like that. Not pictures of me everywhere, but information on what I'm doing. But I also want to include information on other people, and make it A5 size — a little booklet. A really good quality magazine with artists and video makers contributing to it. I think it could be quite good.

It's a good idea, but I laughed because you said before that you cut off all your hair to look like Jimi Sommerville from The Communards and then I thought 'Bugle Boy' for the name of a magazine was a little over the top.

MJ: Oh my God! Small Town Bugle Boy. I only got a little bugle. Yeah, that's a point, you fuckin'...

Did you say, "Conform to deform"?

MJ: No, that was Stevo. Foetus' answer to that was, "Bollocks, deform to deform", which I thought was really good. (laughs)

Do you think that it's necessary to 'play the game' in order to get a large audience, or is it possible to do what you want all the way through, like Foetus for instance, and still get that audience?

MJ: He's doing what he wants to all the way through — he's starving too, by the way, but he doesn't care. I'm doing what I want to do as well, but I'm not starving, so there's a difference. It depends really on how accessible you are. My stuff is more accessible than his at the moment, but I think Foetus is very accessible actually. I must admit, I think he should be massive, he should be the new Elvis Presley, the white Michael Jackson. He could — he's got the looks for it, and he's got the talent for it. I mean, a phenomenon — he could be massive.

Is 'Giant' being remixed?

MJ: Apparently... Yeah.

Who is that being done by?

MJ: Arthur Baker.

Are you excited by that?

MJ: Not really. Well, kind of, but I'd wish he'd get a move on because when I was over there, he just couldn't get it together. And I went up to his studio a couple of times and just messed about a little. He was listening to the multi-track and suggested a few things, but he just hasn't done it. So I wish he'd get on and do it basically. If he does it, great, but if he don't, then...

Get Jim to re-mix it.

MJ: Well I'm going to be working with Jim. In actual fact, yeah, that... what a good idea. Yeah, I'll do that. Yeah, he'd do it better probably. Good idea. I'm gonna tell Stevo that tonight. Tell Arthur Baker to stuff it up his arse. Yeah, good idea! Foetus could re-mix it. What a bit of inspiration... your round as well.

With 'Red Cinders In The Sand' and 'Cold Spell Ahead' you move into an entirely different song halfway through without pause, yet you keep the same title. Why is that?

MJ: Wait until you hear what I'm doing with my new drum machine, fuckin' hell! The reason 'Red Cinders In The Sand' did that was because I recorded a track with that guitar break which is in it, and I thought, "Fuck, I don't like this song really". So I started to record another song, which was 'Red Cinders In The Sand'. Then I forgot to erase a couple tracks, and I listened to them with those guitar things, and I thought, "Fuck, that sounds good". So I started pressing the buttons in and out, I mean this was 1981. I was doing all this hip-hop stuff at the board (laughs) and I thought, "This sounds really good". It was purely by accident, which is how a lot of good things come out. They're just happy accidents really.

On 'Cold Spell Ahead', I had two time sequences. There was the 'Uncertain Smile' one, and there was also the one which was the 'Touch Of Experience', but they were different time sequences. They went so well together, but the only way that they could possibly be together was by having a tempo change — and the amount of problems we had! Because the time that I did that was 1981 as well, and rhythm machines were very primitive. I mean, I've been using rhythm machines now since 1977 which is a long time. In fact, when I went to get the drum emulator, the kid that I got it off was... (laughs) I said, "Can I have a demonstration of the drum emulator?". And he went, "Well, as you can see, it has all the things..." you know, being really cocky. And I thought, I didn't say it, I thought I should say to him, "I was using one of these drum emulators when you were still in nappies mate, don't give me that!" So I said to him, "How do you do the old so and so on that?" — because I knew that he wouldn't know. And he just went all red going, "Oh, I don't know, oh, oh," and he started cursing the machine because he didn't know how to use it. (laughs) Anyway, with the one that I first started using, we had to have the help of some guy. I would go "... Now!", and then it would sort of switch over to get the tempo change. It was very primitively done. I had to do that because the two chord sequences went very well together, but they were in different time signatures and measures.

Do you feel that you're trying to change music in any way?

MJ: I think that Test Dept. and Einsturzende Neubauten are doing more to change music than I am quite frankly, because I work within fairly standard formats. Like a half to two thirds of my stuff is songs, and the rest is often quite innovative and experimental. So in a way, I'm not trying as hard as I should be. I started to realise that I'm being a bit too straight in a lot of my things. And it becomes very easy and comfortable to write a song instead of taxing yourself to think of different ways to do things. So I'm not making a massive contribution at the moment, but I think I have made a contribution because I hear lots of my ideas popping up in other people's records. Obviously some of them are getting through to younger bands and stuff. But that is in a fairly negative way — they're just copying. But I applaud what Test Dept. and Neubauten are doing. I admire them because they're pushing against the perimeters really — "What is music and sound?", and stuff like that.

Both groups are very sincere and love what they're doing, they do it with passion and they do it brilliantly. Now I couldn't do that, so it has got to come from me. I've got to push down and do what is right as far as I'm concerned. I think I could do it by just sounds, just song structure, just lyrical content and vocal style. So many things I can really expand and push the perimeters in, and Test Dept. and Neubauten are doing it in other ways. But for me to just say, "I'm going to do something totally unorthodox just for the sake of it" is fuckin' cheap and dishonest and I wouldn't do that. I suppose with more experience, you develop a higher filter system with which you quickly work out what would be effective and what wouldn't be effective in certain songs or situations, or to certain lyrics which you're going to apply music to. But I'm probably doing about a quarter of what I could achieve at the moment. The amount of effort that I put into it is about twenty five percent, and I've got to learn to put one hundred percent into everything I do, in all areas of my life.

What's holding you back?

MJ: Laziness really. I've been expecting too much, thinking I had a divine right to do things that I didn't. You've got to work at things. It's not good enough just to be good. You've got to work. In fact, there's a lesson to be learned from Martina Navratilova and John McEnroe, the effort they put in and that determination. They are the number ones in the world, but they're still not satisfied with what they're doing. They've got to be better and better. And I find that really inspiring. They're always striving for perfection. People should learn a lesson from sporting champions and give one hundred percent in everything they do.

But I'm fascinated by music, I love music, I've had a lifelong love affair with music. That is why it is still my hobby really, as well as my work. And I hope that it continues. The music business can make you go sour, I just hope it doesn't ruin it as a hobby for me. I love listening to it; I love analysing how it works and I love writing it. I think it's great.

('Two Tribes' by Frankie Goes To Hollywood begins on the jukebox) That really irritates me, that "Ow, ow, ow". If he didn't do it on every song it would be OK. But it seems to slip out. Probably when he's on the toilet, he goes "Ow, ow, ow," (laughs). Actually, I think that Frankie Goes To Hollywood breathed a bit of fresh air into the charts. Frankly, I'd rather have Frankie at number one than Spandau Ballet, Duran Duran, A-Ha, or whoever else, because there's a little bit of aggression in their imagery, and they're quite stylish. Musically, they're more interesting as well. It's a lesson to be learned — the way that they've gone about the whole thing.

Do you feel that it's important to have knowledge of the record industry, or are you embarrassed by that?

MJ: I think it's very useful, in fact, even now I still read as much as I can about it. Because basically, music is my craft, and manipulating the music business should be an extension of

what I'm doing. There's so much stuff out there that you've got to have a better knowledge of, so I try to amass and absorb as much information as possible. I don't think you can ever know too much or should ever be embarrassed by knowledge. Every bit of knowledge is useful in some way or another. I'm still learning about it really. But ah... your round. (Grabs paper with notes on it). Interviewers never like you reading their questions...

I don't care.

MJ: (laughs) Fuck you! (Reads) "Why Some Bizzare?" Because I'm a social outcast. Some Bizzare is a home for social lepers — emotionally constipated people looking for a spiritual laxative. I fit in because I suppose, well, I don't know. They say, "The eye never sees itself".

Who says that?

MJ: Thomas Beckett. No, I don't know who it was, but it was a quote and it was in one of my songs actually. I used it, the eye never sees itself except when it looks in the mirror. Can you imagine that, your eye. I am fascinated by eyes, I think they're great.

I'm sure they mean the "I" that's you.

MJ: No, the eye (points to his eye) never sees itself, because you can't see your eye, can you? Unless you look in a mirror. That's what it means, you can see every other part of your body. And your forehead, you can't see your forehead.

You can.

MJ: No, the eye never... Yeah, I know, but ah, it's like... Ask me a question, you go off and I'll answer it.

Alright. Why is it that the person being interviewed wants to read the questions which are to be asked of him before they are asked?

MJ: And you're going to the bog while I answer it. OK, go on then so you can't hear my answer. (Pauses, interviewer leaves). Well, basically it's because people like me, and other musicians, we get asked so many questions all the time — like these ones I'm holding up at the moment. "Why make a record?" I mean, do me a favour. I mean look, it says, "Why make a record?" I mean what idiot would ask a question like that? "Radio airplay, is it important?", I mean, "Why Some Bizzare?", I mean, do me a favour. We just like to check our questions before we get asked them because you never know what you might get asked. Also, you might get asked some rude questions which, of course, being the professional that I am, I'm not able to answer. Anyway I think that sums up this question, and I hope you've got my soda water and I hope it's bloody cold. (Interviewer returns)... And your questions aren't too bad, I suppose.

Do you feel that your music is direct enough to change something?

MJ: My music tends to be quite pleasant, plays on the emotions and inspires an emotional response. When Throbbing Gristle did it, for instance, it was physical. That is the major difference. In fact, when I met Leonard Cohen, name dropping here, but me and Leonard, well me and Foetus met him actually — we went to dinner with him. And Leonard Cohen was talking about the equal strength between soft and hard. Soft is just as strong as hard, hard being something abrasive like Throbbing Gristle, but soft being something that was more mellow initially, but has the power to move you from the inside. So there's equal strength, it just depends where you lie in the spectrum. I think for me to go and do very abrasive things would be hypocritical and dishonest because it's not what I want to do and I don't feel I need to do that. But I think I can reach people. A thirty year old American would probably respond more to me than he would to Spandau Ballet. I would appeal to a more loyal following and a more long term following than Spandau ever would.

But why do Spandau Ballet and Duran Duran go to number one?

MJ: Why does The Sun newspaper sell more than The Guardian newspaper? That's a circular argument, how can I answer that? I don't know, it's the lowest common denominator. I think that people's intelligence is insulted from a very early age basically. From radios and the media they're given a very low standard and may form quite a low opinion of themselves. I also think with the way Western society works, people don't link into their psychic capabilities and to their intuition. They just work on a very material level, both in news and music. They're not allowed to develop their depth. People en masse seem one dimensional.

Children are very perceptive, but through the schooling process it is beaten out of them. And so people are just conditioned to buy and accept this low quality product to perpetuate the manufacturers. It's very economic and commercial — an extension of commercialism really. The problem lies with the education system more than anything else, in that intuition and the appreciation of good things of any beauty is beaten out of people. The people don't necessarily have a low opinion of themselves, but they're totally unaware of their capabilities. And to say the The Sun sells more is the most obvious analogy between those two, isn't it? The education system should be greatly revised, the teachers should be taught more, and there should be more development of the senses. It's taken for granted that you've got other senses and intuitions and things like that. I know they exist, beyond any doubt, but very few people do — and people are just belittled and shrunken down to be manageable by governments. It gets down to being a very paranoid conversation about authority and stuff, but I don't know if that's true. I don't know whether Mrs Thatcher is aware of the way things have developed. There's just too much ignorance. But everything should be considered multi-dimensional instead of one dimensional. What I'm trying to do with my music is make it multi-dimensional with different layers of sounds, and make my voice up front so it's like a head talking to you with certain things coming around behind you and emphasizing certain things. Putting certain emotional accents on certain things and certain lines to reciprocate a response.

Would you say it was more to illustrate the mood?

MJ: Yeah, I'm giving the mood, and whether the person receives it or not is up to the person who is listening to it. I just put everything into it, and sooner or later, I think people will. "You can lead a horse to water, but a pencil must be lead". I think Stan Laurel said that.

Can you see a move away from Some Bizzare?

MJ: Yeah. I'd like it to be very agreeable, I wouldn't like to see lawsuits or anything like that 'cause I think that friendships, relationships, marriages and business deals run in circles. People are only together so long and then grow away from each other. It's just naive to think that you're going to forge a life long alliance. I mean, how can you fucking align yourself, or form an allegiance which is life long? You might be growing very quickly and you might just grow out of somebody, or vice versa. You can't do that. People have to be aware of their own individuality, their own independence. I'm just going to have a piss actually, I'll carry on with this.

(pause... returning from the toilet) Some Bizzare, or Stevo in particular obviously, have been very instrumental to where I am now. He had real faith in me when other people didn't. He took me to the record companies when everyone else was turning me down. So I'll never forget that. But it would be silly and naive to think that I'm going to be on the label forever, because The The, my own identity, is as strong as Some Bizzare.

Going on to the thing about marriage, I disagree with the establishment of marriage, and I think it's stupid to think that you're going to be with somebody that long, because it means that you're probably having to contain certain aspects of your personality which otherwise would develop. You're having to contain them or compromise. Compromise doesn't necessarily need to be a bad thing. Caring for others and giving to others is a good thing, but I think people should develop their independence — as far as looking after themselves. People now are becoming more independently minded, like males are, but so many men can't cook, can't look after themselves, can't clean the fucking place they live in — and that's really bad. If people are married, or living together, it should be where you both are independent people, you can totally look after yourselves, but you're just coming together making life easier for each other and taking a turn in doing things. I mean, I do the housework. I love hoovering... Well I don't, but I quite enjoy it.

How would you use your intuition...

MJ: In the studio? I just used it. I knew you were going to say studio.

That's because you've seen it written down. Or live?

MJ: Live. I'll answer that first. Live, I find I'm either very meek, mild and shy — or very aggressive. I have to learn to get the balance so I can learn the projection and the dynamics in performance. I do feed from the audience, but I haven't had that much experience. I'm still quite overcome by nerves, and it manifests itself in either being overly aggressive or overly shy. Either like, "Oh my God!", or, "You bastards!" So as far as intuition goes live, I'm not confident enough yet to start feeding on that because I'm too overcome by nerves, it just blocks out the intuition.

In the studio I use a lot of intuition and instincts, just spontaneity. I'm also one for believing every disappointment is for a good reason, i.e. if something goes wrong, or somebody that I want to work with is not available at that time, I think it's obviously meant to be. I put an optimistic attitude on it, and by doing that, things fall into place. A lot of the time, just having the belief in your own intuitions and instincts, as well as yourself, helps things to fall into some order. That's not to say that it makes things all roses, because you get doubts and anxieties and they're also very real, but it makes things more interesting. It gives you a bit of a superiority complex in a way, which is bad obviously, but you feel that you know something that other people don't. You realise the amount of potential that exists there. You just feel things, and I feel very strongly about atmospheres. Sometimes I'm overcome by them actually, I might just see one thing, even a photograph, a scene out of a film, a smell, a piece of music, or a particular light, and it will bring something back to me so strongly that I'm... like on a drug or something — which is really weird. But I use instinct and intuition above intellect in my work because I'm not an intellectual. I'd like to become more intelligent and more articulate, but not to the detriment of my instinct.

I think you've got to get the balance. I mean, I don't know how to read and write music. Originally, it was because it was too hard. I now know that if I applied myself for a couple of months I could do it, but I don't want to because I think that would make it a bit more sterile in a way, that would sterilise what I do. What I do is not based on what you can or can't do, or what an augmented ninth or whatever is. Obviously that's how music started anyway — people like cavemen banging and blowing and making noises. So why should music be shrouded in these laws of what you can or can't do? I think you can do whatever you fucking want to do, whether it be what Neubauten do or whether it be what I'm doing. What I'm doing isn't governed by laws. It's governed by how I feel, what I want to do, chance, and keeping the balance. It's critical to have the balance. Contrast, a very important thing in the stuff that I do, in my own life anyway. Because without the white, you can't appreciate the black.

I think the Velvet Underground summed that balance up.

MJ: That's why I love The Velvets, because of that contrast. You get something like 'Heroin' next to 'Candy Says'. And it's important to have that. To appreciate one you have to have the other. One of the philosophies of my work is to have that contrast and that diversity. I think that's very important.

Do you look at The The as being Matt Johnson?

MJ: Not really. I like to maintain my own identity outside of that, which is why I never wanted to use my solo name because that would mean it would take over your whole life really. For me, I try to develop a personality or life outside of that, because The The is a limited company now. So I see The The as being separate from Matt Johnson, most definitely. And the concept is developing all the time, everything fits into place nicely. I'm a great believer in destiny really, I believe there is a strong invisible beam throughout your life, but you can stray off that. And I've strayed off it a few times, and when you do, you go through extreme inner turbulence where you know something isn't right. You get a disquieting feeling inside that you're straying off your tracks, and you feel something is not right. And then you move back on them and you feel at peace within yourself. I do believe in invisible currents and invisible forces without any doubt at all. I know it, because so many things have happened. When I was about thirteen or fourteen, I used to say to people, "Wow, isn't it strange", and they'd go, "Huh?" But now I don't even bother 'cause I accept it. With other people that I know, it's like an unsaid thing, and maybe it should be more widely said because the potential is there for everybody.

MARC ALMOND
DAVE BALL

Despite the initial success of 1981's *Tainted Love*, Marc Almond has rarely been liked within the music industry. Even though his records and those of his previous group Soft Cell have sold exceedingly well, he has always tried to maintain his identity without succumbing to their marketing pressures. Record companies have repeatedly advised him against working on separate projects, but Almond has always followed his own instincts and personally decided on his own progression. Bearing in mind that Soft Cell sold millions of records and had numerous hit singles in England, pressures to retain an established formula for continued success always threatened.

In addition to Almond's work with Soft Cell, he also formed Marc And The Mambas, whose music was more heavily emotional and extended Almond's musical range to include strings. Almond has also played with fellow business provocateurs Lydia Lunch, Nick Cave and Clint Ruin as The Immaculate Consumptive. In 1984, Almond formed a new band and maintained allegiance with Some Bizzare, with whom he has always worked, while also taking part in *Violent Silence*, celebrating the writings of Georges Bataille. 1985 saw Almond return to Top of the Pops in his collaboration with Bronski Beat, followed by the signing of a lucrative deal with Virgin and chart success in his own right. During 1986 Almond performed in a three piece ensemble, headlining the Soho Jazz Festival, and also recorded further material released by Virgin. His perseverance and drive has earned him many trusting followers collectively known as Gutter Hearts. What they get in return is an emotional understanding in the form of Almond's music — an honest expression without ultimately pandering to them.

Dave Ball first met Marc Almond at Leeds Polytechnic in 1979. The two shared a love of Northern soul and began recording together. While Almond had the knack of sounding in and out of tune simultaneously, Ball had the skills to programme drum machines and play a wide variety of instruments. Capturing the interest of DJ Stevo who was compiling a chart in Sounds, they recorded a track for the *Some Bizzare Album*, which eventually led them to a contract with Phonogram through Some Bizzare. Their songs often contained sexually ambiguous overtones and sleazy imagery, reinforced by Almond's camp behaviour. Soft Cell soon had a string of top ten singles.

However, they also fought the 'pop' system; Almond worked with industry no go's Psychic TV, while Ball spent time with Cabaret Voltaire and Clock DVA. The album covers of Soft Cell progressively reflected their rejection of themselves as selling points, with their first album showing them in full form, *The Art of Falling Apart* partially masked, and the total absence of a photograph on their final album. Soft Cell played their last gig in January 1984, leaving Ball and Almond free to concentrate on other endeavours. Publicly the chatty and visible Almond remained in the limelight, while Ball quietly took a seat in the shadows. Ball's solo album *In Strict Tempo* matched his own gift for rhythms with the talents of Gavin Friday, Genesis P-Orridge and Virginia Astley to produce a compelling, yet neglected study. More recently, Ball has produced The Virgin Prunes.

How did you feel Soft Cell differed from a mainstream pop band that might be featured in Smash Hits, or did you ever view yourselves that way?

DB: I think with any group, you can never believe the promotion and marketing. A record company is interested in selling records, they're not really bothered about how you see yourselves, they're just bothered about exploiting what they've got to the maximum potential. We sort of thought of ourselves as working in the pop area, but tried to do something different with it. I mean we did a few things that were, I suppose, considered a bit "outrageous" and "naughty" at the time, but it's very difficult to really make any changes. Like if you've moved an inch, you've done a lot. I don't think anybody really believes their own marketing and advertising, and if you do you're a fool. Maybe there are a few people that believe it, but that was one of the things that used to really upset us. It was a conflict between us; whether we wanted to be completely sold and marketed or still retain our artistic ideals. I mean it's very difficult to do. I don't think we did it successfully but I think we made a good attempt.

Do you think you could have done it without Some Bizzare?

DB: I think when Some Bizzare started it was a new thing and Soft Cell was a new thing, and I think we helped each other. I don't think Some Bizarre would have made what it is without Soft Cell and vice versa. It was an exciting time because it was like an independent label but it wasn't. It was like having independent control but using the power of a major, which was quite new at the time. Before then, all you had was independent or major labels with nothing in between. I mean Factory and Rough Trade were becoming more like majors, but you didn't actually have an independent controlling a major, although we probably didn't have as much control as we liked to believe.

Do you feel real change can come through music?

DB: I think if you want to change things, then become a politician or a terrorist. That is real change. You don't change people's lives by releasing a record. You might get them interested in different things, but that's the most you can hope for really. If they hear you doing a song that has something in it that they think about, say some of the words mention a particular subject, it may make some people go and read about it, but that's all. People have to teach themselves. I've never really learned anything from a pop record. All that pop records do is catch a feeling that you want to have or just echo something that you've done. It's all second hand information and second hand experience. It has been neutralised, it has been turned into a product.

Is that what started happening to Soft Cell in any way?

DB: I think that it happened at the beginning and we gradually tried to fight it. When we started off, we didn't know a thing about the industry, and we just had all these catchy tunes and sort of "naughty songs" and did them. And then we started thinking about it, and the second album was a bit more serious. And the last album was very serious, compared to the first, it wasn't just a pop record. I mean, just the titles went from 'Non Stop Erotic Cabaret' to 'The Art Of Falling Apart', which was in between, and then 'This Last Night In Sodom' went to the other extreme. Usually, people start off being extreme and then evolve into a pop band. We did it the other way round, probably because we got it forced on us so much in the early days. It was a runaway success that no-one was ready for, no-one expected. We were just like, "What hit us?"

Is there a current theme that runs through 'In Strict Tempo'?

DB: That album really isn't an album in the sense of a finished concept, it's really more like a scrapbook of ideas, and I almost felt that it was overplayed. When it came out, there was too much expected of it. The record company thought it was going to be a big thing, and I didn't do it as that. It's just bits and pieces of ideas. I put them together and I thought it was quite interesting, but it wasn't like a major thing. And a lot of people took it the wrong way, they took it too seriously. But then again, you can't justify why you're doing something. I suppose it's self-indulgence in a way. I mean it got terrible reviews because I think people looked at it in the way that they normally look at a finished album, I don't think they knew what to make of it. The only themes running through that album are just various ideas, approaches and juxtapositions. That was what I was interested in when I did it.

Do you feel that some of your music, for instance 'American Stories' — where you were using tapes rather than the voice, lacks soul?

DB: That part of the album was really about lack of soul. It was about that particular aspect of America — commercialism. Do you notice what the tapes are saying? One of the tapes is an advert for a brothel in New York that I took from cable television and it's saying, "Everyone, everyone can be a playboy, come up to The Pleasure Palace", or whatever it's called. And also there's a tape which is an interview with Charles Manson playing at the same time. It was the conflict of, "Everyone can be a playboy and everyone can do this", and having Manson going on with this American TV music that's getting all distorted. But because they're on telly they both have the same importance.

It's the same with newspapers, but it's not as exaggerated. It happens so many times. I remember in The Sun, the top half of the page was about the Yorkshire Ripper, with a photograph of him and a photograph of a dead girl, but the bottom half of the page was an advert for carving knives. It was totally tasteless. Another one I saw the other day was about this sex fiend that's on the loose, The Fox or something, and it was going on about that, and the page opposite was the Page Three Girl. It's a real conflict, I suppose it just confused me, but it really intrigues me, the way that everything is reduced to one level.

Have you found that your musical experiments have been working?

DB: I've got some details and some information about frequencies and levels, and that's really what it's about. There's this New York company that installed these little black boxes into supermarkets saying, "Do not steal", or, "I will not steal." They reckon when they install those, the shoplifting goes down by about seventy percent — and yet you can't actually hear it consciously. And Gen told me something interesting too. The CIA, I think it is, have their suits impregnated with a particular scent that an animal produces when it's afraid, and it has that effect on people. Like, when a CIA person comes near you, you're frightened, and you don't know why. It's because the suit is actually impregnated with this musk.

I'm sure that Michael Jackson's albums have got subliminals on them. I'm convinced about that. Have you listened to those albums on headphones? A lot of the grunts and groans are very sexual, but just the frequencies; there is something in the sounds that you actually can't decipher. When I was doing the soundtrack for the film 'Decoder' with Gen, we were doing some experiments with muzak tapes, which we shouldn't have had but we got hold of, and we analysed them on a spectrum analyzer and the levels all stayed the same — just straight. With normal background music, the LEDs were just going up and down. Muzak is just straight across, it didn't move. Basically it's just totally compressed because it's music put together by scientists.

Do you feel there is a function in your music besides entertainment?

DB: I like it to be entertaining, but I suppose there's a function in terms of approach. It's very difficult to say that it actually has a function and purpose, it's very difficult to justify. I suppose it's just a view of the world. I can never answer questions like that honestly, because I don't really know the answer. I don't really think that music affects people's lives, except that it's an art form I suppose, that's all it really is. I can't really say more than that. You've got me there.

———

How would you define 'pop' music?

Marc: I wouldn't define pop music. I don't really know anything about it and I don't wish to. It's something that defies defining, and I wouldn't dare. I'm not qualified.

Do you think that most people look at you as operating within the field of 'pop' music?

Marc: I think they probably do. People probably look at me and see me operating in the field of pop, but I'm not there to argue with them. I let other people put up the barriers by giving them names and titles. I'm not interested in putting up those barriers by myself. People can give me whatever pigeonhole they want to if it makes them happy, but I'm not likely to agree with them.

The word that it makes me think of, when I think of pop records and pop stars, is something that is utterly disposable and valueless. And it really is, it's so trivial and valueless, and meaningless. I like to set my aims a little deeper than that. I can't really do what is called good 'pop' because I don't get my records played on the radio all the time, I don't fit in, so, you know...

How do you view performance art?

Marc: Performance art I always knew as moving sculptures and moving forms using the human body. Using living three dimensions as it were, the living, breathing, talking, whatever. And even when I did at one time what some called performance art, to me it was never really performance art, it was more like little cabarets or dialogues. Again it's something that I don't really know anything about. I'm not qualified. (laughs)

I always thought you were involved in performance art in Leeds.

Marc: People called it performance art but it wasn't really what the experts on performance art would call performance art. I was up in Leeds for three years doing a very free fine arts course which let me do whatever I wanted within the framework of that course. It threw me into a pit and told me to survive, and it didn't give me any guidelines, it just gave me the facilities and a home for three years and said, "Right find yourself, do what you want, find what you want to do and who you are" — and so it was sink or swim. I was determined to swim, and swim I did.

I was never very good at painting, and I tried all sorts of things, I mean I said that you've got to try everything, that has always been my motto, I'll try whatever there is to try. I tried painting, I tried sculpture, I tried all these things just to put myself to the test as it were. But I felt others could do a far better job at it than I. I felt the main things that I had to use were myself, my body, my voice, whatever. So I decided to use my actual person as a catalyst for these things. I looked at it as being my living diary, little cabarets more than anything else. Entertainment has always been important to me as well as education, the two go hand in hand for me. I take my inspiration from people who are pure entertainers and from people who aim to educate.

What are some of your opinions on the record industry?

Marc: I think it's basically a cesspit. It has built itself up to this huge great thing of importance that it doesn't really deserve to have and shouldn't have at all. A lot of very unimportant people doing very unimportant things, like making hit records and trying to formulate hit records. It's a business and my mind goes blank when I'm confronted with things like business. Creating things is what I'm interested in, creativity and destruction both hand in hand. But the record industry is basically something that is sinking, just crawling up its own arsehole into oblivion...

It seems to be getting stronger in some ways though.

Marc: It's getting stronger in some ways, but the foundations are getting weaker and weaker. I mean, I hate the way that it has reached new heights of sickness, when groups release five, six, seven, eight mixes of one song, release the same song in seven or eight different covers to exploit their fans into buying each one of those records because they've got a different cover of their favourite pin-up. And they basically buy the same thing five times over. I know they say, "Oh well, we're not doing it intentionally, people don't have to buy all those mixes", but they know fans, they know how fans love to collect everything by their idols. It becomes sick when these are the games that you have to play to compete in this world of current pop music.

Do you find that you play any of those games?

Marc: I try very hard not to and I don't think I do really. People have tried to make me play those games and I've lost out because of it. I get dismissed by radios. I get treated like an idiot within the record industry because I will not succumb to these games, I will not play to them. They think I'm a fool for not doing that. I feel that I don't want to exploit the people that like me and the people that are interested in what I have to say. It's ridiculous, I don't need to do that.

Have you found that you've lost any of your passion for making music after gaining an understanding of the record industry?

Marc: No, I've always kept very tightly to my roots and I never felt that I should act like people in the business would like me to act — like a 'pop star' or have that attitude. I've always kept very much to the realistic side of things. I don't have any value for things like money. Money to me is a disease — often terminal if you take it too seriously and it starts to become the meaning of your life. Things like that don't mean anything to me at all. What money has meant to me is that I've been able to travel more and explore more. And it has opened a lot of doors for me, but it's meaningless really. If I didn't have those doors open, I'd find something else. I would never be stopped, I wouldn't let money be my answer to anything really.

The people I've mixed with have always been the same friends that I had before I had success and the same friends that I'll always have. I never see any glory in sitting by a swimming pool reflecting on how successful you've become. Successful people are very boring usually. I've just tried very hard to always be myself and to always go for the things that I believe in, the things that I enjoy and the things that I love. And that has created a lot of conflicts in me over the past few years because it's very difficult in this business to do that, to hang on to what you really are and to your roots. People want you to be something else and they try to steer you into being something else — and they insult you if you're not. It's more difficult to hang on to yourself really, but you've got to be very strong and do it. You've always got to hold on to your self-respect. In the end, that's all you'll have left.

How autobiographical was 'Fun City'?

Marc: I write a lot of songs about other people or about characters that I know or that I've met or watched, so I always think everything is a little bit autobiographical. Something like 'Fun City', for example, is almost directly autobiographical. It's like when I first left college and first came down to London, I had no money so the only way that I could do it was by selling myself! (laughs) I did it to get behind the doors in various circles as well.

'Bedsitter' was also a very autobiographical song. It was written when I was living in that situation and watching all my friends living this daytime and night-time existence and looking for glamour in the squalor if you like. That has always been a thing that has run through a lot of my songs and lyrics, this glamour and squalor, this glitter and grime. The two hand in hand, heavily seeped in a lot of romance. Everything that I do is very romantic because I'm quite a romantic person. I see a real romance in grime and filth and that sort of thing.

Is it possible for that to happen?

Marc: As long as you realise it's a real side. I can see the very real and the very hard side, often the very sad side, and I can see another side as well, a very romantic side, like the romance of the streets. Someone like Borel, for example, is very romantic. He wrote about very gritty things and very real things and painted very gritty pictures, but they were very heavily seeped in romance as well. And it's similar with someone like Genet as well. It's this real filth as beauty, or beauty as filth, filth and beauty side by side.

What does success mean to you?

Marc: There are different levels of success. I mean what is success? One level of success is where somebody gets a number one hit record; another level of success is when you feel it's great that three hundred people will stand in a hall and listen to your songs. That to me is success. I've not actually reached my point of perfection yet and I never want to. I always like the imperfections. When I've recorded an album I always think, "I'll listen to that album in a few months time and I'll find a lot of things wrong with it, or things that I could have done better", and that's what I like. I never want to reach that pinnacle. It's the experiences that are the most important, not whether you get a hit record or a slap on the back. The different experiences of learning, of developing as a creative artist, in my singing, writing, songwriting or whatever I have to do.

Why does sleaze interest you?

Marc: People talk about this interest in sleaze, but what interests me is the loner, the loser, the misfit, the survivor and the underdog of society. What goes on behind the door, what goes on deep in somebody's heart. Sleaze is just a very small part of it. When you think of sleaze, people tend to conjure up this image of whips and leather. And I'm not saying it doesn't interest me (laughs), but it's a very trivial thing to be interested in really. It's a very tiny area of what I write about. But I like to write about things that the majority of people may be shy of writing about. It has become very trendy over the last few years to write about filth and grime by people who really haven't got a clue basically.

A lot of my songs are just love songs really. I look at them as just plain love songs. Or often as I say, they're just plain love and hate songs — love for myself and a few hand picked individuals, and hate for the rest of the fucking world! (laughs) It's just that often the losers, failures, misfits and loners are the real gems of society, they're the real diamonds amongst the shit as it were. I like to watch and observe strange and bizarre people sometimes and imagine their lives. Or imagine I'm having an affair with one of them and just sort of use it.

Do you think that people get an accurate depiction of Marc Almond through what they read in the press?

Marc: I haven't seen one single accurate depiction of me in the press. I've seen a few that come a little bit close or hit home on a point, but the thing is, like Matt Johnson wrote in his song 'Giant', "How can anyone know me when I don't even know myself". I think that's a really good statement because I don't know myself properly. I mean who does? So how could other people know me? I mean I'm the only authority on me, and I'm not much of an authority at all.

Do you get upset by the coverage the press has given you?

Marc: I think so, because I try to be very hard — but I'm not. I'm a very sensitive person and I get hurt very easily about nothing. It's taken me about three or four years to become harder about it. Now I see some of the things and I just laugh, I find it more funny than upsetting. But who doesn't get hurt if you care about what you do and you care about your work, who doesn't inside get a little upset when they hear or read something that is totally derogatory?

I'm not above criticism at all, there's a lot to be criticised about my work, and I'm the first person to criticise it. I'm the first person to make fun of myself as well, and I often ridicule myself in songs and other things. I set myself up something rotten. Sometimes you see the real venomous, low sort of comments from somebody you have never even crossed paths with, somebody who has somehow been terribly offended by you. But I like that in a way because it's good to get up people's noses and wind people up. And I feel glad for someone who writes so strongly about me in that I have touched their life in some way — I have affected their life.

When did your Spanish/romantic interests develop?

Marc: I can't really remember, it just developed. I collect a lot of music by Eastern singers from places like Egypt, Morocco and the Middle East. I really wanted to go those places because I loved the music so much and I wanted to actually taste the culture. I always think that there's nothing really English or British about me whatsoever. I don't really like Britain, I don't really like what it has to offer. I don't really like British people all that much and I don't like their attitudes. I do enjoy living in London, I can just about tolerate it. It's enjoyable because I'm lucky enough to have good friends here. I mean that's the main reason for staying here. On other levels it's just barely tolerable. When you pick up a newspaper like The Sun every day and look at it, you think, "Why the fuck am I in Britain with garbage like this?" But there's nothing really British in my outlook, the way I think or the things I like.

I like things that have a very exotic flavour — Spanish and Middle Eastern stuff I really love, that type of culture and music. But it is something that has just developed from listening to music, listening to records and visiting places. I love somewhere like Barcelona. It's a wonderful city because you have all the back streets and alleys which are full of bars, clubs, cafes and all sorts of interesting life, incredible characters and incredible people. On the other hand you have beautiful art nouveau architecture everywhere.

British people are spoiled so much by everything. They're complacent about music because they are spoiled by it. They have everything thrown at them and they lack romantic vision. I'm not saying all of Britain, I'm saying the general atmosphere and feeling I get from the whole British way of life. When you go to Spain or somewhere like Morocco, they really use their culture. I mean a British person would say it's because they're backward (laughs) — typically bigoted as ever — but they use their culture in a really passionate way. They're not afraid to dance and to use music and sing, and there is so much colour and so much of a fiery passion, it's almost like the fist beating on the breast if you like. But I love that fire and that passion which I seem to find nothing of in Britain.

How would you define the word 'soul' when talking about music?

Marc: Well, I wouldn't necessarily limit it to black music. Soul is really just a genuine cry, feeling and emotion from the heart and body. Flamenco music has soul, all sorts of music, it's not necessarily limited to funk and black music. I'm finding a lot of black music now really soul-less, as opposed to soulful. A lot of black music is falling into this clinical middle of the road pit.

I think a group like Swans have an incredible amount of soul.

Marc: I most definitely agree. Music that affects you emotionally and physically in some way.

Contrary to some of the things at the top of the charts which are sold with a fashion created by a record company.

Marc: Yeah, it's like fake soul, it's plastic soul. It's like they've sat down and said, "Let's make this sound like a soul record, we've got to make it soulful, so therefore I'll sing it like it's meant to be soulful". But it's not something you sit down and consciously think about, it's just something that happens naturally. You've either got it or you haven't as they say. And it's a very natural feeling, it's not something you can contrive at all. I mean George Michael is plastic soul. The man on the street would think it was soulful, but...

It's a joke.

Marc: Yeah, it is definitely.

What do you think your music does to other people?

Marc: I would like to think that it makes people laugh and cry — sometimes at the same time — that it makes people feel emotional, entertains them and educates them... It paints new pictures, gives new insights and makes people look at themselves and other people in a wider light. To broaden people's horizons, just an inch, a fraction. But I'm not going to dictate what it does to other people. I don't mind what somebody gets from a song. They can laugh at it in absolute ridicule if they want, as opposed to with it — it doesn't matter. That's just as well as far as I'm concerned because it has evoked a reaction within them. People often laugh at my songs. (laughs)

What is your biggest fear at the moment?

Marc: I don't really know what I fear, really. To be old and to be totally useless and senile. I wouldn't want to live to an old age. I think once I started to lose the faculties of my mind and limbs, I'd wish I could just pop off, you know?

Do you have any artistic fears at all?

Marc: Of drying up, yeah. Waking up one day and not being able to do anything. But I think that you learn a lot from fear, I think you need fear. It's not really of things like death, because you come back anyway as something, your soul lives on as it were. My fears are quite normal fears, like fears of going blind, fears of losing my limbs, fears of just being made a prisoner in some way. I get terrible claustrophobia, literally and almost metaphorically speaking as well. I hate that feeling of being trapped in my bed or in a house, or trapped in a hospital — that's the old age thing. I'd hate to be trapped to a totally useless frame that has senile mind.

How do you feel when some of your followers mimic you in their appearance?

Marc: I've always believed strongly in people being individuals and looking for themselves and trying to find themselves. And it's very strange to see people dressing up as you, especially because I never thought that I'd be exactly an icon of fashion to follow. I mean quite the opposite, I never win any polls in that respect. But it's very odd, I wish people would sort of find their own individuality. But if they're finding their individuality by dressing as me, then hopefully that would lead them to finding their own individuality. If they need to be somebody else before they can be themselves, then that's fine, as long as it doesn't become a lasting fixation. Dressing up is so surfacey and superficial in a lot of ways, I mean it's mainly just done to please yourself — I just dress to please myself.

It's when people want to actually be you in a lot of other ways that it becomes ridiculous. When they actually want to copy the things that you do because they've read about it, I mean the more irresponsible things that you do. And I never want to be responsible for people. I'm quite honest about things that I do, I don't try to pull the wool over their eyes, but I'm not going to be responsible either. Because I don't want to treat them as children, but I wouldn't want anyone to actually try to be me because I wouldn't think that I'm a particularly good example to follow. (laughs) But they're not doing any harm to me — I just hope that they're not doing any harm to themselves.

Have you found that since people recognize you in the street, your lifestyle has changed that much?

Marc: I suppose it forces you to really. I've become a lot more shy than I used to be about going out to clubs, going places and being seen around. I don't like to be seen around. I very rarely go out and I don't like people taking photographs of me in clubs and taking photographs of me in the street because I do value my privacy. I need it. There are lots of times I just need to be invisible.

Do you think that being successful has affected you, in that you can't go into an underground or illegitimate place for research or entertainment purposes because people will recognize you?

Marc: I find that in a lot of those places people really couldn't give a shit anyway. They may say, "Oh whisper whisper, it's so and so", but at the end of the day they really couldn't give a shit. I've never found many problems like that. Especially abroad when you go into places, nobody knows me from Adam so it doesn't really matter. And when I lived round Soho, everybody knew me around there anyway, it was no big deal to see me. It's no big deal to see me, as far as I'm concerned I'm like anybody else.

What was it like meeting Andy Warhol?

Marc: Very dull. But I mean it usually is dull when you meet people who you've often admired. They're ordinary people and you can just tell he has his 'Andy act' to put on when people come round. He gives you a signed book, takes a couple of polaroids, talks with you about trivial things and all that, has a cup of tea and that's it. He just does an 'Andy act' for everybody that goes around. But I didn't expect anything more or anything less really.

Why do you feel that experimentation is important?

Marc: Who wants to be safe and contrived and know that everything is going to work out nicely and brilliantly? Experimentation is important because if you didn't, you would never learn anything. It doesn't matter really if it turns out a disaster, because a disaster is just as valuable to learn from as a success. It's just important to take risks, to be a little bit adventurous and step out on a limb occasionally.

THE BIRTH

It was his brother that tore the caul on that, the morning of their birth and as if that sole act of assertion was to set an inverted precedent for inertia within his life to come, Euchrid, then unnamed, clutched ahold of his brothers heels and slopped into the world with all the glory of an uninvited guest. The noon-day sun spun in the sky like a molten bolt and hammered down upon the tin roof and tarred plank sides of the shack. There, inside, at yonder table sat Pa surrounded by his ingenious contraptions of springs and steel, sweating midst the bleeding heat while greasing his cruel, cruel traps and trying, in vain, to closet his ears from the drunken ravings of his wife who lay, sprawled and cat-a-wauling, in the back seat of the old burnt out Chevrolet; pride of the junk-pile, that car, sitting on bricks, out backer the shack, like a great shell, shed in disgust by some out-sized crawler. There, in the squirms of labour, his bibulous spouse shrieked against the miracle that swelled and kicked inside her as she sucked on a bottle of her own White Jesus, rocking the Chevy on its stilts and moaning and screaming, screaming and a-moaning, "Pa! Pa-a! Pa-a-a!", until she heard the shack door open and then the shack door shut, where upon she took leave of the morning and passed into unconsciousness. "Too pissed to push", Pa would tell Euchrid later. Prizing the liquor bottle free of her grubby clutch, for even out cold she hung on and hung on, Pa broke the bottle carefully on the cars rusted tail-fin. Taking intuition as his mid-wife and a large shard of glass as his cutter, he spread his prostrate wife-with-child and dowsed her private parts in peel liquor. And with a chain of oaths spilling from his mouth, and with all the summer insects humming, with the sun in the sky and not a cloud in sight, with a hellish shriek and a gush of gleet, two slobbering bundles come tumbling out. "Jesus! Two!", cried Pa but one died soon.

The first sickly yellow morning spent a damn long day dying. The night wore black but her weeds dripped with trinkets; a shameless moon and a lot of vulgar stars — The Merry Widow of the Valley. Plain trash! Inside the shack two fruit crates lined with newspaper sat side by side on the table. The animal traps had been moved and hung around the walls. Two boxes and in each a babe. Pa peered in. Neither made a sound and both lay quite still upon their backs but with eyes wide and wandering. Naked as the day. Pa drew the nibbled stub of a pencil from his trouser pocket, then squinting a little, leaned toward the little one's writing on the foot-end of the firstborn's crib thus, "1", then, licking the tip, wrote "2" upon Euchrid's crib. Then he stood back and stared one to the other and one and the other reciprocated earnestly. Their's were strange almond eyes, identical to each others, with slightly swollen upper lids and next to no lashes, yet unblinking it seemed, their pupils blue but so pale as to almost verge on pink; intent, eager, never still, even when fixed on something or, indeed, someone as they were then, rather, they seemed to hover, these weird chattering eyes, hover and tremble in their browless sockets. Little Euchrid coughed, short and sharp, his tiny pink tongue lapping at his lower lip then curling back inside. And as if waiting for a signal and recognising it to be Euchrid's timid hack, the brave little first-born closed his eyes and fell into a slumber from which he would never wake. And it was at that moment that Euchrid knew, in his child's heart, things that would be a crime to waste on cunts like you.

"Goodbye, brother", Ah told him as he slipped away and for a full minute Ah myself thought that Ah too was going under, so fucken' cold was his dying. And me, in pluris naturalibus!

Then, a solemn moment passed in lieu of his martyrdom, but solemn moments and solemn thoughts are short-lived aboard this ship of fools, for sailing through the still night came the raucous fray of her bitchship, my mother, Ma, screeching in horse malediction, through the very anus of obscenity, while banging on the side of the Chevy and going, "Wha-ars mah boddle! "Wha-a-ars ma-ah boddle!!"

Extract from the novel "And the Ass Saw the Angel" by Nicholas Cave to be published by Black Spring Press Ltd.

NICK CAVE

When The Birthday Party came to London in 1979 from Australia, they expected the city to be a hive of extraordinary musical activities — a not uncommon myth. Instead they found British audiences and London itself cold and rigid. The began as The Boys Next Door in Melbourne and gradually progressed into something more abrasive and confronting. Through the music's innate violence, The Birthday Party gradually broke down the normal barriers of the band/audience relationship. Subsequent releases were met with higher and higher critical acclaim, but the band split in 1983, leaving singer Nick Cave free to explore growing infatuations on his own, namely the American South. On *From Her to Eternity* Cave took on numerous written voices, from itinerant preacher to ship's captain.

The subsequent albums saw Cave immerse himself further into his rural obsessions; however it became obvious that it was not simple mimicry, but a return from his own visions. In his first novel, *And the Ass Saw the Angel*, Cave creates a time and place which draws from his various interests and fantasies, inventing a land distinctly his own. Cave's band, The Bad Seeds, include Blixa Bargeld of Einsturzende Neubauten, Mick Harvey formerly with The Birthday Party and Tommy Wylder of Germany's Die Haut. Together they embody the randomness and adventure that The Birthday Party held sacred, while Cave himself somehow remains detached on stage.

In addition to his recent novel, Cave has also written 50 One Page Plays with Lydia Lunch, still unpublished and unperformed. He took part in The Immaculate Consumptive, and has given readings of his work on numerous occasions. In 1986 Cave released an LP of cover versions entitled *Kicking Against The Pricks* followed closely afterwards by an LP of his own material *Your Funeral My Trial*.

What was the reason for your recent stay in Los Angeles?

Nick: I've been writing a film script for an extra-curricular idea that I've been working on for the last two or so years. In fact, it's for a feature film for two young film-makers who are going to make this their first feature. They're involved with rock video stuff in LA, and they're, at the moment, the darlings of the LA rock video set. They made the 'Nick the Stripper' video which is really excellent.

Have you been writing that by yourself?

Nick: I was staying in the house of these two video-makers who are making the film. I was basically asked if I would go over to LA and stay with these two boys and write this film script and work on the idea with them. It was a lot more than I had bargained for. The particular people who were making the film were verging on the insane, and their very clever form of insanity managed to take over my entire life. Like all my money came into his bank account and he issued it daily and kind of allowed me use of the car every time he had the whim to do so, which was rare. Consequently I was in the situation where I was forced into sitting at the typewriter every day and every night just writing my arse off. Which is what I did, and this really great film script came out of it.

When will it be made?

Nick: The last time I talked to Evan English he was talking in terms of selling it which sort of made me raise one weary eyebrow and consider "Why?". Or ask myself, "How is this person able to sell my script?" But I don't know, maybe if the right person wants to buy it, then it might be a good idea. I think these two people could make it into a really excellent movie, they're really clever boys. The film script as a work of art is really brilliant I think.

Do you want to add anything about it?

Nick: Well, it's quite a disciplined thing for me, it's not unusual for me to get involved in something like this, but I think it is unusual for someone in my unfortunate genre to be involved in. But it is a straight narrative film in the sense that it has an extremely strong, complicated, intelligent and intense plot. It's a 'tragedy' of sorts, in the classical sense of the word, and there's no way some people might think that I'm involved in it. It sometimes worries me that people would think that I would be involved in perhaps an alternative sort of cinema. It's drama in the classical sense, but an extremely good one. And basically it's a stew for all the particular fetishes I have, which I managed to work into one cohesive story.

Do you think you will reach a different audience with film?

Nick: I haven't got that far yet. The audience I've had so far with film is one — two video-makers. They're the only two people who have had anything to do with the film script whatsoever. It seems to me that to be a film-maker you would have to have incredible patience. I'm very much used to fast art in a way. And even though it takes me a long time to write a record, it doesn't take that long to record it. The film, if all went well, would emerge in two years or something like this. The thought of an idea that I've had now coming to fruition in two years time is quite terrifying. If I think of the ideas I had two years ago staring me in face for the first time now, I'd be floating in a river somewhere.

What appeals to you about America that you can't get elsewhere?

Nick: There's something romantically inherent in America that is duplicated all over the world, but it's not authentic. I find it a country that's really centred around an incredible number of forms of escapism which I find I embrace very quickly. I find I can't embrace those things in other countries except maybe Australia which has a similar sort of romantic notion. I find it very easy to become quite lost and obsessed in the cliche of America, and the myth of America. I'm perfectly aware of its horror and bullshit, but its indulgences I enjoy very much.

You seem to be increasingly interested in the blues of the American South. Have you spent much time there?

Nick: No I haven't. I've been to Georgia and played one concert, and spent the night in a little town out of Georgia, that's basically it I think. But I do have intentions of spending a lot more time there. It may seem as though I'm obsessed with it and I'm sort of dwelling on it a lot. It has been uncomfortable for me at times to be spending so much time with my writing using a lot of the imagery of the South when I've never been there. So in a sense, I guess, it's all borrowed or second hand, although I can never say where it's borrowed from. I don't really have any desire to go to the South to make what I write credible. I don't think that's necessary. I have been criticised about it, you know, "Why is this Australian rock singer writing about the South and writing about it with real authority as well?", which I tend to do, like I know a real lot, bending round a lot of facts and figures and that sort of stuff.

For instance, I've written something that I'll be reading in Amsterdam tomorrow night and part of the next day at the World Poetry Festival. There's a really long piece that I wrote called 'Blind Lemon Jefferson', it's part blues verse, it's part kind of documentary style stuff, it's just a lot of different pages of stuff that constructs a certain period of his life. I mean the whole thing's totally bogus. It talks about being back in Clarksdale in 1935 or whatever which is basically all out of a hat. It doesn't interest me really, that side of it, although I dwell on it a lot, but it's for far more perverse reasons that I do it. There's just something about it which allows me to write a certain way, like an actual language style which happens to be inspired as much by the South as it is by Shakespeare or The Bible or whatever. But it allows me to write in the first person, and say I felt this way. And I can write 'Ah' instead of 'I', like, "Ah may go see the preacher".

Do you feel that what you write can always be transformed validly during a performance at a concert, so that people understand how you feel?

Nick: Uh, I don't know, I'm changing my opinion about this line of thought. I've been trying to work out what makes me never want to hear the 'From Her to Eternity' record. I think it's a really good record, along with all the other records that I've made, but I just can't find the desire to listen to it whatsoever. I think the reason for that is some sort of over-emphasis on the language. I mean those songs that I wrote on 'From Her to Eternity' really took an incredible amount of time. 'Saint Huck', that one song, took three months of not writing any other songs. And what is read in the end, squeezed out of it, is one track on a record which is seven minutes long. I think I just subconsciously became too intent on making people understand what I was singing, being able to hear the words and that sort of stuff. The whole thing becomes a bit pompous and I think maybe that's the reason. The writing in a sense is all too 'good', there are no errors, basically, in it. I mean I'm interested in rhyming and always have been, using a fairly conventional form of songwriting style, but it's all too 'clever'. The new songs I've written consequently aren't as clever as that I guess. They're just a lot more spirited than those other ones, not 'epic' masterpieces.

Is that a reason for doing a reading or a performance, like in Amsterdam or with The Immaculate Consumptive in America, where the focus is put more on the words in the piece rather than the music behind it?

THE COMPLETE STATE
OF NICHOLAS CAVE

Nick: Yeah, obviously it works a lot better, I mean it works perfectly to read something that's literary, and that really has to do with language, which is what my songs mostly are. I think obviously to read them and to have them read to you are far more effective ways of being subjected to it than to hear it put to an incredible barrage of noise. I've always tried to combine the two, but maybe that just doesn't work, or I haven't been able to make it work, I'm not sure. I'd like to find a more happy equilibrium with my music, where the words don't overpower the music and vice-versa. You're not going all gooey over a line, and whether there is music behind it or not, one thing works with the other thing a bit more. This is what I'm trying to do.

Is there anyone you know of that has reached a happy medium between the two?

Nick: Well, we did a Bob Dylan song tonight that I've always liked. I could count on one hand Bob Dylan songs that I thought were great and still do, and they've always been the very simple songs that he has done. I've got a book of German translations of all his songs up until 'Nashville Skyline' — and it's just this incredible amount of songwriting, and a large proportion of it is throwaway lyric writing I suppose. But I found all my favourite Dylan songs are just ridiculously simple when you read them on paper. They really look like they have been written out very quickly, and reading that has affected the songs that I've written for this record, as much as listening to blues music or whatever. Spontaneous blues music in particular, where someone says to John Lee Hooker for example, "Sing a song about Abraham Lincoln", and he just writes "He Done Got Assassinated", sort of rattles it off the top of his head. I think the songs that we are listening to now (John Lee Hooker) are really excellent. Just an idea, going through it, and saying, "Next".

Do you get frustrated sometimes at other people looking at your work further than it was originally intended?

Nick: No, it's not really an age when that sort of thing is fashionable anymore. All the critics have come around to the idea that it's unfashionable to do that anyway. So I don't really worry about that sort of thing — where I sit down and read that one of my songs is supposed to be about so and so. I think they're fairly self-explanatory. It just doesn't happen a lot, and when it does, I find it amusing if anything. I like people doing that, just because it can't help but be a total abortive attempt at a different viewpoint.

I am aiming at one particular thing when I'm writing my songs. They're not songs that are a lot of words trying to create an atmosphere — it's up to you what you want to make of it. I suppose as my songs go, I don't hold by that, my songs mean something, and every word is written for a reason, to put forward or across something that I'm writing about. I'm not throwing words and lots of colourful images or scary imagery to do whatever. I just hear so much stuff, particularly new wave stuff, which is so nauseating for that reason. You hear all this incredibly fierce use of imagery, but it's just so obviously vacuous. And it's done with such kind of cockiness and arrogance, you know? But there is no need for anyone to justify what they write about. It has just unfortunately given out a licence to a lot of shit writers who can't write very well.

How important is it for your writing to be seen or heard?

Nick: There are a handful of people who, if I write for anybody apart from myself, it's for them. The only rewards I get from other people appreciating what I've done come from those people. And that would just be, I don't know, five or six or whatever. I don't get any sense of feeling that I've done something worthwhile, nor am I persuaded to think that what I've done is good or bad, by the voice of the critic in the newspaper or by the collective voice of a couple of thousand people at a concert. I mean that sound leaves me totally cold. I think that there would probably be very few people who could say that it doesn't matter what anybody thinks about their writing, you know, "It's great, I like it, it doesn't matter". I think that, but I know that if one of the five or so people said, "What you've written is a bunch of shit", it would really upset me.

What are you trying to accomplish with your music now?

Nick: I would like to be able to put across, somehow, a purer, more basic, emotional feeling. Something that doesn't rely on me as a craftsman. Something where I can sing some basically inane lyrics, and give them all the meaning in the world. I mean that would be nice. Then I would perhaps start listening to the records.

When you're performing, how would you describe the feeling which is coming out of you? Would it be as pain, or anger, or something else, and is it directed at anybody, or is it directed at yourself?

Nick: There's no rule for that, it really depends on the situation. When I'm performing at my best, it would be when the audience has shut up for long enough or when we're playing well enough that I have forgotten about them. Then I can deliver whatever I feel about that particular song that I'm singing, rather than just a battle of me trying to maintain some sort of application to what I'm doing. That's the hardest bit, it's just this constant distraction. It's really hard to be sincere about what you do when you're just being made a fool of basically. I'm sure I hear a lot more and I start to imagine a lot more. But when I'm actually singing, when there's all this noise coming out around me, I can still hear people. And when I think about it, I'm sure I probably can't — but there's this effect they have on me that's really hard to shake.

What would be an ideal performance for you?

Nick: I don't think there can be an ideal performance, because the very act of performing defeats itself anyway. I think it's just a self-destructive act to perform. I've never felt elevated — ever, after coming off stage.

Do you think it will change, is that why you keep doing it?

Nick: That's the obvious question, why do I keep on doing it? And I can't answer that, I don't know why I keep doing it.

Do you think it's possible to get your written ideas across to people at a rock concert?

Nick: Yeah, I think it's possible to get through to some people because when I'm singing them, I can see that they're getting through to some people. I'll sing a line and I can see people laugh or smile, which is what I usually do when I hear somebody worthwhile. If I go to a Fall concert, for example, and I can hear what's going on — sometimes it's just great. You're just bowled over by Mark Smith's wit and so forth, and the band help to elevate it and put it in an even more absurd situation. But I'm not interested at all in people enjoying it, it doesn't really bother me one way or another. People try to comfort us when we obviously go down like a lead balloon, and I just don't give a shit whether we do or not. And it's the truth, I really don't.

I feel a certain responsibility to the other members of the group. I think that's one of the inane reasons why I still perform in the way I do, even though each concert sort of tempers itself more and more I guess. People feel more and more disappointed with each concert because less and less happens. But one of the reasons why there's still some action on stage physically, physical movement, is because I feel so sort of obligated to the other members of the group. And I'm always tempted, because it's a really easy way to sucker people in and it's a really easy way to get people to like you.

Financially me being in a group is just a total joke. I'm in no better position financially than I was six years ago when I left Australia. I might as well be on the dole now as in this group really. I just have a more expensive lifestyle in the sense of what I need money for to kind of make it, it's horrible. So I'm certainly not doing it for the money, I don't see that I'll get any money out of this in the future, and I don't really care about whether I'm popular or not any more.

I'm not really interested in perfecting myself musically any more anyway. I think the statements that I will be remembered for have been made, and I could make another ten records and they won't be remembered. I enjoy making records, that's something that I obviously like doing, particularly with these people that I'm doing it with, because I think they're really great. (Pause) Sorry, I've forgotten what I was saying.

What are your feelings about the audience?

Nick: I don't have a particularly bright opinion about the audience, or a bright sort of love for the audience. I have an incredibly narrow opinion of them, and I know it's a really stupid opinion, but it's just the way I think about them. When you ask me about an audience, immediately a handful of really obnoxious faces come to mind. This disgusting guy with blond hair and a red neck who just kept screaming things at me through the entire concert, the most obnoxious sort of attempt at being hurtful or humiliating or whatever they were trying to do. That's basically what I end up seeing when you mention 'audience'.

text to ;   C.R.E.E.P.   by The Fall
                    ────────────

    HE reads books; of the list book club
    And after two months-his stance is a familiar.hunch
    It's that same slouch-you had the last time he came around
        His oppression abounds,his type is doing the rounds
        He is a scum-egg; a horrid trendy wretch
        C.R.E.E.P   CR E. E. P.

    BLACK saucers at the back of your neck
    Interruptions,from the side when you talk
    n the prescence,of this ugly gawk,
     is offending,make sure you're not absorbed
    (With hideous luck-he'll absorb all your talk)
        CR E.E.P. C.R.E.E.P.   X 3

    FROM the bright sun,he came one fine morn
    "Populist"- well in his class at least
    But then came REAL AGE, and for that we all must pay
                            (and for that we all do pay)
        c.r. e. EP.   C.R.E.E.P.
        C.R. E E P   C.R.E.E.P.

    CR E.E.P. - cr E.E.P.   CR E.E.P. - CR E. EP x2
        And he wants world peace ! (and for that we all must pay)
        He likes ABC !   (C.R.EE.P.)
      C.R.EE.P.   CR. E.E.P.   X"2
                    CREEP !

    ── ───────────────────────────────────

MARK E. SMITH

In mid 1977, writer and science fiction fan Mark E. Smith formed The Fall in Manchester, England. The following year they began releasing records and gathering a devoted audience, inspired by the astute lyrics and casual manner of Smith and the relentless drive of the band's guitars and drums. Despising rockist fashion with an equal scorn to being classified with any musical movement, The Fall have cloned various permutations of rock and roll with their ideas to form a sound which has been described as 'Northern rockabilly' or 'Modern folk'.

The technical merit of the music is often distorted by the way The Fall choose to record themselves, many times leaving background noises and mistakes in, thus adding to the initial rawness of the music. Smith's lyrics often bear no rational symmetry to the actual music, and at times he becomes a storyteller addressing things obliquely rather than directly. These allegories are often best consumed through album covers and sleeves, usually scrawled with segments of lyrics or other printed matter. Since 1983, Smith's wife Brix, has played an increasingly important role within The Fall, releasing singles in her own right as The Adult Net. In 1984 The Fall increased their coverage by signing to Beggars Banquet.

In December 1986 Mark Smith directed his own play *Hey Luciani* at Riverside Studios in London. The play, loosely based on the life on Pope John Paul, used few regular actors and was punctuated by several numbers from The Fall. Smith was insistent that the play was neither historically accurate nor anti-religious, but through the use of different time and place location, back projections and music, created a plot about the life of the one month Pope and those who surrounded him. After a string of increasingly accessible singles, The Fall entered the top 30 in 1987 with a cover version of R. Dean Taylor's *There's A Ghost In My House*.

Do you think that music has become less powerful than it was at some point in the recent past?

MES: It's funny, 'cause when I was moving house I found a New Musical Express from 1981, you know, those times were like the intellectual times of music, weren't they? And like reading the singles reviews, they were written in heavy foot, philosophical sort of stuff, you know, but now it's like a complete reaction against that.

Brix had this Smash Hits on the train you know, and I was reading it, it had like Lou Reed and stuff. But the girl who was reviewing the singles was called Mary Duff. I mean you know what Duff means in English slang, like duff means like really rubbish, and she was reviewing this Lou Reed thing and going like, "Lou Reed has influenced everybody from Ian McCullough to Frankie Goes To Hollywood," as if this was something to be held against the guy, you know, like the only people who will listen to this will be people in sunglasses and black leather jackets, which is like the ultimate simplification of Lou Reed's work, you know? Imagine if you were him reading that, it would break your heart, you know what I mean? And compared to like what somebody would have written three years ago, it would have been equally full of bullshit, but it would have been all philosophical bullshit, you know?

Do you think that musical criticism can become too educated?

MES: I just think it's interesting to observe and sort of like, you know, I think there's more to it. It's like The Fall are now dismissed as some sort of old cranks who have got to be respected. But I don't like that, I don't think that is. When The Fall were analysed and that, it wasn't satisfactory in any way at all. In a way, I like it better like this. I just like bad reviews now, I think it's good.

Why do you think they're good?

MES: I mean they're idiots, they always will be idiots. One thing about today, I think it's completely illiterate, but I don't know if it's more or less illiterate than it was.

Do you think it is important now to sell a product?

MES: I think it was, always has been. Now it always reminds me of, like one of them, like futuristic books you know, that everybody's much the same and everybody's like... You see the bands now, they're all like wearing stuff. See I always notice that, I was thinking the other day, the thing with The Fall is they always act opposite to that. Now everybody's going very scruffy, we're sort of going very smart, it's weird. It's strange, we're always like the inverse of that, isn't that strange?

Would you say that The Fall has an image?

MES: No, not really. Looking at sort of the people in the group nowadays, they're all very underground people who don't really take it that seriously, you know? I always wonder why it can never cross over and that — but I mean looking at it, you know the people that like us and stuff, it's all very underground, which is an old cliche, but it's true you know, every time.

Do you find that having that underground or cult status is confining sometimes?

MES: It's only confining if you let it be, you know? (long pause)

I mean do you sometimes feel that because you are an underground band and you've been around for so many years, that you don't get the publicity you should?

MES: Oh, definitely. I mean this is what's happening now, yeah. I mean the easiest thing for us to do now would be just to change the name.

Have you considered that?

MES: No, you know, it's ah, even people who want us to be commercial don't agree with that. You know it seems sacrilegious that, I don't know what it is, just that word, it's like that's the great thing about us really. You know I mean I thought of calling us The New Fall, and I thought, "Well no, nothing's that different, it's nothing to be embarrassed about". But it's true, you know, like you get these fucking groups with weird names getting publicity, but I mean that's the nature of the market, it's the way the fucking whole thing is organised. I mean this is all they do, isn't it? I mean this is all Stiff Little Fingers do or anybody like that, they just break up, don't they, after two years, you know, reform under a new name, pick up on the trend that's happening and divert it that way, you know? And somehow it's very interesting and new, but what we're doing isn't. (laughs)

How would you define commercialism within music, or being commercial?

MES: I don't know, you see it all seems dead obvious. It's like you feel it in your bones, it's a very sort of physical thing that you can sort of learn to hate after a while, you know? I mean like the Frankie thing, I think it's good but I mean... All the advertising is Wyndham Lewis, you know, which is very close to my heart, I hate to see it used for something like pushing a sort of rebellious pacifism, (laughs) you know what I mean? 'Cause I mean like Wyndham Lewis would've really hated it, you know, it's fucking populist and it's horrible, the whole CND thing, and it's like how bad America is, and how bad Russia is, you know? Like using Wyndham Lewis, who was like the archetypal man, you know, when the First World War broke out, Wyndham Lewis was all for it and everybody hated his guts for it, you know, and they always did, and the man died in poverty because of things like that.

Like Celinean people, like that's the same story, they always went across the grain and were always persecuted by jerks who, for years later, plagiarised their whole art. I mean I identify with that stance a lot. I think it's happened to me a lot you know, and sometimes you sort of despise the fact that you were an innovator once, because people just take it and sort of distort it into something a lot weaker.

How important are the lyrics within the music of The Fall?

MES: It goes up and down, you know, over the years it's very interesting that sort of constant sort of writing thing. Most of my stuff over the past two or three years I just haven't used in songs, which I never used to do, you know? Nowadays I try and keep it simple and try and do things that are going out to annoy and are going out to break new ground, I think that's important. Whereas when I started, you know, I'd use everything I'd ever written, I mean I seriously would, you know, I mean it's obvious. I mean this is interesting about other groups, is that other groups actually dry up completely, whereas we never have. I mean to me, the last two years we made a conscious effort to stop thinking we've just got to keep writing. But then again, who wants to hear about it, you know? We could have brought out twice the amount of LPs we have done, you know, easily, and it would have all been pretty much as good standard as what was brought out. In fact, I always get letters all the time about, "Why didn't you release this bloody track you used to do, you used to do this great song", you know, and it's songs you can't even remember the lyrics to, I've chucked 'em out.

Do you consider yourself more of a poet or a musician?

MES: I mean what's a poet, you know? To me, poetry stinks, you know? This is what I'm saying, that like if somebody's a poet nowadays in music, it's like pulling some kind of revelation, like some kind of great talented guy, when in fact they're just writing lame poetry, you know? I mean I like to think of myself as beyond that point even, beyond the pop lyric. I think this is why the pop lyric is appealing to me, because you can distort it and shoot it that way more than going out to be a poet, you know? You know what I mean?

Do you find your lyrics become too literary and confining in that sense sometimes?

MES: My stuff once was, yeah, I mean about '80-'81, not that anybody complained about it, but you know, you just end up getting up on stage and singing your diary, you know like I mean a few bands do that now and do very well out of it.

Why did you feel it wasn't working?

MES: 'Cause when you write you should do your best, you know, not just like some kind of deep, self-centred monologue that is boring to everybody. I always try and put a little crack in it, and I always try and put lyrics that mean nothing and like jumble it all up and you know mess around with it. I like to, like, you know, get people off on the strange words, you know, not strange words particularly but slang words and stuff like that.

I was looking up some lyrics from a while back and they were really good. I can't remember, totally escapes me now, I think it was from, like you know, a mid-sixties thing or even a seventies thing, and the lyrics, I mean nobody could have understood them, you know what I mean? And ah, they're really good but they're really wordy compared to the songs now which are like — like if you look through Smash Hits, you never even get the word receive, you know? Like receive is a big word — did you ever get that thing where you forget how to spell words? Like on the train, I forgot how to spell receive, so I got Smash Hits and I was looking at the lyrics for receive, and there wasn't any, or anything with an I and an E in it you know, 'cause I got the I and the E the wrong way round. (laughs)

I before E except after C, 'cause I always used to get them mixed up, and then somebody told me that.

MES: (Pause) Yeah, right. I remember that. That's the thing you learn at school isn't it? I learned that at school and forgot it, yeah. (laughs)

Why do you think expressing yourself with music is more powerful than simply the words written on a page, or do you?

MES: Well now I've come around to that point. I mean I've said this like loads of times, but I'm gonna actually get down and do a sort of short lyric book, you know, of about 12 songs, I mean I'm doing one for the Germans which sort of appeals to me.

Why the Germans?

MES: Well particularly non-British people, 'cause non-British people, you know, it's the old story, you know, funnily enough, it's other people who aren't English who are really interested in my lyrics.

Why do you think that is?

MES: I don't know, I was ah, I had this interview with Record Mirror a while back, and this lad was going you know, like doing me this big favour, "Like Record Mirror is even interested in you Mark!", and all this, and Brix was saying, "Oh well in New York, you know, they really like his lyrics and stuff", and he was going , "Well I can't understand that, you know, I mean uh...", and I was saying, "Yeah, well in Belgium and in Germany, you know, people are more interested in...", and he was going "Well they can't understand the lyrics, how could they possibly understand them more than English people?" And I says, "Well you know it goes back, you know, why is fuckin' Shakespeare bigger in fuckin' Japan than it is in bleedin'

England", you know what I mean, which is the truth, you know, people are interested. And I get mail from German schoolchildren which I find incredible. I got this letter from a class, the whole class signed it, and like they wanted to know the meaning of 'Jew on a Motorbike'. (laughs) I never wrote back to them though, because they said, "You better write back fast because we leave school next week", and it was too late.

But anyway I know this lad who lives in Berlin, and he's got a printing press and shit he's an artist and he wants to, he thought it would be a laugh to translate, 'cause what he does when we tour there, he translates the lyrics really freebase you know, he just like abuses the Germans really. I mean he knows everything about The Fall, but it would be just too boring for him to write, "Well the first album was 'Witch Trials'...", so he writes other things, you know, and it sort of appealed to him, it's his sense of humour to see like my lyrics in German. So what we got talking about is doing something like that.

But to get back to, I mean, I think a lot was missed of my past lyrics that wouldn't have... I suppose I still don't like the whole of them printed on the sleeve or anything, 'cause that would go around the whole point. I mean I think it's up to a person to take what they get out of the lyrics. I mean I still think like, you know, music's much more interesting when you don't know what the lyrics are. 'Cause there is that sensation. If you're into words, you know, if you're a reader which I am, I'm like, I've got to read once in a day, I've got to read something, even just a paper. So if you buy an LP, which is an investment, if I ever saw a lyric sheet, I mean it would spoil it for me 'cause I'd read all the lyrics before I even put the record on, you know? I mean I know that like ninety percent of the people don't do that, I mean you know, they look at the lyrics a few years later, don't they? But if we're talking about the lyrics I'm gonna print, I'm gonna do one or two sort of present ones, but mostly old ones like, you know like 'Marquis Cha Cha', I mean I think that looks really good written down, it's like a story you know?

Do you think your lyrics work well on paper or do you think they're greatly boosted by a musical backing?

MES: Some are and some aren't. I like to think they all stand up on paper, I also like experiments where it's just like a sound experiment. In a way I find that I did that with something like 'I Feel Voxish', I just wanted a vocal tune going — but the lyrics in that are dead interesting actually, like the throwaways and that, it's the sort of thing I can't even remember to write down, but it would look good written down.

When The Fall first started, what was it you wanted to do?

MES: I don't know, it's just that, the music, as it was, looked like it was dying out to me, and then the 'New Wave' happened, which was really very good, but when I went to see the bands, I mean I saw them all, and I just, it wasn't like everybody says now, "They thought they could do better than that..." — everybody knew that. What it was with me is it was like, the possibilities. People forget this now, all those, like smart arses in the rock world and that, they forget that before like '76, you just didn't! I mean we had a group, me and these two other lads, and the mere idea of getting up on stage was just like, you know, you just thought it was against the law and it's hard to imagine them days now but you did, you know? If you knew anything about music, you know what I mean, like Top of the Pops, the music programmes, even if you hated the guts of the people on them, you'd never dare try it without a million pounds, you know what I mean, which is what it's getting back to now in a way.

So, when I saw that New Wave, that Punk thing, it was good, but I mean lyrically, it wasn't satisfying and stuff like that, and like it wasn't respectful to the influences, you know?

Mark E. Smith: A name which inspires dread and respect, Mark E. is the most feared man in the full colour dream state of Poprock Britain '84. Age 22 - 37, he was born to the strains of 'Stranger In Paradise'. A self taught intellectual, his lyrics have restructured the course of the Wests' musical underground. Incorporating history and cold first person narratives through the groups' random musicianship.

Everybody says the Velvet Underground and all that, I mean this Velvet Underground thing is a joke, I mean you used to get things like the The Pretenders and The Buzzcocks and that, you know, they're good in their own way, but you know, they were nothing of the spirit of the Velvets or The Stooges or anything like that in mind, you know? That's what was good about the Velvets was they were literal you know, and nobody else was. We're literal, but we're never seen to be literal, which I think is great.

Originally did you want to become more literal than the predominating supergroups?

MES: No, I just thought you know, interesting things could be written about. A big inspiring thing was early Can stuff, when they had Damo Suzuki. He wasn't even singing lyrics in fact, he didn't even know what he was singing, the Japanese guy, he was just like, he was learning English, and he was just saying words, you know? And that's what inspired me. They used to have like, there's a Can track called 'The Empress And The Ukraine King', and it's some mad story about, you know... I don't know what it's about but it's really like, it's just so stimulating compared to like, you know, anything else that was. The music was good too. I mean I also, I must make this quite clear, I also hate that sort of songwriter-poet thing, I mean that's shit, you know, the way the music is some kind of piano or two piece guitar band, like now you're getting that routine, like well sort of even Costello type of stuff, where the music is contemporary, but it's not like... great.

Why do you hate that?

MES: Because the singer-songwriter thing, it's a self-important thing of being taken as a poet and stuff, I mean it stinks. And it's crap, you know, it's bad. It seems like bad poetry to me, written down it looks bad, it's not the mark of a genius, you know? But I mean you meet these people, like Ian out of the Bunnymen, I mean, you know, he used to say to me, "You're no poet, I'm the poet", you know, "You're a wordsman". And I went, "A wordsman?" you know, what are you talking about, you know? You see his lyrics written down, and you know, he's doing his thing, you know, and he's successful at it and it's good, you know, but his lyrics don't hold up when you see them on posters and that. I mean they're a joke, I mean I burst out laughing. I saw one in the train station and it had, "If all soldiers are going to war", or something, no, "If my heart is a war, it's soldiers are dead", you know what I mean, what the fuck are you doing, is this like English literature class or what? You know, fucking art class at primary school, you know, "Write a poem today kids".

Would you say the motives behind The Fall have changed?

MES: Well, now they have. I mean like recently the pure motive of the band was to get money because we were hugely in debt. We just had this bad luck that dogged us, badly, with tax and shit, you know? I mean this is why bands break up after two years too, you know, it's clever, you know, it's the right thing to do. That's why bands emigrate and stuff, it's the English way, you know? It stinks.

Do you think your sound has become more accessible?

MES: No, 'cause what happened to me was this dimension where you get to the point that you don't give a fuck anymore, you know? I mean all it is a matter of expressing yourself fully when you do business, you know? This is what I've found. I mean our single on Beggars Banquet wasn't particularly commercial, they didn't want us to do a commercial single, you know, they just said, you know, we'll push it, whatever you want.

Do you think it's important to be original in what you do?

MES: For myself it is, yeah, just out of pride, you know, not that many people really notice that you're being original. In fact I think you get a bit heckled for it, you know, you have to wait two years until some band makes a big career out of the sound that you had two or three years back, you know, know what I mean? I think that's true in The Fall's case you know, anything off 'Slates' is as well produced as anything these guitar bands are turning out, you know, it's got a lot more punch and it's a lot more interesting, but at that time it was just ahead of its time, you know? Um, it's important to me 'cause I get embarrassed if anything sounds like something else. I get very spiteful you know, I just hear the band, if they just write some music and it sounds a bit like something else, I'll go, "We're not going to do it", you know — really. I mean in a way it's wrong, you know, but I mean I'm ultra-sensitive about it. I think that generally people don't know that they're doing it, sometimes, you know?

Like I don't think The Alarm genuinely think they have been influenced by The Clash. I was talking to the sound-mixer about this a while back, that a lot of these bands now, these so called 'underground bands', like the independent bands, they all sound like, very much like the old, what I used to call 'weirdo' bands, like Black Sabbath and Jethro Tull and that. And I said to the mixer, "You know what I think it is", and I think it is true, "Is that when bands start out, they've been listening to records from when they were like thirteen or fourteen, and that is like at the back of the brain, but when they form a band, they've got to be contemporary, so they like follow the mold, but after a year or two they sort of subconsciously go back to what they started out listening to". And I think that's what is happening now, you know, and I don't think they're conscious of it.

I mean I heard a single the other day by Gene Loves Jezebel, I could have sworn it was like a track off a Black Sabbath album. I mean there was nothing different from it, I mean it's really good actually, 'Shame'. But if you went back in a time machine ten years ago and played it to somebody, a Black Sabbath fan would really get into it. You know, so what's what? And I mean, a lot of bands now, you know, they sort of sound jazzy, rocky, you know like, and very English, this horrible sort of English music that turned up around '69-'70, what I used to call weirdo music. I mean Duran Duran sound a bit like that now, do you know what I'm saying? Like did you ever have old Jethro Tull LPs and that?

Yeah.

MES: Yeah, well they were good, I mean his lyrics were good. Some of his lyrics were great. Very indirect.

It could be the start of another revival, after neo-psychedelia...

MES: Yeah, but I mean I still think it's there, you know, they all laugh at those groups, which

I think is dead dishonest, if they can't recognise the similarities, you know, in their own work. I mean I wonder what they're in it for, you know, why are they in it? To be like people that have gone before?

Why are you in it?

MES: To be like... The Stooges (laughs). No, it's ah, it's just the writing bit, I think it's good, original.

Why do you think it's important to stay away from trends in music?

MES: You can do things, but it's a temporal thing, I mean you can only do things once or twice without getting fed up. I've turned my back on the audience because, you know, I like to concentrate on my lyrics sometimes, and I've read lyrics off paper and it's because I can't remember the lyrics sometimes — that's all. I mean that's the thing, you know, that's what stinks about the 'rock' thing, you know? You're supposed to take the whole show around and it works very well, you know, it's like the old thing about Jimi Hendrix, you know licking his guitar and it's the old boring thing, it's even boring to talk about it, see you're yawning already. (laughs)

Sometimes we play, you know, and I can see people have come because they expect Mark Smith to get annoyed with the audience, or the Mark Smith who's going to be absolutely brilliant tonight, you can see it, you know what I mean? I mean to force anything like that would make me physically ill, 'cause like when sometimes, like when I've gone through the motions once or twice on heavy tours, I've never felt well after it, and people have been raving about it and stuff, and I've never liked it.

Do you think it's important to play live?

MES: Yeah, it's important for us in two ways, one is we can actually earn money playing live, which we do, we can always get a few weeks wages out of it, you know. So I mean that instantly means that when you're recording and stuff, and you're dealing with record companies, you can say, "Fuck it", which was like the situation with Rough Trade, you know? Like they just wouldn't give us any fucking money 'cause it was all going into other groups, you know, but we were selling well. But I mean quite rightly they said, "Well, you get your royalties in three months", and I said, "Well our last company went bankrupt right, so we have had no royalties for the last two years, we have no money", you know? And I'm not going to go in there and say, "Look I'll do this and I'll do that if you give me the money up front", you know, which I could have done, it would just take a bit of mental application, but I didn't want to creep to people who I regard as my inferiors, you know?

So I mean what we did was just arrange five dates, you know, people want to see us, they enjoy it, you know, we enjoy it, we'll get new songs sorted out, we travel and shit, you know, it's a grind, you know, but it's worth it, you know? I like it you know, I mean, 'cause some of the live tapes are great, you know, I mean the best, some of our best stuff has been worked out like that, just accidents. Like we played The Hacienda, and the live tape from it, some of the versions of the new songs were just definitive, it'll be hard to top them in the studio, although the other three dates were a bit shaky.

Do you feel The Fall experiment much within music?

MES: Um, I think you have to watch being self-consciously experimental, you know? I think I am. I don't think the group is really. What we needed after 'Perverted by Language' was actually to tighten it up, not to tighten it up playing wise, but just to tighten it up so it's a bleedin' sound instead of a complete like, as you said, it tended on the monotonous, you know? There's a difference between monotony, and like you can play the same note over and get a syndrome, and like it's really good. There are so many groups now that just play the same things over and over, and this is why I had to get rid of a lot of people in the group because they felt that was it, they've mastered their instrument and they think, "Oh well, I can play the same chord brilliantly for six minutes", which is, ah — you should get a bleedin' machine to do that. You know, the thing is to play it with an inflection.

In what ways are you being experimental now?

MES: With the lyrics I think, 'cause I'm surprised, some of the new stuff that I've been writing is really weird. I've got a great song about Scottish groups, and it's uh, I started out trying to write about how shitty all Scottish groups are and how Scottish groups always lecture everybody on how they are from Scotland, and how hard up they are, and I just tried to make out that this is just a part of the national character of everybody, and you shouldn't take it seriously, don't feel guilty about it, you know? I started writing it like that, but then it started going on about the price of Scotch Whisky, and then it sort of goes into this weird thing about how I can attain to the sky and stuff, and it was really weird and really good. I'm sorry, I don't want to talk about it anymore 'cause it's a really good song you know? And the riff is just like, it's like something the Sex Pistols would do, it's really good. (laughs) The riff is like completely you know, just not what you'd think from something like that. I mean if it's going to be a satire it would be something like The Bluebells or something, tinkly things, but the music is just like, how the boys came up with the music is just like, I don't know, you know, it was one of Brix's tunes actually. When you heard the music you would have thought, you know, "I'm in hell, I'm living in hell", do you know what I mean, a sort of like direct, very simple thing, but the lyrics are really, they get more and more complicated the more I do it.

You mention a lot of other bands. Is it important for you to know what else is happening musically around you?

MES: It's a funny thing, I think a lot of it is, to just talk about The Fall and myself, I can't do it, you know what I mean? Like you say, what is there to The Fall, I just see a vacuum, you know, which isn't true. It's one of those cases where you wished you had said this, you know what I mean, just like the brain isn't connected to the mouth at all. I know what The Fall is and I don't think there is much you can do to explain it, which is why a lot that is written about us is absolute gibberish, 'cause there's nothing you can actually say about it really, without it being there, which is why I think we're valuable. I know it's funny, I think it's just that little kick that keeps us tight.

It's not that I'm really interested in music or anything, I don't really, you know, Brix is always reading music magazines, and I go, "Get it out of my face", you know, "I don't want to see it" you know? It irritates me, which may be the secret to it, you know?

Would you like to be commercially successful?

MES: Yeah, I think the boys deserve it you know, but what I'd do with it, I don't know. And I don't see how anybody could take us to their hearts, like a nation or a generation, which I think commercial success is all about. 'Cause we have actually sold a lot more records than a lot of people in the charts, 'cause we've sold records over quite a few years, which is a weird thing, you know? But people always say, "I bet you're feeling bad that you never made it", and I usually say, " Yeah I do", but then, you know later I think, "I can't complain, it's not as if we've been brutally treated". But I mean there's never enough money there, you know, of course, but I mean everybody's like that.

Would you say that you've compromised much during The Fall's career?

MES: Um, no, 'cause I'm the sort of person who people don't approach with compromises. Maybe it's a bad thing and a good thing, though I've found for the potential we've got, you know, nobody here would even think of coming up to me and saying, you know, "Could I suggest this?" I mean nobody ever says it to me, you know, they just don't say it, it's a funny thing. Sometimes we'd wished somebody had said something like that, maybe things would have been a bit more interesting, but I don't think so.

When listening to 'Perverted by Language' one hears a lot of fragmented noises and odd sounds which are incorporated with the music in a unique way. However, The Fall aren't usually looked at as being great experimentalists, are they?

MES: Well you know, people who see those things know them and feel them, you know? But no, I've always tried to do that. Yeah, a lot of 'Perverted by Language', like I had a cassette of the demo tape that we did in the room of the track, you know, played on an acoustic, out at a different time and everything. I'd have it going in the studio, so it sounds like a background. It's almost like a weird echo.

What would be the purpose of something like that?

MES: I just think it's real interesting, you know, I hear it, you're witnessing the last version of the song and the first version, even though you don't know it, only I know it or something. I do a lot of vocals live too, well on that I did, I do a lot of the vocals with the group so you get the overspill which I always try to keep on, which means from my mike you're going to get a feedback from the guitar that isn't necessarily going through the guitar or the drums. So that's why a lot of the vocals are muddled.

How much are the band a vehicle for your lyrics?

MES: Um, I think there as good on their own, you know, without me. I think it's important for them to know that. They're only a vehicle for things like that actually, when I am experimenting at their cost sort of thing — I mean so people say. I think they like that in a way 'cause it gives them a lot less responsibility and they never get attacked for anything they do seriously wrong. And also, a lot of the time when you have that sort of thing going it's good 'cause sometimes just emotionally, they'll just like go apeshit on a track, you know, and like completely express themselves better than they ever would have done.

You've only got to hear people who have been in The Fall when they make their own records, there's like something seriously missing there. And, "It's Mark Smith's Fall, it's his lyrics" — it's not, it's not that at all. It's the last thing I think is missing. What's missing is that actual oppression that sort of gives rise to freedom in a funny sort of way. They just take the mechanics of it, and try to, you know...

Do you think it's important for your product to be heard?

MES: I think it's important for us to be heard. Like I don't think 'rock' on TV is important, I just think it's important that, you know, maybe a snatch of us is heard on television, that's good enough for me, you know? Surprisingly, it's very hard, you know, it's such a fucking corrupt business. It's not corrupt really, I mean it's just a lot of people have got instant careers to move forward, you know, so they're obviously a lot more desperate than me.

On request,
Rolling the toilet roll down the stairs, I turn my head to see a moth flying towards the flame. He hops out of the room.
Right is everyone <u>Yes please</u> "Rubbing a sponge" <u>Liar</u> or an optimist.
<u>Unscrew</u> "Turn off clock, feed philanthropy" <u>Greed</u> (when in need)
<u>Exploit</u> "Put a pistol to the suckers brain"
<u>I can get some more out of this but I won't bother</u> "After all he's got a car" (I'm planning on some wheels)
Pre-conditioned <u>I was asking</u> the child dances in the presence of the horrified fool (is there a handle on the door you slammed?)
The official book of nothing sensible. They never knew the wiring, but they know how to charge for it.
Structures to please your movement I hope you choke to death (he is a fun kind of guy)
At this point he leaps in the air and lands on a guests stomach.
No, of course I'm not frustrated. I don't need a portion of a days work to project a false smile which ends up permanent.
Self-inflicted Diarrhoea face.
It's not a fact of being strong, I just thought you might overlook the word condescending <u>content</u> until and I hope it will never happen and I can't do what I want.
Never take it in consideration what other people want because if you can't please yourself, you can't please your soul. So to get back to the beaurocratic ladder climber of a lifeless lie for what security who lost that on the entrance. International companies and we've heard they don't share. Squeeze them like a sponge, there is nothing wrong with using and abusing as long as you say you do.
Chuck a penny in the wishing well.
Who is picking up the coppers.
<u>Stimulation</u> is being confronted, inspired by hearing a structure you have not been through. To the pre-conditioned it is intangible. Tangibility is shut off by the ignorant. The ignorant always wisen <u>up</u>. So I've got plenty of time. I'd rather shout at an echo rather than lie that someone's listening.

STEVO

Some Bizzare is a record / management company based in London which has variously presided over a contrasting stable of groups; Marc Almond, Cabaret Voltaire, Test Department, Psychic TV, The The, Einsturzende Neubauten and Scraping Foetus Off The Wheel. Its public face is Stevo, originally from the East End of London, who managed Soft Cell when he was seventeen and compiled the *Some Bizzare Album* whilst working as a Futurist DJ in a nightclub in Retford, near Nottingham. This led to the formation of Some Bizzare, whose initial aim was to act as a middle man between individual groups and a major label, thus retaining the group's artistic control while gaining a widespread distribution through a major. Stevo does not conduct business by the established rules. Rather than sending a tape to a record company and checking on its reaction a few weeks later, Stevo is more likely to burst through the door of the company president, slam a ghetto blaster on his oversized desk and play the tape at an incredibly loud volume, while simultaneously doing a handstand in the opposite corner of the room and spouting gibberish. Because of his past success within the industry, Stevo is often afforded the upper hand.

However, his erratic behaviour has made him notorious within the business for upsetting their safe, structured marketing campaigns. Stevo has also been known to speak at the New Music Seminar in New York while wearing antlers or a judge's wig to upset the convention's formal mood. Whether wacky, mad, imposing or threateningly extrovert, Stevo prefers to fight from within the industry than from the outside, aspiring to "remain content with himself artistically". This drive has more recently attracted Stevo to video, where he edits a Some Bizzare cable TV show in America and compiles footage to be released in the UK.

In general what is Some Bizzare?

Stevo: Some Bizzare is a commodity name for people to relate to anything which *is* basically. But for Some Bizzare to be followed as a cult is a contradiction of a cult, for the simple reason that if you cross over Some Bizzare, you don't cross over any style, you cross over diversity.

So what would be your definition of a cult?

Stevo: Tribalistic instincts of people. But we try to cross over and hopefully never have the same transient music cults which have been around for the last thirty years.

So it's basically trying to create something new.

Stevo: It stands for the innovator, the one that inspires others, and not the parasites that are inspired.

Some of the records on Some Bizzare are distributed by other companies. How does that situation work?

Stevo: Well, I don't believe in signing away my destiny. Some Bizzare is an independent label for the fact that no-one owns the name Some Bizzare. And we have label identity, but we go through lots of different outlets. So we're not owned.

Would you consider bands like Einsturzende Neubauten and Test Department to be part of a movement?

Stevo: I don't particularly. I mean, yes, surely there is a certain amount of cross over from Neubauten to Test Department, maybe some people might class that as a movement, but I mean as far as I'm concerned, Test Department and Neubauten haven't really anything in common at all.

Other than the fact that they use similar type percussion?

Stevo: Well no, not really. Test Department are four people more rhythm orientated, and I would consider Neubauten to be more destructive.

So are you against categorising certain bands?

Stevo: Try categorising the unknown. If they can be categorised, categorise them!

Do you find that the albums sell well six months or a year after their release?

Stevo: The albums on Some Bizzare are not transient at all, the signings are inspired by longevity and durability. As far as I'm concerned, you will see the albums in the racks in thirty years time, when you will not see something that has been in the charts for twenty weeks, or something on the strength of radio reaction. If a band relies on radio to sell records, that band is in a pitiful position as far as I'm concerned. Basically in this country there's one station, and if they play something, it'll sell records. If there's one hit from some garbage band, they'll sell lots of albums on the strength of it. But at the end of the day, if they're not doing something which is original, they're not going to last. Or if you're selling records on a fashion — fashions die. At the end of the day A&R men have to justify their job, and they can only get that kind of quick reaction on something that is basically uninspiring and unoriginal. They do not bring you art, they bring you sales.

So rather than signing a band to commercialise and capitalise from it, you obviously have a different motive.

Stevo: Our aspirations are sincere and artistic.

At the Neubauten Concerto at London's ICA, do you feel the response from the audience was forced upon them?

Stevo: First, we did that performance under 'The Concerto for Voice and Machinery' presented by two members of Einsturzende Neubauten and not Einsturzende Neubauten. It was a hundred percent against the verbal arrangement and was a conceptual, theatrical performance of destruction. The ICA is supposed to be a radical arts centre. We showed them up for how 'radical' and interesting they really are. And the reason why we jumped out into the audience with the cango guns was because, if the excitement is on stage, it's intangible. But as soon as it jumps down into the audience, then it's on your doorstep, which does create a reaction. And we won't mention the nuclear shelter under that place for the aristocracy...

Would you consider 'The Concerto' as a device to promote chaos within the audience?

Stevo: I would consider it an artistic cry of disgust.

Was it supposed to be ten or fifteen minutes long, or was it planned to go on for a longer period?

Stevo: As far as we could have gone down to the nuclear shelter. The aristocracy, The House of Lords, and the Head of the Military in Britain's whole shelter system is beneath the ICA. It's just the idea to keep going until they stop you.

What do you think of this one thousand pound bill that has supposedly been levied against you for damages to the ICA?

Stevo: I said I'd see them in court.

Do you think they would bring you to court?

Stevo: I would make a mockery of the court, stand up going, "Art... Not Art... Art... Not Art". Because one of the arguments he said is, "I'd hardly call it art chucking a microphone in a cement mixer". I said, "I'll argue that".

When they talked to you about getting Neubauten to play there, did they know there would be a certain amount of damage?

Stevo: Well, I don't know. It's their job to find out, it isn't my job to tell.

Would you call 'The Concerto' music?

Stevo: I don't know what music is for a start. 'Rock and roll' is not just a style, it's an indoctrinated, instinctual thing which is bred into people. Basically, people are preconditioned. I think as soon as you smash down that instrumentation, that bass guitar, lead guitar, drums and vocals, the whole perspective gets a lot wider. The initial thing is to break it down so you're open to experience a lot more.

How do you go about finding bands like Test Department or Neubauten?

Stevo: I don't look at all. I honestly think that people that are doing interesting things, true artists, want to be with something they feel can understand what they are doing. They find me.

Could you explain why the Test Department gig at Waterloo Station was cancelled.

Stevo: Cancelled... Pretty radical cancel! I was out of the country, I was in America. The place was an illegal drinking place and the police raided the club because it didn't have a licence to sell drinks.

Whose fault was that?

Stevo: If you go to a club where there are barmen and bouncers and lights and a disco and it's all decorated, you don't ask if there's a licence. In fact I did hear while I was in America that some people thought I organised that, which I found very... bizarre.

What do you think about America?

Stevo: I like New York. It's most probably one of my favourite places in the world. I like New Yorkers. I can't really talk about America because I haven't experienced the whole of America. I don't like California very much. The place stinks of who has got what, and not who they are.

You don't find the same thing in New York?

Stevo: You find that thing in every capitalist country in the world, but I find that it smells and it's more obvious in Los Angeles than anywhere I've been.

What do you think about your music selling in New York, do you feel there's commercial potential there.

Stevo: I find that New York, as far as my experience goes, is a lot more open minded than a lot of other places in America. But again, you've got to realise that what people cannot see, hear, or read, they cannot think about. I mean then it becomes a whole situation of apathy, and the safe bet is the wrong one. I mean if something causes a reaction, it's a lot better than it just being subliminal, going in one ear and out the other.

We don't plan for a starter. It's the same with Psychic TV, Cabaret Voltaire, Neubauten. When they go into a studio, they rely on their psychic force to present them with opportunities. It's when you're in the studio that you open yourself to fate. They don't contrive anything until it comes together in the studio, and I think that's the best way to work.

Has the business been profitable?

Stevo: For Some Bizzare, not really. But you like the music, so at least some people are getting something out of it.

Has it been profitable for you?

Stevo: I mean I get by, but I'm not a materialistic sort of person at all. I just want to live the standard of living which I've got used to, which isn't that high obviously. What's more important is, if Some Bizzare closed down tomorrow, then a lot of people's optimism would just collapse, because a lot of people consider us the last standpoint of sincerity.

What was the first thing that interested you in Throbbing Gristle? What were you listening to before that?

Stevo: I wasn't. I mean I've been a TG fan for a long time. I could have signed up the Throbbing Gristle back catalogue, and there's quite a few things which I consider very artistically credible, but I will never go back. If you compare Psychic TV with Throbbing Gristle, there's no comparison. If you compare 'The Crackdown' with 'Sluggin' Fer Jesus', there's no comparison. And if you're a Foetus fan, compare his old albums to his new material, there's no comparison. I could carry on... To me, what Some Bizzare produces is not the same as the past, but I still respect the past.

In that way, do you want every album that comes out by a certain band on the label to be very different from their other ones?

Stevo: It stands to reason that it will be. I know there's no-one treading on anyone else's toes artistically. That needs not be said. All you have to do is listen to the music. But I do agree with clarity and separation to make things hit harder.

Are there any other labels or musicians that you admire?

Stevo: Not a lot. I do like Ralph records. I do enjoy self-indulgence. But I think The Residents are rolling a ball along a long corridor and they're not taking a side door, so at the end of the corridor there's a brick wall. It's a shame because they should get away from their limitations.

In listening to 'The Some Bizzare Album', the music is very different to what's coming out on the label now.

Stevo: I can't even listen to it now. It was recorded for about fifteen hundred pounds. The only drum machines then were, "Boom Cha Cha, Boom Cha Cha". There was no such thing as a Linn, or an Oberheim or whatever. The Soft Cell track was recorded for about seven pounds, the Blancmange track was recorded in a basement and The The was recorded in a garage, so it's pretty rough.

What was it that made you lean in a direction away from electronic music, which mainly comprises 'The Some Bizzare Album'?

Stevo: I only release what I like. If I get goose pimples, then I like it. I like electronic music with a grit or with the right frequencies. I don't like things which plod along nicely. I have no respect for artists who contrive hit singles. The approach is wrong and untrue.

Are there any other labels that you respect besides Ralph?

Stevo: I don't really know too many. I would like more contact with people who have the right attitude. I mean it's very difficult for me to ever get letters which are sent to the office anyway because I've got a kind of filtering system. Everyone is overworked. Some Bizzare is on the verge of collapse — collapse in the sense of nervous breakdowns. That office, as soon as you walk into it, has got this aura of chaos.

Do you like that image?

Stevo: I don't think it's contrived. (laughs) But I find the best music is projected from insecurity. So on the good aspect, it's the actual end result on record. But on a day to day basis, everyone involved with Some Bizzare, including myself, is very obsessed. Some Bizzare is like a self-created padded cell.

Do you find that certain images shown at a live performance might be harmful for some people in the audience?

Stevo: I believe in absolute liberation, and I think people like to be confused. I think that actually creating something to get people paranoid, or to cause a reaction, manipulation, indoctrination, is good. You've got your choice. You don't have to go to a Psychic TV gig, but if you do, then you have to face the consequences. If you open yourself to fate, as soon as you become aware of that, things will happen. I mean it's weird when you open yourself to it, because it's going on around you even if you haven't noticed it before. If it has happened to you, then you're lucky.

Do you find music political at all?

Stevo: The frustration of censorship, visual, sound, that kind of general apathy creates a certain amount of disgust, and I don't believe in hiding that.

How political are you?

Stevo: I'm very against dogmatic attitudes. I don't mind who sits next to me with whatever extremist views, as long as they don't try and ram it down my throat.

When Matt Johnson signed, didn't you sign the contract in Trafalgar Square?

Stevo: This wasn't contrived. The managing director's secretary at CBS said, "Oh Mr Oberstein would like to meet you at some restaurant in three days at so and so a time". And I said, "No, no, no. I'll meet him in my time, which is twelve o'clock tonight at Tottenham Court Road train station". So surely enough, it was raining and he walked past me about four times and he finally came up to me and said, "Stevo?" And I said, "Yes... you're late". He said, "I've got a car". I said, "Hard luck". He said, "Where do we go then?" I said, "Trafalgar Square...". It was the first place I could think of and I just jumped on the line. If he wanted to speak to me he needed to follow me.

Have there been any other things like that with other bands that have signed?

Stevo: I done Test Department's deal on a rocking horse — Horace. I get sweets every week for the rest of my life from Phonogram. The Teddy Bear over there was sent to a meeting dressed as Robin Hood to get Soft Cell a deal. And the brass dildo has all the record company names on the top of the penises, like saying, "Go fuck yourself". You see, international companies are a pyramid, the shareholders don't share the profits with the mass that makes it tick. Now, if they did, there would be no hope for free enterprise. And also if they did, that would be the end of capitalism, which is not a political statement, that is just reality.

Also before I signed Psychic TV, I heard Gen's voice in this house saying, "Stevo... Stevo", in the bathroom, which was like the final thing to convince me to sign Psychic TV. And also I heard 'Red Cinders in the Sand' by Matt Johnson on a plane coming back from New York in the toilet, and I was slapping myself around the face and pinching myself and chucking water, but I kept hearing this. Those are the only times I've actually heard something. And with Neubauten I got this weird card which was all in pieces and it went together to form a spanner and a hammer. It was just addressed to me. And a good friend gave me this, which is an iron fist, which is the first thing that inspired me to sign Neubauten. So there's a spiritual guidance behind Some Bizarre.

How did you start Some Bizzare?

Stevo: By getting loads of tapes sent to me. I was doing a chart in the papers called The Futurist Chart. I was a DJ, but I was banned from about four or five different clubs. I was chased out of a club by about thirty people through fire exits once, 'cause I was just repeating, "Yes, hello, hello, yes, it's highly psychological", and mixing Mickey Mouse into Cabaret Voltaire at half speed, and actually doing things that they were not used to. I also DJ'd with six desks, mixing the same record, all the different titles, so it was like the most intense thing you ever heard.

Did you get that on tape?

Stevo: No I haven't got any pictures either. I don't send postcards, I don't write letters, and I don't keep any memorabilia at all.

Did you have much capital to put into Some Bizzare before it started?

Stevo: No, it was all done on credit.

Are you pleased with the position that you're in now?

Stevo: No, I mean we've chipped away such a small amount. I don't actually sit back in a content manner. I can honestly say I don't ever look back at all, because forward is the only thing. I mean as soon as you sit back, then you're going to be destroyed.

What do you think of restrictions created by society?

Stevo: I don't think there should be any restrictions at all sexually. If two people are willing to do whatever they want, there should never be any restrictions. I believe in total negation. I mean if you talk about a psychic force or a spiritual fate or force behind you, people just think you're a paganist — which is looked upon as evil. Religion to me is full of hypocritical and financial power.

Do you read much?

Stevo: I've never read a book in my life. I couldn't read and write when I left school. I didn't have any qualifications whatsoever, and I couldn't speak properly until I was about thirteen. I mean if you're honest with yourself and follow you're instincts you will never go wrong.

Have you ever thought that you had made a wrong choice?

Stevo: No, I'm very anti-culture, nostalgia and diplomacy.

What would happen if a band on your label started doing things that were against what you personally believed?

Stevo: I would sway a certain way, unless I felt it was aimed to irritate me.

Quotes of yours appear on certain albums. Is that just so other people can understand some of your own beliefs?

Stevo: Yes. I mean at the end of the day, I will be out of this business and into films, and I will write a book. There's a lot of it already written. Nothing has ever really been printed of what I write down because it's multi-schizophrenia on paper, and the more times you read it, the more things it tells you, and within five hundred words, it would basically cause such a reaction, you'd have to go back, and back, and if you can imagine a book like that, it would be pretty heavy going.

Do you consider that genius?

Stevo: No, it's not contrived, I just write, and I put things in inverted commas, I put things in brackets, I underline things, I put things in capitals. And basically if I'm saying something, I will contradict it or show another angle in capital letters. But when I actually take out all the capital letters and put them on one page, I sometimes can't go to bed at night because I've got goose pimples.

How did the name Some Bizzare come about?

Stevo: So me.

What makes Some Bizzare different from other companies?

Stevo: We're bigoted, because if we look and see what's around, then that's our reason for it. At the end of the day, we must stick together to smash down that wall, and when you feel that you're banging your fist against a wall of ignorance and naivety, the only thing that keeps you going is people that come up and actually say that it's important. We have a lot of allies in the media, on the street. I think that a naive person can open his eyes to life, but someone with his eyes open can never end up naive. And Some Bizzare basically puts out records for the people who have their eyes open. So it can only be increased by the people who haven't yet, and I don't think we should degrade our intelligence by going to their level.

A DEAD MAN

A WOMAN

He's looking down my dress. He can see my breasts. He wants to hurt me, hang me with the noose that's in his hand. He's mocking me with it, swinging it in front of my face, showing me that if I go with him he'll hang me with it after we fuck. I'm not sure if I want him to hurt me. I know that when he pushes his cock into me it will hurt when it hits my uterus. His cock fills me up and makes me another person, subject to his desire, his violence. He's going to call his friends over and invite them to gang rape me, then hang me while they masturbate in harmony with my suffering. I'm prey. I'm constantly hunted. I keep my head down trying to obscure myself, trying to sink into the wall. They always smell me. My ass gives off a scent. I can't get rid of it. Men smell me. They want to fuck me and obliterate me once the smell has reached the nerves inside their heads. They want to fuck me, rip me to shreds. I have to steal myself, be more clever than they are. I use my scent as a lure (a kind of weapon). I lead them to a cliff, then I push them off. As they fall they can't believe what has happened to them. They scream in stupid male agony. They've been had. Sometimes they get the better of me. Then I'm tortured, cut, disregarded after being used. Someone's going to hang me. Some man will follow me and string me up in his shed. He may as well kill himself, because once I've been wiped out I'm of no use to him — and he needs me. He needs my smell in his head. When I die my smell will shift into decay and choke his desire. His desire is putrid, selfish, ugly. Mine's justified, because my cunt has to be filled. My cunt smells like death, because it was made to choke cocks. I deserve to be hanged, eviscerated, my feet and hands cut off, because I'm a woman. My body should be left hanging in a dark room until it gets ripe, until the smell is physical and solid. When he comes in and puts his hands on me, cuts me down and lays me out on the floor, my corpse mouth will moan for him to fuck me. My smell will press him into my corpse while he fucks me and the words I lick into his ear will kill him slowly while he fucks my body.

A SCREW

I don't trust anyone. I'm trying to guard myself. I hate these creeps. Their dirty penetrating eyes see every humiliating flaw. I know I'm better than anyone I've ever seen or met, anyone I've ever worked for, anyone that has ever seen my face when I'm exposed. I'm hiding something. I'm holding it in. I'm hiding because I'm better than they are. I'm transfixed. I'm staring at my naked body in the mirror. I've had it shaped according to what I want to see. Slabs of fat cut away, my breasts uplifted, reduced to the perfect size and shape. I've worked on this body. I've put myself under the knife for it, I've sweat for it. It's mine. I control it, use it for my own gratification. It provides me with perfect sex: Self inclusive, contained, rigid, unrelenting, punishing. It's mine. I'm perfect for myself. The smell of my sweat, the feel of my muscles tightening, satisfies me, fucks me. I'm perfect. I fuck myself. My image in the mirror is fucking me. I turn myself on. Everything else is superfluous. I'm self contained. I'll eliminate anything, any creep, any ugly living flesh that gets in my way. When I look in the mirror, I make time stop. I need nothing, no-one. Nothing can fuck me like I fuck myself. No regrets. I've worked myself into what I want to fuck. I'm fucking myself now.

© Michael Gira

COIL

Coil was conceived by John Balance in 1982 as a concurrent project with Psychic TV, with whom he was working, playing bass guitar, vibes and various Tibetan instruments. In 1984 he began concentrating full time on Coil together with the co-founder of Psychic TV, Peter 'Sleazy' Christopherson. In addition to his role in TG and Psychic TV, Christopherson was also a member of the Hipgnosis design group who executed covers for many 'supergroups' of the seventies, including Led Zeppelin, Yes and Pink Floyd. John Balance has previously worked with David Tibet and Fritz Haaman in Current 93. On the Coil album *Scatology*, they are variously joined by Clint Ruin and Gavin Friday of Virgin Prunes. Coil have also written the soundtrack to the feature film *The Angelic Conversation*, directed by Derek Jarman, while the video for their version of *Tainted Love* is on permanent display at The Museum Of Modern Art in New York. In 1986, Coil released a mini-LP with Boyd Rice, and in 1987 an LP entitled *Horse Rotorvator*.

What is Coil?

Sleazy: Loosely, it's what we do musically. We do other things apart from music but it is the term for our musical experiments. Although it's basically me and John, we do get other people to help as well. In that way, I suppose it's like Psychic TV regarding the set-up and collaborative aspects. Coil is also a code. A hidden universal. A key for which the whole does not exist, a spell, a spiral. A serpents SHt around a female cycle. A whirlwind in a double helix. Electricity and elementals, atonal noise and brutal poetry. A vehicle for obsessions. Kabbulah and Khaus. Thanatos and Thelema. Archangels and Antichrists. Truth and Deliberation. Traps and disorientation. Infantile, inbuilt disobedience.

Where is the term Coil derived from?

J Balance: I chose it on instinct and since then I've found that it actually means a noise. And there are things like the spiral, the electrical coil and contraception. The spiral is a repeating micro/macrocosmic form. From DNA to spiral galaxies. A primal symbol. It's a nice little word.

The Black Sun that we use is a surrealist symbol from Maldoror by Isadore Ducasse. It has 10 rays (2x5). Coil are essentially a duo and five is the number of the aeon of Horus — the present time. We have a private mythology completely in tune with symbols and signs of the present aeon. We don't believe that it should become an important part of our public image — as misinterpretation, and unnecessary and incorrect replication would possibly occur. Silence and secrecy. After all, the image of Horus most appropriate to the new aeon is of a 'conquering child' with his finger to his lips — the sign of silence.

What is the significance behind the title of the album 'Scatology'?

Sleazy: Scatology in the medical sense is an obsession with human shit, or as the old fashioned dictionaries used to say, "An obsession with animal lusts and base instincts". So it's a combination of those two.

Why do you feel that's important to incorporate in the title?

Sleazy: In as much as 'Scatology' is more to be listened to as entertainment, the titles of those records normally try to attract people in a slightly outrageous way and at the same time, give some indication of the atmosphere of the record. I think it's a good title, and a lot of the songs on the record refer, either in their lyric or in their moods, to the most base of man's instincts. It seemed quite appropriate. It is what Dali in 'The Unspeakable Confessions of Salvador Dali' calls "The Humanism of the Arsehole".

What do you see as the importance behind a ritual?

Sleazy: Most people's lives are basically devoid of anything that adds meaning. That sounds so patronising to say, but I just think that the fulfilment I get from doing things that have no immediate everyday need while at the same time fulfilling other needs, certainly indicates to me that it would be interesting for other people to try them too. And you can only use yourself as an example for how you think other people should live — rather than saying in the way that religions do, "You must do this", or whatever.

Is it important for the ritual to be designed by the person that practises it?

Sleazy: I don't think so, millions of people benefit from catholic rituals.

J Balance: Or The Japanese Tea Rituals. It's the Zen philosophy that every movement means something. I think that way of living is far richer and it gives them an awareness of what and where they are. But ritual in the West is monopolised by the church, especially in Europe and the United Kingdom. People carry out rituals all the time, the English parlour obsessions with table turning, clairvoyents and wishing wells. All these exist and are practiced, but people seem to be somehow ashamed of them and would rather be represented by the church. I suppose that's because it's a rich organisation with ostentatious shows of power and wealth.

How would something like the Japanese Tea Ritual differ from something that the church has organised?

Sleazy: They're not at all different in what they achieve in the person. Where they differ is that the organised church has exploited its knowledge of ritual to control people and enhance their own political end. Certainly in this country in the last thousand years the church has been a political machine that has done what it has for profit and for the advancement of the people in control. And I think it's a pity that the church leaders have exploited their position that way because it has fucked up a lot of people in Northern Ireland, the whole of South America, Spain and most of the Far East.

J Balance: To take a blatant example like the Aztecs, their whole society was controlled by priests who knew the language and knew the way to stop the sun from dying, and so they had complete control over every member of the population. If people didn't do certain things, they believed they'd die. The system was highly developed, very brutal and based on human sacrifice. But they believed if the Gods didn't get their blood, then the sun would not rise and the world would end. And it's just the same here except it's far more insidious and hidden.

Sleazy: All that you really need for your own rituals to be valid is a belief in their abilities. The only problem is that it's easy to have self-doubt about what you're doing. And if you have a body of other people doing a ritual that somebody else has designed, then it's more easy to believe that it might have some power.

Is it possible to use rituals for negative purposes, to bring out evil or destructive things?

J Balance: Oh yeah, but what's the point really? The Tibetan Bon-Po shaman priests still do this. They've been called the most powerful and evil magickians that ever lived. I've got an LP of part of a malicious, destroying ritual.

"The first low-keyed monk's voice marks the beginning of the Mahakala prayer. The chant begins with an extended description of Mahakala as well as his different emanations. The chant continues, calling upon Mahakala in his various forms to come down to earth and receive the offerings of the participants and to devour marigpa". 'The Mahakala Prayer' — Side 2 of Lyrichord Disc LLST 7270.

They go on for days and cause plague in a whole village. The energy and powers exist to be able to do that sort of thing, but what's the point?

Sleazy: The gutter press, National Enquirer sort of mentality, use basically the same argument when dealing with more or less anything, whether it's a nuclear bomb or a ritual. Sexuality, for example, they frown on because it is a way of having a powerful experience. Not exploiting, but using the power of human nature to do something. And if it has a possible negative power, then they immediately say that the medium is at fault.

Does the energy of the ritual come from within the person or can it be drawn from other sources?

J Balance: It doesn't really matter where it comes from. The point is it works, that power can be summoned, generated and you can harness, manipulate and channel it, so you never need to know where it comes from.

Why do most people view a ritual or magick as being evil?

Sleazy: It's fear of the unknown. Basically it's because the church saw other people who were doing rituals as a threat to their control.

J Balance: They try to keep a monopoly so anything else is bad or evil and you get thrown into hell for it. It's Christian propaganda basically. England has strong pagan roots and the church has always attempted to stamp these out. Originally by neutralising pagan temple sites and then building churches on the same sites, then by burning witches and religious persecutions. If they couldn't kill them, they used ridicule and fear tactics to deter people from the pagan heritage. The devil is only a Christian adaptation of a neutral nature deity; Pan, Cernos, the horned gods — which are phallic. The Christian church has never been very sexual, except where the pagan undercurrent has been allowed to emerge because it was too strong to suppress completely. The devil is a representation of pagan sexuality, which is why people are attracted to it even when seen as a Christian invention.

Sleazy: At the moment we're sort of going through a right-wing backlash against the freedom of the sixties and seventies, certainly in terms of sex. And I wouldn't be surprised if in ten years time there was a religious resurgence of interest in the church.

Were the angels symbolic of a larger concept on 'How to Destroy Angels'?

Sleazy: All of what we do is symbolic on several different levels at once, so you can interpret angels as being a number of things, whether it's the controlling influence of the church, or whether it's an unnecessary desire to retain virginity.

J Balance: When I thought of the title, all these things went through me. It was a record to accumulate enough power to destroy theoretical angels — Christian gossamer angels don't seem hard to destroy. It was a curious matter of fact title, almost like a manual, a handbook you'd come across which could be the key to immense power and change.

Do you think that Coil will vary to a large extent from TG live?

Sleazy: Yeah, the trouble with playing live is that everything has to be done on the spot more or less. And nobody in TG was a particularly great musician. Basically that narrows down your options as to what you can do live. You can rely very heavily on backing tapes, you can just do your best, or you can bring in other musicians. And none of those options are very acceptable to me. Just doing your best and trying to work out sounds that one could reproduce competently and that sounded interesting was really what TG were doing. It got to the point where we couldn't go any further and that's one of the reasons why we split up. And the Psychic TV dates that we did in the Summer and Autumn of 1983 didn't really go any further than TG had. We had Alex playing, who is a good musician in that he can play proper guitar, but jams even with good musicians tend to sound like what their influences are. And so a lot of Psychic TV stuff ended up sounding like The Velvet Underground, which didn't seem to me like it was advancing anything.

J Balance: Although the ideas were interesting live, it became more brutal and relied on the noise element while the ideas got swamped. I mean it's alright for people who had heard the records before and knew what we were about and they got energy off it, but it wasn't much more than a sort of controlled noise with a cause behind it. Which on reflection seems pretty reasonable, but something wasn't right. Genesis would probably say it was our attitude.

Sleazy: Well that's alright, but the reason why we haven't really done any live dates is because we haven't actually solved this problem of what to do. Certainly we could rely more on backing tapes in the way that a lot of groups do, but people really want that sort of dense atmosphere and rely on that adrenalin rush and I don't know if you can get that from backing tapes.

What did you see as the function or purpose behind Throbbing Gristle?

Sleazy: To see if it was actually possible to get people to react physically. And also we were just trying to advance our intellectual and artistic aspirations in a new way, because prior to that we hadn't been doing music at all. And also to have fun and attract young people who we could fuck. All the reasons people normally have groups. (laughs)

Is there such a thing as inaudible sound?

Sleazy: Pardon? (laughs) The theory of all that stuff is that if you actually play something at a lower level or backwards or in flashes on the screen it's absorbed by the subconscious mind which acts upon it immediately. But I've never had any information or evidence that it works. People say The Rolling Stones album 'Their Satanic Majesty's Request' has reverse masking and it says, "Come to Satan", or something. I mean it's all bullshit, it doesn't work in my view.

J Balance: Records are very crude as far as recording and playback quality goes and there is no way that scientific experiments can be done in this medium. I think holophonics are far more interesting anyway. Stevo gets accused of doing a big hoax and so does Zuccarelli who developed the system. With holophonics we were able to get atmospheric subliminals and record a particular feeling including the spatial limits of a room or a cave and the movements of people in it. But I remain very dubious about back masking and inaudible sounds having profound but subtle effects.

Sleazy: Coil are interested in subliminals of another kind — delirium subliminals. Avatistic glimpses of a grand chaos — surfacing in flashes of black light — in darkest Dali, Jarry, the Moomintrolls, The Virgin Prunes, in the face of Edith Sitwell, Boyd Rice's humour — emotional subliminals. Psychic information, partly deliberate, mostly instinctive.

Do you think that ghost images in a visual picture have an effect on people?

J Balance: I think they possibly have more effect. Apparently 'The Exorcist' originally had dead animals subliminally put in and they had to take them out. I mean there was a huge reaction about people being sick because it was the first high class splatter movie. It has more chance of having an effect if you see adverts many times — and they're not subliminal. If you see adverts for ice cream, next time you're in the shop, you go, "I'll have one of them", because you've seen it on telly. It just works on a crass level like that.

Sleazy: But there are lots of things that happen with films that could be exploited more, just things that you see in the background that you don't notice but are actually there.

J Balance: All of these subjects — subliminals, back-masking, cut-ups, the Industrial group's subjects — culled from Burroughs' 'The Job' and 'The Electronic Revolution', have been done to death... And not very well. Sonic research is very hard to do properly on a Rough Trade advance or whatever. It maintains a pseudo-science, it has a wishy-washy quality that I don't particularly want to be associated with. I'd rather been seen as a perverse noise unit with decidedly dubious musical leanings. I admire the intentions of all these groups, but the purity or scope of the possibilities are diminished by huge amounts in the translation to vinyl. Z'ev and NON seem to remain pure — as do Sonic Youth, but they're coming from a different area as far as I can tell. In the end, the intentions alone can be appreciated — golden conceptualists and dull records type of situation.

Do you think that music is the best medium to get your ideas across to people?

Sleazy: No, I think film and television is by far the strongest because it's a way of really affecting all of us. If you could affect the senses of smell and touch as well, it would be stronger still.

Is there a difference between chance and fate?

Sleazy: I don't think there's such a thing as fate really. I don't think there's such a thing as chance either, but that's different. Fate implies that a certain thing is bound to happen, but I don't think that's the case. To rely on logic, then obviously whatever's going to happen is going to happen. But at the same time, the implication that it's out of your control is obviously rubbish. At any point you have a myriad of choices, whether it's running and jumping out of the window or not. Obviously things happen as a result of circumstances that one could not possible foresee and that is what one calls chance.

In the studio, does the recording process differ much with how you've worked previously?

J Balance: With Coil we lay down the backbone ourselves, and if we want to we collaborate with other people. With PTV it was more of a jam, things spontaneously arose out of rehearsals.

Sleazy: But all the PTV records that we were involved in were fundamentally done in the same way that we do now, which is to set down a rhythm and just lay things on top of it as they seem appropriate.

Do you think that you can change society through music?

Sleazy: No, I don't think you can change anything with music particularly.

J Balance: But then again, a group like Crass might say it's not necessarily their music, but the message that's coupled with it. We're very cautious about having one heavy message, but we do have a life style and I do want to change a lot of things. We're obviously not like Ultravox where their album and the way they view life may be quite separate.

Sleazy: I actually don't know any members of Ultravox personally, but my suspicion is that the content of their lyrics actually isn't very deep and doesn't concern very many of the things that I'm interested in. So that's one of the reasons I don't buy Ultravox records. Music is just an expression of the taste of the person that's doing it, and that is ultimately why you buy a record — whether it's Johnny Rotten or Captain Beefheart.

J Balance: If you hear a record you like and you suddenly find out that the people responsible do something that you're really against, then you probably won't listen to the record in the same light.

But shouldn't music be judged on its own merit?

J Balance: I don't think it should just by the song. They should have a sense of realisation that people do tie the two things together.

Sleazy: That's a very difficult question because having been around the 'business' for a long while, I've met people whose music I've respected but whom I discovered I didn't respect as people. And certainly that changed my perception of their music and their work.

Do you think that is elitist in some ways?

Sleazy: I think we are elitist. I know that I am a bit of a snob in some ways. I mean we're

talking about politics now and that is about how much self respect you have and whether you think your opinion is actually better than somebody else's. And the important thing to remember is that one's own opinion is the best there is for you but not necessarily somebody else. It has got to do with whether you are big headed enough to think that your own opinions are the ones other people should hold. And I think that's very dangerous. I have certain very strong views about particular things that other people would certainly think were elitist, unusual or unacceptable. But I only hold those views for myself and I wouldn't necessarily expect other people to enjoy the things that I enjoy. And likewise, I would expect them not to force me to live in the way that they do.

Coincidentally we have touched upon a very common misconception — which is that elitism is a bad thing. It's also an old misconception that it's important to do a particular kind of music at a particular time. I mean you can look back on certain songs as being 'classic' or completely different from anything else at the time, but it's all temporary. I think it's worse in America where people tend to accept commercial dogmas more readily. In England, the eccentric is part of the history of the country. There has always been the village idiot.

J Balance: Does that make us the village idiots?

Sleazy: No, but there's the whole tradition, Oscar Wilde or Quentin Crisp or whatever, as being acceptable as the local weirdo in a sense. And the people that do that in America are far more out on a limb until they get some commercial success. I mean New York is a cultural island relative to the midwest — where the people that do weird records have a difficult time. At least in England people are prepared to listen to something new with an open mind, so it's that much easier. It may be crazy, but I still have an optimistic hope that free thinkers will be allowed to continue to do so because most of them are not threatening to society even though society might feel that they are. That is why we're lucky in Britain in that we accept eccentrics and people that do things out of the ordinary as being a healthy and contributory part of society's existence.

J Balance: But you make it sound like it's idealistic and that all these things are allowed to happen. There are huge backlashes all the time against those who appear to deviate. But society needs the deviants in order to change. There's this thing, "Let them grow up so far and perpetuate some sort of change and then beat them down again". It's as if society, like an organism, allows mutation in order to improve itself but keeps a tight rein on how much actually occurs.

Sword imagery creeps into several Coil tracks. Is that simply a phallic symbol?

J Balance: We didn't mean it as a phallic symbol. If you get Freudian then it's definitely a phallic symbol, but in magick it's not. The sound of the swords on 'How To Destroy Angels' represents Mars, as in martial, the God of Spring and War, who cabalistically represents dynamic, positive change. The sword is a symbol of willpower.

Sleazy: Although I certainly wouldn't describe us as militaristic, we recognise that man has an aggressive streak. I don't think the peace movement, for example, has got any real hope of succeeding. You have to recognise the nature of man, accept it and use it.

J Balance: It's the way things happen isn't it? Its created force is what we're aiming at, rather than militaristic, crass and obviously masculine, sexist type things. Rough Trade actually said that the cover notes to 'How To Destroy Angels' were misogynist, which I find ridiculous — just because it dealt with masculine qualities.

Sleazy: They stocked the record and it sold out, but I don't think they were too happy about it. And they didn't put the poster up either because it was too extreme for them. In many ways the people that are supposed to be spearheading the libertarian view are just as limited in their view as the gutter press and the more conservative elements.

J Balance: Their ideals often disagree with the practical way they work. They'll say, "Oh yes, we support free thinking and things", but when you actually bring a copy of it into the shop, they'll smash it if it disagrees with their personal sensibilities.

Sleazy: You're bound to come into contact with hypocrisy when you step out the door really. The only thing you can do is to try and make sure it doesn't take place in your own home.

What inspired 'The Sewage Workers Birthday Party'?

Sleazy: It came from a story of the same name in a magazine called Mr S&M, a Scandinavian publication which is basically fetishistic in its content. It's an area I'm interested in anyway. We wanted to try and express it in musical form, and I'm personally quite pleased with the way it turned out. It's an interesting piece of music even if you don't know the original story and where it came from. I'd have liked to print it, but I don't think the people doing the covers would have actually accepted it.

Does it seem strange doing dance music now?

J Balance: Are we doing dance music?

Sleazy: When Throbbing Gristle did 'Twenty Jazz Funk Greats', it was the intention to do something that was more conventional in that form, but it wasn't totally successful because we didn't really know how to do it. We still don't know how to do it, it's just that we wanted to make some of the music a little more up tempo, aggressive and rhythmic. But it's certainly not a considered attempt to do a dance record, because I think if we tried to do that it would be a disaster.

I can't speak for the intentions of others, but I get the impression that The Art Of Noise were really a very considered attempt to do dance music in a way that would be artistic and fashionable. And it feels to me that the results are sterile and not very interesting.

J Balance: It all depends on what dance you're going to do. I think that The Birthday Party were dance music, but it wasn't the kind of thing that got played in discos very often.

Do you think that anybody has added a great deal of depth to a song which is also very entertaining and commercially accepted?

Sleazy: It's very hard because you don't know what people's reasons for doing the records were. 'Endless Sleep' by The Poppy Family, 'Tainted Love' by Gloria Jones, 'Seasons in the Sun' by Terry Jacks, and 'Emma' by Hot Chocolate, to name a few, seem to work on lots of different levels, but I don't know whether that was the intention of them in the first place.

I mean from The Beatles onwards, some records have struck at exactly the right time for them to be amazingly successful and also interesting from some other philosophical or inspirational point of view. I think that's true for films as well. That's probably one of the most satisfying things for a creative person to do, because that spiritual or philosophical side stands or falls for what it is.

What do you think about cults that develop around certain bands, such as the mimicking of haircuts and dress that became noticeable with TG and PTV.

J Balance: Thoughtless and crass mimicking of anything is worthless.

Sleazy: It's one thing to dress a particular way and to meet other people that have by their own route arrived at similar conclusions. But to wear things because one's hero or idol happens to wear them is really weird and a bit unhealthy — and slightly distasteful. That whole thing of Marc Almond clones — even though Marc's terrific. It's the same with Bowie clones. It's ironic as well because at the time we were in PTV, one of the messages of the group was free thinking and independence from that kind of thing. I can't speak for what they're doing now because they're going their own way and I wish them well, but there's no way that I personally could continue to be a part of that.

How important is image to Coil?

Sleazy: We haven't established an image for Coil as such. Although we obviously have interests slightly apart from the norm, we haven't particularly gone out of our way to create an image. In many ways it works against us because that means when we do occasionally give interviews, people don't really know what to ask.

J Balance: We've got the added problem that we could easily rely on ex-PTV and play up all the same things, but we make a conscious effort to play down those things even though some of the aspects we're still very much involved in. We're making a conscious effort to be isolationists. I think it might become our image in a way. I suppose some people might try and pick up on the fact that we're gay and associate us with that — like Bronski Beat who were only ever thought of in that context.

Sleazy: It's a question of really not allowing ourselves to be reduced to two dimensional objects. Although sexuality is fairly important part of what we do, it's by no means the only part and I don't see it as a restriction.

Why are so many people scared away by some of the imagery that TG and PTV made use of, such as skulls etc.?

Sleazy: I think that it must be that we have a different threshold, a different interpretation upon imagery. I mean it's a cliche to say this, but I've been at home and felt happier in fairly desolate and lonely sorts of places. And if people get scared by photos of the Berlin wall or something like that, then I just can't perceive of the life they lead and how they could find it scary, because it just seems natural to me.

A vast proportion of what we do and the way that we live our lives would probably freak out the majority of civilised people, simply because it's out of the norm of their experience. It would certainly freak out my mum. We don't have any wallpaper, we've got rat shit everywhere, it's just a completely different way of living. But the reason that people get frightened is because of their interpretation of those things, not because of the reality of them. It's easy for a person to interpret a photo of you holding a skull, but it doesn't necessarily mean that you are a devil worshipper or a necrophiliac. It's their interpretation which is at fault. If my mum was living here, after a while she would probably think it completely normal and would have a much more realistic scale to determine whether I was a nice person or not.

It's a very dangerous thing that some of the newspapers and the media do because it's so easy for them. And they're going to sell newspapers for being outrageous and saying, "Naughty Vicar", and "VD Hospital", shit. But outrage has always been a commodity. I mean Boy George, The Sex Pistols and everything are all manufactured, totally. But none of us, even Gen, has ever done anything really to make mileage out of being outrageous, it just comes naturally. Which is quite different I think. Although you see people on the subway with whom you feel you have absolutely nothing in common with and possibly even dislike just because of the kind of people they are, I'd rather have nothing to do with them. I don't think it's even worth going to the effort of outraging them. I just wish they weren't there.

Is there anything else that should be known about Coil?

Sleazy: We have talked quite a lot about ritual and I'm not sure if that gives a true picture of what we do. Because although it is part of our lives, it's not something that we would particularly be interested in having a name for promoting amongst young people. The Temple Ov Psychic Youth was an attempt to bring ritual to other people. I wouldn't really want to be seen doing that still, because I don't feel it is my job to tell people how they should live. But if they want to ask me, that's fine.

```
*******************************************************************
```

O.K., O.K., O.K., OKOKOKOKOK, Mister Charles McFuck SUCK ON THIS shit
HEAR!
HEAR!
here
i sit
grouchier 'n a mofo.. 'n ready to buuuurrrrrrnnnnnn.......
Smokin' cigarette after cigarette after cigarette... with (a) vengeance...
Like a non-stop lifeline...lung to lung
Nicotine stain up to the elbow
Mouth like an old leather purse (fulla wooden nickels...)
In the head an' heart an' bowels an' heels of the week
Wanna lock the doors; swallow the key; not utter a peep
NONONONONONONONONONONONONONONONONONONONONONONONONONONONONONONONONONO
I live in the foolish pools of the 90% who shit in their own nest...
They've long since learned to SIT in it... I guess
People who live in ASSHOLES shouldn't throw stones
People who live in ASSHOLES shouldn't stow thrones
I'm bad and mean and mighty unclean... afraid of no-one 'cept the man
With the divining rod... fuck you,baby................
Complaining bout ma cam-pain for ma personal decency
I don't pretend excuses bee-cause all them rules is MINE
Them rules is wrapped in BAR-BED WIRE-laced with busted glass...
WHAT's MINE IST MEIN
_____FUCKYOUBABYYYYYYYYYYYYYYYYYYYYYYY
KILLER STILL AT LARGE................
_____FUCKYOUBABY_____
I don't like what eyesee and eye wears glasses thik as milkbottles
Every step a pupil takes is on the bridge of sighs..
Trippin' over cataracts like folds of sewerflesh
Centipede in tinseltown just stepped in a pile of fucking JEWFAT
BLACK FUCKING JEWGLUE ON SHOE NUMBER ON WRIST
INGROWN FOREHEADS TO THE LEFT OF ME-INGROWN FOREHEADS TO THE RIGHT OF ME
IF THERE'S ONE THING I CAN'T STAND IT'S BEATING ROUND THE GODDAMN BUSH
AND I'M ON MY WAY TO BEING A QUEER BASHER WATCHMEJUSTFUCKINGWATCHM
E***AND NO JURY FUCKING WORLD--
NO JURY IN THE FUCKING WORLD COULD CONVICT ME!!!
tarzan on a rumble................d'ya feel lucky, punk?
CHRIST THESE VOICES ARE DRIVING ME INSANE PLEASE DRIVE THOSE FUCKS OUTA
MAHOUSE!!!!!!!!!!!!!!!!!!!!!!
if you spent half the time you do with theory you'd find you'd made
your practice perfect.
past won't make future happen/money don't make world go round/
PUT YOUR TRUNCHEON WHERE YOUR MOUTH IS BEFORE I PUT MY FOOT IN IT
OFF THE SOAPBOX/INTO THE DIRTBOX/FUCKYOUFUCKER
IF YOU CAN'T STAND THE HEAT GET OFF MY GODDAMN STOVE DON'T TELL ME...
...WHAT I ALREADY KNOW
```
*********************************************************************
```
I'LL DISCIPLINE OTHERS SO DON'T REMIND ME IF I CAN'T DISCIPLINE MYSELF,
                    --MOTHERFUCKER!!!!!!!
IT IS BASE BORING AND INSULTING TO ASK ME TO ENDURE YET ANOTHER DAY
OF THIS FUCKING FUCKING LIFE, "LIFE" , LIFE RITUAL. MUST I REALLY LOOK
LOWER (!) THAN YOUR COMMON DE-FUCKIN-NOMINATOR??????SHIT!!!!!!!!!!!!!!!!
IT'S CASTRATION, IT'S CASTOR OIL, IT'S OILY,GREASY & NONE TOO FUCKING EASY.
               GIMME A FUCKING BREAK. START AT THE NECK
chain smoker on a chain gang..bruisin bloodeyed black & blue
I'se waging a secret war and the enemy is YOU..
I'M A BRANDED MAN..I AIN'T BLANDED, MAAN don't expect no apology, YOU FUCK
                    yours, J.G. THIRLWELL
                    c/o Sado, Massachusetts

               ----------GO DIE--------


```
*********************************************************************
```

CLINT RUIN

Jim Thirlwell first graced the English shores in 1978 when he moved from his native Melbourne, Australia to London. Financing himself by working at one of the Virgin retail outlets, he started Self Immolation records and began putting his plans into action with a series of varied releases.

FOETUS UNDER GLASS consisted of two Brazilian statistics collectors, their penpal Frank Want (who hails from Athens, Georgia) and temperamental singer Phillip Toss. Phillip left the band during the recording of their single due to negative press reaction (he had previously released an LP on EMI America which sunk without trace) and went fruit picking in the South of France, where he is currently working on a book about car accident victims. The band, always a turbulent collision of personalities, dissolved after an assassination attempt on one of the members by a Brazilian terrorist group. Undeterred, Want moved to San Francisco, and the rest, as they say, is history.

PHILLIP AND HIS FOETUS VIBRATIONS were put together as a one-off when Self-Immolation A&R man Drake Buck lured back Toss from his reclusive sojourn for a single backed by You've Got Foetus On Your Breath. The result *WOMB KX07*, was recorded immediately after the DEAF sessions, and ironically reflected Toss's inner turmoil and bitter personal vision. Toss has since returned to the wilds.

FOETUS OVER FRISCO is an occasional aggregate of musicians composed of YGFOYBers Want, Ruin, Rank and Serf abetted by guest San Francisco musicians (whose names cannot be disclosed due to contractual reasons). In their first manifestation as Foetus Over Frisco they married percussive power with systems disco, musical punnery and wry lyrical venom. In their second form, as Foetus Uber Frisco (on *Finely Honed Machine*) they match disco narcissism with neo-contructivist self-discipline, transposing Le Corbusier's concept of the house as a 'machine for living' to the self, and retaining a devastating funk base. A third project in the triumvirate of twelve inches is planned, this time as Foetus Uber Alles.

FOETUS IN YOUR BED consisted of Want with YGFOYBers Satan, Kowalski and Haldt, exploring meditative, though Foetified, post systems territory, lulling the listener into a false sense of security before battering him/her with dissonant elements.

YOU'VE GOT FOETUS ON YOUR BREATH are / were, of course, Self Immolation's raison d'etre / mainstay / ultimate. A catalogue of claustrophobia, violence with finesse, positive negativism, aesthetic terrorism, black humour, they are now, perhaps sadly, no more. Frank Want recently disbanded YGFOYB on account of 'wimpiness' and now, along with fellow founder member Clint Ruin, has conceived the even more awesome creature Scraping Foetus Off the Wheel.

SCRAPING FOETUS OFF THE WHEEL is Want's new brainchild, conceived as a reaction against what YGFOYB could have become, while simultaneously clearing out YGFOYB's deadwood before comfort and the establishment of their name became functioning elements. SFOTW consists of Want and fellow founder member of YGFOYB Clint Ruin, along with other musicians from Sado, Massachusetts. Want describes SFOTW as, "…using lateral dynamics and more desperate motives, having fits of cackling borne of the taste of death and tantrums borne of futility… realisation and disgust of the intrinsic stupidity, futility and absurdity inherent in our semi self-perpetuated socio-business medium. We wallow in aggressive ignorance of currently accepted and embraced media values, preferring violently disaffected expression. And violence".

Having since signed with Some Bizzare and releasing the LPs *Hole* and *Nail* as Scraping Foetus Off The Wheel, and a twelve inch single *Foetus-Art-Terrorism*, Thirlwell gave birth to Wiseblood, featuring his own racing vocals combined with the relentless pump of former Swans percussionist Roli Mosimann. The Foetus family continues to extend, hoping to ultimately release Foetus On The Beach, a gargantuan project consisting of a full length motion picture musical, a triple soundtrack LP and an E-Z Kleen fotonovel — as Frank Want says, "My last hard laugh". 1987 marked the return of the Foetus incarnation, this time as The All-Nude Foetus Review.

Are you going to New York?

C Ruin: Yeah, I'm going on Tuesday, I've had to arrange about ten thousand things in the last week. So it's been total madness. I'm going basically 'cause I hate London.

How come?

C Ruin: I think it's a dive and I just prefer New York. I drained London for all it could give and Lydia's over there so... And I'm doing a couple of gigs there, just with backing tapes, at The Peppermint Lounge and Danceteria, then possibly putting together a live group for a little while. Just a sort of experiment really, like an all percussion group, just percussion and vocals.

I've been mulling over putting together a group for so long because I really like playing live, but basically the actual format is so difficult because I don't really find much validity in the use of backing tapes. I think it does have its moments, for instance with The Immaculate Consumptive it worked really well. But basically it does lend a certain amount of sterility to the entire affair which one tends to either undercompensate for or overcompensate for — which is a problem. And I like the chance element of working with a group where you're working on basic song structures but there is room for — not improvisation 'cause I hate that word — but chance elements, mistakes, inspiration and spur of the moment things — and still keeps to a very condensed, powerful format as well.

Why did backing tapes work with The Immaculate Consumptive?

C Ruin: Basically, because that was like a one hour set within which you had four featured lead singers as well as duets and collaborations, but the music was fairly diverse and not disjointed. It did have a thematic continuity to it through all of our basic intentions about the whole thing, and to a lesser extent I guess, the subject matter — which is a slightly belaboured point about us four. But the stuff that we all did, no-one really expected us to do. It was pretty unpredictable. And even though we were working with backing tracks, it had a great sloppy feel to it — sloppy is the wrong word — it was like organised chaos basically.

Did you feel that The Immaculate Consumptive was successful?

C Ruin: Yeah, definitely. I'd have loved to have been in the audience.

Why did you decide not to do it in London?

C Ruin: Ah, veto reason. It was more conceived and done as a fleeting sort of thing, three performances were enough, you know? We'd made our point at that stage. Also, it's too simple for us to have done that here, it's too boring really. I mean I think we're thinking of doing it another time, but we don't want to do it in New York again. We're thinking of doing it in Tokyo.

How did the fascination with Foetus come about?

C Ruin: Ah, I can't really remember actually, it's so long ago, it's just something that stuck with me from an early age. I mean it's hard for me to really say at this point in time because I've worked under that name for so long that I can't really feel an emotional... I mean if someone hears the words or the phrase, "You've got foetus on your breath", then they're going to have a lot stronger overt emotional reaction to it than I have because I'm so bloody used to it. And by the same token, to me it's not shocking or anything and it was never really supposed to be. It wasn't conceived for shock value.

Do you think it's important for you not to change it, bearing in mind that record companies won't sign you with that name?

C Ruin: Yeah definitely. I'd rather be poor and proud than rich and guilty. I mean I don't really think in terms of sell out, but I could change my name, to say Clint Ruin as opposed to You've Got Foetus On Your Breath tomorrow, and probably pick up a deal, but I don't see the point. The actual names are intrinsic and inseparable to the music. Not that the music wouldn't exist if I wasn't called that, but I don't see any reason why I should play their game. I think they should play mine.

Would a label actually not accept you with that name?

C Ruin: The major labels, yeah, they really shun the name. They just know we're not going to get any radio play with a name like that and also, they sort of find it bad taste. I know I'm too close to it to find it offensive, but to me it's such an abstraction. Everyone has been a foetus, it's so abstract to say, "You've got foetus on your breath". I mean, the name The Sex Pistols was tasteless. When I was in LA I was talking to Chris D from The Flesh Eaters, and even they had a lot of stick trying to get gigs because of their name. The Flesh Eaters! I mean that's really quite mundane, it's like having a group called The Vegetarians.

Is your music progressing parallel to your own progression, or does it have a life of it's own?

C Ruin: I don't really think in terms of me, but I definitely see my music as progressing. The actual execution and the finished product that I come up with is going to be a lot more concise, a lot more powerful and a lot more hard hitting than it was three years ago. Also, the music that I'm doing now is a lot more violent and direct — which to me is highly desirable. But as far as me and my music goes, I mean it's my wife and it's my life. My music's progression is my progression — as opposed to the other way round. I don't really have an overview as to how I'm progressing as a human being, socially or whatever, but I do have a concept as to how my music is progressing. I mean I'm more interested in my music than I am in me.

Do you think it's important for that music to reach people?

C Ruin: No. I don't care whether it reaches people or not. Basically it's enough for me to have actually done it. I've made the statement — that's enough. I've purged myself of what I wanted to say there, and I don't care whether it comes out or not... At the end of the day, I make the music for myself and not the audience. I don't care if they don't hear it because I've got cassettes of it.

Why bother pressing the records when you can just have the tapes?

C Ruin: Yeah, well I did go through that conflict with myself several years ago and someone talked me out of it. I can't remember what their argument was, but it was a good argument at the time and I thought, "Yeah, well, I better press 'em up". But I don't see any reason to just throw any shit at the wall. Whatever actually is released I have belief in. Basically my original reason for ever actually releasing records was because of the turnover thing. I was holding down a full time job to subsidise Self Immolation and every time I had any time off, I went straight into the studio. I'd been saving up money all this time and poured all of it into recording. To release it meant that I could go back into the studio after I had sold X amount of records. That was the original reasoning.

Just before Some Bizzare approached me, I was totally bankrupt. They really gave me a lot of opportunity in terms of the facts that firstly I could record this great backlog of material that was building up and I had a great passion to record, and secondly I got the opportunity to work on 24 track which I had never done — and you can really tell the difference. I mean there were great limitations that I had come against just working with eight tracks, because I might end up putting fifty overdubs and then bouncing them down, so eventually they ended up on eight tracks. I've since amassed a lot more experience. The more I work in the studio, the more I have a grasp on how to do things that I want to do more effectively and how to eliminate the extraneous elements and make the most direct interpretation of my idea possible.

What do you think would have happened if Some Bizzare hadn't come along?

C Ruin: I dread to think, I probably would have killed myself. I was totally bankrupt and I didn't have a job, I was totally demoralised from the reaction 'Ache' had, I had no prospect of going back into the studio, I was stuck in a house that I didn't want to live in, I was in an absolutely terrible position and there was nothing I could have done. In retrospect, Stevo saying, "Do you want to be on Some Bizzare?", was like a Godsend really. They're really perfect to work with because they don't put any restrictions on me. Whatever I want to do, I do, they don't have any say in it.

How do you feel you differ now that Some Bizzare is handling you?

C Ruin: Well, when I got together with Some Bizzare I thought, "Thank God for that", you know? There was me running a record label full time, recording all the music myself, and taking copies around to the music papers and stuff like that. And I thought, "Fantastic, I don't have to have a full time job, I can concentrate one hundred percent on writing and recording the music and I don't have to do things like promotion and stuff like that". Basically, I've relinquished the responsibility of being a record company so I think I'm within my rights to say to Some Bizzare, "OK, go be a good record company, go sell records".

Do you see a time in the future when you feel you'd like to expand into something else besides music?

C Ruin: Well, I don't have a grand plan in terms of the next twenty five years or something. I know that I'd like to diversify and I know I'd like to continue striving for that ultimate statement. But I think each time I do something, I'm aspiring to make the ultimate statement within the format and structure and limitations of what I'm saying.

But there are projects that are flashes of things, which is why I do those things under different names. Whereas, the LP 'Hole' by Scraping Foetus off the Wheel I find ultimate and fairly rounded. Well, rounded is probably a bad word for it because it's not round, it's very jagged, but it's not a total experience to listen to. I'm talking about what I view as a fairly wide variety of emotions, subjects, feelings, lusts, and at the same time encompassing a fairly broad spectrum of music without making the whole thing disjointed. I see it as a total statement, and that is what I'm aspiring to each time. But I can do a lot better in an album format making a total statement about a wide variety of things.

What I'm aspiring to is making an LP which is the ultimate, pre-apocalypse LP. Like you listen to the LP and then they drop the big one. It's the last statement — ever. I think the closest I've ever come is the new LP which no-one wants to release. But I think each time I do an LP I get closer to dying because I really drain myself and throw myself into it one hundred percent, spiritually, emotionally, and physically. And probably there will be a point where I make an ultimate statement like that artistically, just finish mixing it and the next day — die. And I'll be happy to have done that because I will feel that I have fulfilled my purpose.

What do you feel like the night before you go into the studio?

C Ruin: I don't sleep, I just sort of wrestle with ideas all night. And at that time my mind and body have this terrible argument whereby my body wants to go to sleep, yet my mind goes, "Ah you're going into the studio tomorrow, so I'm going to give you a really hard time" — which it invariably does. So physically I feel like shit, but at least I know what the hell I'm gonna do...

For me recording is like a religious experience, the actual act of creation. And it's the time I'm happiest, it's the time I'm most at one with myself and like myself best, and the only time I really feel at home.

Have you ever tried expressing your feelings in a different form besides music, or do you find music is the best way?

C Ruin: Well at this point in time, music is the best way to do it. I mean I don't think I could do it through prose or poetry because I have a fairly fascistic view of the different mediums of art, which I haven't quite reconciled with myself yet; I don't think they're totally valid. Personally I don't really like prose and poetry as a consumer. Doing it through music is to me the greatest purge, the greatest way of getting it out. It has always been dear to me.

Do you have any external references that you use before you go into the studio or when you're thinking about ideas?

C Ruin: I like to think in terms of the actual creative process. I know there's the cliche of ten percent inspiration — ninety percent perspiration, but before I actually go into the studio, which involves a lot of perspiration, I like to let the actual creative process be more like ninety percent inspiration. I don't like to ever force things, but I used to impose fairly rigid restrictions upon myself. Like if I knew I was going into the studio on a Saturday, I would stop listening to records on the Thursday before so that I had a blank mind — I wasn't letting ideas infiltrate except for my own, so they were like turning around in my mind. And obviously, any input of culture is going to become a part of your perception. I do make a lot of musical quotations and try to evoke atmospheres, not due to a shortage of ideas, but due to the fact that if you use a well worn musical phrase out of context, it can evoke things to a listener. So you've got say a really aggressive percussion song, and then in the middle of it 'A Walk in the Black Forest'. It ain't because you can't think of a melody there, but because you're throwing things out of drive.

Lyrically as well, the concept of quoting lines, transposing phrases and throwing little things in I refer to as aesthetic terrorism, which can be interpreted in a lot of ways. I mean I would also say that Einsturzende Neubauten are aesthetic terrorists, but in a different way to me, because basically I'm drawing on more populist culture as source material, whereas they're starting from a blank sheet. I'm starting from a blank sheet of paper but sort of drawing in something from 'Singing in the Rain' and something from an Albert Camus novel and just amalgamating things. To expound on that suggests that it is something that I do constantly, which I don't. It's not as if every song has a musical quotation in it. Very few of them do these days.

How do you work in the studio?

C Ruin: I usually have copious notes about what the song is and have all the lyrics worked out. With regards to structure I know exactly how it's supposed to sound. When you're hearing an entire song in your head and then track by track getting that down on tape, the combination of the first three things you put down can be evocative of some new thing that you hadn't thought of at the time. So I like to think in terms of striking a happy medium between letting the song write itself and keeping heavily in mind the original conception of the song. I don't see it at all in terms of a collage, but I do see myself as a sound sculptor. I think fairly texturally, and when I do a song, I encompass myself in it one hundred percent and find every atmosphere. I know every note backwards and walk around in it and mould it and stuff like that. But it's not collage in terms of sitting down with a magazine and constructing a collage of found material, because basically it's coming out of the subconscious. I think the sort of stigma which is attached to collage has the idea of randomness to it — and my stuff isn't random, it has reason to it. I might all of a sudden quote from something because it relates perfectly lyrically — or it may not at all, but it's there for a reason. It's not as if there are no random elements, but they're more musical. The songs have definite intentions. I'm not a jammer, I know what the intention of each song is.

Would you like to be popular, not in a fashionable way, but just for your music?

C Ruin: I don't care really. I mean as far as that extends, all that I would like is for the records to come out. I don't think that's a hard bargain to drive. I don't care if they don't sell. I've never sold many records anyway. I would like to see them come out, but I mean it's not going to make them come out any faster if I worry about it. If people like it, that's just a mistake, I haven't designed that song for them to like. If it's catchy then that's an incidental type thing. I never try to make a song catchy, but I do whatever I want to hear at that particular moment in time. I don't care if it doesn't become popular, and I never expect to make any money off music.

What inspires you outside of music to create things within music?

C Ruin: I don't really draw on particular sources, I'm not a movie buff or anything. Only in retrospect could I say that I'm influenced by this group or that movie or whatever. I mean life in general. I mean you can take in culture whether you like it or not, just walking down the street and seeing a billboard. I couldn't really say anything specifically. Maybe in ten years time I'd be able to answer it.

How about music, what do you listen to?

C Ruin: Uh, fairly little really. I like particular records rather than bands or solo artists because I think most of them come up with so much dross. I think Neubauten are really fantastic, I always liked The Birthday Party and I like Nick's new stuff. What else? I like Swans, Sonic Youth.

What's your favourite Neubauten album?

C Ruin: I haven't got one really. I'm biased towards the Mute one because I helped them compile that and I think it is a good representation of what they're like live, whereas 'O.T.' is a good representation of their moody qualities.

Why were you so interested in getting them exposed?

C Ruin: Just the fact that they're so intense and they seemed so relevant, and good, and fantastic, I don't know, it's hard to say — their great intensity, great vigour and great conviction. They couldn't give a fuck, they were just doing something which was really fantastic. The first time I saw them was in 1982 — the first time I went to Berlin — and I just said to them afterwards, "Do you want to have your records out in England?" And they said, "Yeah, OK", and I went round to a couple of labels and realised it was a fairly fruitless task. So I set up a subsidiary label of my label, initially to re-release a twelve inch that they had put out, and that turned into putting the compilation LP together. Then Stevo came along and asked me to be on Some Bizzare and I said, "Well. Yeah, OK". But ultimately after a lot of humming and hawing and pacing and stuff, I said, "Yeah, but you've got to take Neubauten as well". So they did. And they were supposed to release that compilation album, but at that point Neubauten were half way through doing 'O.T.' and Some Bizzare started financing that. And by the time that had finished, the deal had just come through and Stevo wasn't really interested in doing a compilation album any more because it was more past history. But me and Neubauten still had great belief in the compilation album, so we took it to Mute and worked out a deal which was OK to everyone.

How do you think the general public views music?

C Ruin: Um, I don't know really. Don't really care, I mean I don't have any respect for the general public. I couldn't give a fuck. Define general public, I mean if that's defined by the mass of people who buy Duran Duran records, I mean God knows. I think my stuff is going to be more recognisable probably to those people as music per se than Neubauten's stuff is, but I think that is not really an issue. I regard Neubauten's stuff as music — great music. It's like saying, "Is Stockhausen's stuff music?" It doesn't necessarily have notes in it.

Do you think if you did something under the name Clint Ruin that it would possibly get into the charts?

C Ruin: I don't think so, I think my stuff has too much of a sick edge to it really. I mean it might sort of come across superficially as catchy, but at the end of the day it has a certain sick edge which pervades it. Everything I do has this sort of inbuilt blackmail element — blackmailing myself against success — which I don't build in deliberately. Maybe one or two elements are just slightly too sick or slightly too aggressive. Or maybe the vocal is too violent or maybe something else is too depressing as subject matter or whatever.

Would you ever see yourself as doing a cheerful song, or what would be seen outside as being cheerful?

C Ruin: Yeah, I think a lot of my songs are cheerful. I don't know really. I don't think in terms of cheer, but I don't think in terms of doom and gloom either. I just sort of do it. I can't ever see myself as having a summer hit, you know?

What do David Byrne's shoes look like?

C Ruin: Oh, they're those black lace up ones, not very pointy, and preferably really well polished. (laughs)

Can you see yourself going back to Australia some time?

C Ruin: No, never, no, it's the bowels of the Beelzebub. I hate it. It's a hole. It takes too long to fly there, it's too bloody hot and I haven't got any friends there — I just hate it. Just because it says that on my passport doesn't mean that I have to like it.

What did Brian Eno think of The Immaculate Consumptive?

C Ruin: I don't know, he wasn't there as far as I know.

Did you borrow one of his pianos?

C Ruin: (laughs) Well, two people independently said, "Look after this piano because it's on loan from Brian Eno". Anyway, upstairs in Danceteria, we raided the attic and got all these props down. We got three pianos on the stage, including the particular one they said belonged to Brian Eno.

Stevo: (entering) So you smashed it up right?

C Ruin: Yeah! (laughs) I didn't really smash it up, I just danced on it with my boots, on the keys. It made a really good sound actually, but sort of wrecked it a bit. The problem was that Nick was going to play 'A Box for Black Paul' on that piano, and after that all the mikes were missing.

How did the audience react to The Immaculate Consumptive?

C Ruin: I don't know, I think they liked it, I didn't really notice. Some of them were a bit horrified I think.

Was there a sizeable portion that was there to see Marc Almond thinking that...

C Ruin: No, actually I think most of the people were there to see Lydia, and then the next lot of people were there to see Nick, and then the next lot of people were there to see Marc, and then, you know, maybe there was like...

Stevo: Three people.

C Ruin: Half a person to see me. (laughs)

Did you find the audiences very different between New York and Washington?

C Ruin: I don't know, I never really pay any attention to the audiences. I don't know if they clap or not and I can never remember if they like it or not. The only time I couldn't tell the difference was when I did something with Soft Cell and there were a bunch of angel dust casualties in the front sticking their hands out all the time. But that's the opposite extreme.

Do you have any contact with your parents at all?

C Ruin: Oh, occasionally, on and off.

What do they think of Foetus music?

C Ruin: Oh they dig it. (laughs) Heavily into it. My mother bought a thousand copies of the first album, she bought them all from chart return shops. Stevo, say something about Foetus.

Stevo: Well, Foetus is on the verge of collapse but it keeps itself together. It's very self-destructive, it's like high speed running from the speakers.

Is this the music or Jim?

C Ruin: Both.

Stevo: There's not one producer that's worthy of licking Jim's feet in structures, and it's like just so unbelievable. Sometimes I can be a little, let's say, aware of the ignorance around and I'm a bit depressed by it, and if I put Foetus on at any time it kind of lifts me, I just get goose pimples down my arms. And I just bow down artistically to Jim. I mean I've been involved in a few projects — but I've never actually been tapped on my back to such an extent like, "You've got to get Jim a deal", like people just tapping me on the back...

C Ruin: People like my mother...

Stevo: Really, I mean the difference between Some Bizzare and most A&R departments is basically that we work from our gut, and when I play Jim's music to people, their gut reaction is like, "Wow!". But then they suddenly stop and think, "Well, You've Got Foetus On Your Breath... uh?", and so they don't actually follow their instincts.

C Ruin: Some Bizzare works from its heart instead of its wallet, and A&R departments work from their wallets instead of their heart.

Stevo: But I think from the wallet point of view that it's going to be on a longevity kind of situation. How much is Warner Brothers catalogue worth? Ninety nine percent of it isn't worth fuck all a year after they've released a record or at least three or four years after. But with A & R men's insecure positions, they've got to justify their jobs and they don't have to look at anything on a long term basis. And that's where the arguments always end up.

KILLER

KILLS ALL

'85 BATTLE OF THE EYES

I'M AN INFANT, I WORSHIP HIM

I'M A PIG, AND I SMELL BAD. MR. SMOTHER IS MY GOD, AND THAT'S WHAT HE SAYS. HE'S ALWAYS RIGHT. I KISS HIS ASS. I SUCK EVERYTHING DOWN INTO MY GUTS. I NEVER SHIT. MY BODY'S GREEDY (THERE'S NOTHING I CAN DO ABOUT IT). I'M BLOATED, I'M SOFT. I WEIGH 349 POUNDS. I'M FAT SCUM. I DESPISE MYSELF. I'M SITTING HERE IN THE PINK PYJAMA BOTTOMS MY MOM GAVE ME WHEN I WAS 15. THEY STILL FIT. I HATE THEM, BUT I WEAR THEM. THEY'RE CAKED AROUND THE CROTCH WITH VARIOUS FOODS THAT I DRIPPED, AND OLD SPERM I NEVER WIPED UP. MY SPERM'S SWEET. A LOT OF THAT SPERM'S THERE NOW BECAUSE OF MR. SMOTHER, SO I LIKE IT. I LIKE TO BREAK IT OFF IN CHUNKS AND GRIND IT BETWEEN MY FINGERS THINKING ABOUT HIM. THEN I FEEL DISGUSTED WITH MYSELF, BUT I LIKE FEELING THAT WAY FOR HIM. I'D LIKE HIM TO TAKE A SHIT ON MY FACE WHILE I LAY BACK ON THE SIDEWALK AND HAVE PEOPLE CROWD AROUND AND LAUGH. HE'D POINT DOWN AT MY FACE AND TELL THEM HOW I DESERVED IT, AND THEY'D LAUGH AGAIN IN AGREEMENT WITH HIM. I'D FEEL GOOD. I LIKE TO FEEL GOOD. I LIKE TO TOUCH MYSELF, ESPECIALLY WHEN I PRETEND I'M SOMEONE ELSE. SOMETIMES IN A RESTAURANT I LOSE MYSELF, I FORGET I EXIST. I SNEAK MY HAND UP UNDER MY SHIRT AND RUB IT ALONG THE HAIR THAT COLLECTS AROUND MY BELLY BUTTON. THE HAIR'S SOFT LIKE THE HAIR ON A BABY'S HEAD. I GET HOT AND I CAN SMELL MYSELF. I'M BEING SMOTHERED IN MY OWN ARMPIT. THEN I COME, BUT I DON'T FEEL ANYTHING. I DISCOVER A PUDDLE OF SPERM IN MY CROTCH. I HURRY AND PAY, THEN I LEAVE, AFRAID THEY'LL NOTICE. WHEN I COME, I DON'T GET AN ERECTION. I LOVE MYSELF, BUT I ALSO HATE MYSELF. I SHOULD BE DESTROYED. PEOPLE LOOK AT ME AND THINK I'M REPULSIVE. THEY HATE ME. I LIKE THEM HATING ME, BECAUSE THEY'RE RIGHT TO DO SO. I GET AN ERECTION WHEN I THINK ABOUT A SPECIFIC PERSON THAT HATES ME. THEN I GET AN ERECTION, BUT I CAN'T COME. OTHERWISE I JUST COME, LIKE PUS DRAINS OUT OF A SORE, WITHOUT GETTING HARD. I NEED THEM TO HATE ME, TO BE SICKENED BY ME. THEN I GET WHAT I DESERVE.

MR SMOTHER IS MY BOSS. HE GAVE ME A JOB, EVEN THOUGH I MADE HIM SICK, EVEN THOUGH HE LOATHED THE SIGHT OF ME FROM THE START. MY SMELL SURROUNDED ME. I SMELL LIKE PUTRID MARMALADE. HE SHOULD HAVE THROWN UP IN MY FACE, BUT HE HIRED ME, EVEN THOUGH HE HATED ME. I DESERVE ANYTHING HE DISHES OUT. I WANT HIM TO DISH IT OUT. EVERY DAY I FIND WAYS TO MAKE HIM DEGRADE ME, WITHOUT BECOMING SO SICKENING THAT HE FIRES ME. I'D DIE IF HE FIRED ME. I WORSHIP HIM. I NEED HIM, BECAUSE HE CRUSHES ME. HE DEMANDS THAT I LIVE UP TO HIS REQUIREMENTS, AND HE PUNISHES ME WHEN I CAN'T. I DON'T KNOW WHY HE HASN'T FIRED ME, BECAUSE I'M WEAK. I ALWAYS MAKE MISTAKES. I LOVE HIS HAIRY ARMS, HIS HAIRY CHEST, HIS HAIRY BACK. I DREAM ABOUT CHEWING HIS HAIR WHILE I MASTURBATE. THEN, WHEN I DON'T COME, I FEEL GOOD, BECAUSE I DIDN'T DESERVE TO COME. I ONLY COME FOR HIM WHEN I'M NOT MASTURBATING. WHEN I COME FOR HIM IT'S BECAUSE HE MAKES ME COME, WHEN I DON'T EXPECT IT, SO I'LL FEEL BAD. BUT LATER, WHEN I'M LYING IN BED THINKING ABOUT IT, I FEEL GOOD. HE KNOWS HOW TO USE HIS AUTHORITY. HE MAKES ME FEEL LIKE A FAT DEFORMED CHILD: I'M SITTING IN THE CORNER IN MY DIAPERS, AND AGAINST MY WILL I SHIT UNTIL IT FORCES ITS WAY OUT ONTO THE FLOOR. MY PARENTS COME IN AND SCREAM AT ME AND BEAT ME. THEN, WHEN THEY LEAVE, TO SHOW THEM THAT I WANT TO BE GOOD, I SCRAPE IT UP WITH MY PUDGY HANDS AND EAT IT. I PROVE TO MYSELF THAT I CAN GET RID OF IT AND BE GOOD. THAT'S HOW HE MAKES ME FEEL. I WANT TO FEEL THAT WAY. HE DOESN'T PAY ME MUCH MONEY, I'M A FAT SLOB. I DON'T DESERVE TO BE PAID WELL. I WANT TO HIDE IN HIS WORLD. HE FEEDS ME. I NEVER WANT TO LEAVE HIM. I GET DEPRESSED WHEN I HAVE TO GO HOME FROM WORK, AWAY FROM HIM. HE MAKES ME FEEL GOOD.

HE'S MY BOSS, HE MAKES ME DO THINGS: I'M BACK IN THE STOCK ROOM GETTING A CARBURETTOR OFF THE TOP SHELF, AND THE LADDER BREAKS UNDER MY WEIGHT. I FALL DOWN LIKE A SACK OF ROTTING GELATIN. I HATE MYSELF. I DON'T GET HURT, BECAUSE MY FAT PROTECTS ME. I DON'T GET UP. I ENJOY BEING ON MY BACK, LOOKING UP. I'M AN OLD COW, DYING BESIDE THE ROAD, WAITING FOR HER MASTER TO COME DRIVE HER TO THE SLAUGHTERHOUSE. I WANT MR SMOTHER TO COME AND INVESTIGATE THE NOISE, AND FIND ME ON MY BACK. THEN, WHEN HE SHOUTS AT ME, I'LL FEEL GOOD BECAUSE I'LL BE ON MY BACK, AND I'LL FEEL STUPID. HE COMES IN SHOUTING AT ME BEFORE HE'S SEEN WHAT'S HAPPENED. "WHAT'S GOING ON IN HERE! HURRY UP! WHAT'RE YOU DOING!" HE COMES UP AND KICKS ME IN THE SIDE, AS IF TRYING TO DETERMINE IF I'M ALIVE OR DEAD. I'M IN A BEAUTIFUL DREAM, LOOKING UP INTO HIS HUGE ANGRY NOSTRILS, HIS COLD BLACK EYES. UP INSIDE

HIS NOSTRILS THE SNOT IS HARDENED AND CLINGS TO THE HAIRS IN LARGE CRYSTALS, LIKE SUGAR. I THINK HOW WONDERFUL IT WOULD BE TO CRAWL INSIDE HIS NOSTRIL AND CURL UP, EATING THE SUGAR, WARMED BY HIS BREATH. "I'M SORRY, MR SMOTHER. IT WON'T HAPPEN AGAIN. I'M SORRY". BEFORE I HAVE A CHANCE TO FINISH APOLOGISING HE SAYS, "YOU ALRIGHT?", AND WALKS OUT TO THE FRONT COUNTER WITHOUT WAITING FOR AN ANSWER. I LIKE THE WAY HE LOOKED AT ME: I'M A BAD DOG. I GET UP AND HURRY TO THE BATHROOM LIKE A FAT POODLE. I PULL DOWN MY PANTS AND STAND THERE FOR A SECOND, LISTENING TO HIM YELL AT A CUSTOMER. THE CUSTOMER IS WHINING, COMPLAINING THAT A PART THAT HE HAS BOUGHT FOR HIS CAR DOESN'T WORK. MR SMOTHER REFUSES TO BELIEVE IT. HE TELLS HIM TO GET OUT OF HIS SHOP, NOW. I HEAR THE DOOR CLOSE. NO-ONE CAN RESIST HIS AUTHORITY. I'M PLAYING WITH MYSELF, THINKING ABOUT THE SUGAR IN HIS NOSTRILS. I HAVE A TINY PENIS. I CAN HOLD IT BETWEEN TWO FINGERS WHEN I JERK IT. I PRETEND I'M MILKING A LITTLE COW. IN ORDER TO TREAT MR. SMOTHER WITH RESPECT I HIT MYSELF IN THE FACE WHILE I JERK. MY NOSE STARTS BLEEDING, BUT I KEEP GOING. THERE'S A LITTLE PIECE OF SHIT STUCK TO THE TOILET BOWL. I GET DOWN ON MY KNEES, STILL JERKING, AND LICK IT WITH MY TONGUE. NOW MR. SMOTHER IS BEATING ON THE DOOR. "COME ON! HURRY UP! WHAT ARE YOU DOING IN THERE? GET BACK TO WORK!" I HEAR HIM WALK AWAY. I WISH HE WOULD'VE BROKEN THE DOOR DOWN. I WANT HIM TO KNOW THAT I'LL DO ANYTHING FOR HIM. I ALMOST COME. I'M GLAD WHEN I DON'T. IT WOULD BE A DESECRATION. IF HE FINDS ME IN HERE WITH SHIT ON MY LIPS HE'LL BE DISGUSTED, MAYBE BEAT ME UP. HE'LL FIRE ME. MAYBE HE'LL CALL THE COPS. I LIKE COPS, BUT I'M SCARED OF THEM. IF THEY PUT ME IN JAIL EVERYTHING I DID OR THOUGHT WOULD BE UP TO THEM. THAT WOULD BE GOOD. BUT I WOULDN'T HAVE MR SMOTHER ANYMORE.

I'M WALKING HOME FROM WORK. I SMELL LIKE SYRUP. I WANT TO EAT MYSELF, IN ORDER TO DISAPPEAR. MY SLIME IS SOAKING THROUGH MY CLOTHES. PEOPLE LOOK AT ME. THEY LAUGH TO THEMSELVES, MAKING THEIR DISGUST OBVIOUS. THEY CAN SMELL ME WALK BY. I LOVE MY SMELL, BUT I DON'T BLAME THEM FOR HATING IT. I'M REPULSIVE.

IT'S GETTING DARK. I DON'T KNOW WHERE I'M WALKING. I'VE FORGOTTEN ABOUT GOING HOME. I STOP AT A SCHOOLYARD. I'M STANDING AT THE FENCE, LOOKING IN, WHEEZING. I CAN'T BREATHE. WALKING TIRES ME. I NEED A REST. BECAUSE IT'S ALMOST DARK I FEEL SAFE HERE. I WON'T BE NOTICED. THERE ARE SOME CHILDREN PLAYING HANDBALL IN THE SCHOOLYARD. I HATE THEIR SHRIEKS. THEY DISGUST ME. THEY'RE TOO UNRULY. IF I HAD MORE COURAGE I'D GO AND CUT OFF THEIR HEADS WITH MY POCKET KNIFE. BUT I'M A COWARD, AND I WOULDN'T BE ABLE TO CATCH THEM BECAUSE I'M TOO SLOW AND FAT. THEY'D LAUGH AT ME AND SPIT AT ME. I'D DESERVE IT, BUT I STILL WANT TO KILL THEM. WHEN I WAS YOUNG THEY USED TO HOLD ME DOWN AND SPIT SNOT IN MY MOUTH. THEN I'D THROW IT UP, AND THEY'D FORCE ME TO EAT MY VOMIT BEFORE THEY LET ME GO. WHEN I GOT HOME I'D THROW UP IN THE BATHROOM WITHOUT BEING TOLD TO, SO I COULD PROVE TO MYSELF THAT I COULD TAKE MY PUNISHMENT, AND NOT CAUSE MORE TROUBLE. BUT I STILL HATED THEM, BECAUSE THEY PUNISHED ME WITHOUT THINKING, JUST TO PLEASE THEMSELVES. THAT'S NOT HOW IT SHOULD BE. IT SHOULD BE DONE WITH A SENSE OF DUTY. IF YOU ENJOY YOUR DUTY IT'S ALRIGHT, BECAUSE IT'S YOUR PLACE. MR. SMOTHER IS GOOD, BECAUSE HE PUTS ME IN MY PLACE, AND HE KNOWS HIS PLACE.

THERE'S A WINO ASLEEP IN THE CORNER OF THE SCHOOLYARD. THE CHILDREN DON'T SEEM TO NOTICE HIM. HE'S A PILE OF RAGS AND MEAT. HIS MOUTH IS OPEN, A HOLE IN THE PILE. HIS MOUTH LOOKS LIKE IT'S DEMANDING TO BE STUFFED, OF IT'S OWN WILL, WITHOUT HIM KNOWING. NOW ONE OF THE BOYS NOTICES THE WINO. I KNEW THIS WOULD HAPPEN. THAT'S WHY I'VE STAYED HERE WATCHING. HE GETS THE OTHER KIDS' ATTENTION. THEY CROWD AROUND THE WINO. THEY'RE SCARED AT FIRST. THEY MOVE UP CLOSE, THEN JUMP BACK SUDDENLY, GIGGLING, THEN MOVE BACK IN AGAIN. NOW THEY'RE NOT SCARED ANYMORE. A FEW OF THEM ARE SPITTING ON HIM. HE DOESN'T BUDGE. THE FIRST LITTLE BOY IS ENCOURAGED. HE THROWS THE HANDBALL HARD AT THE WINO'S HEAD. THERE'S A SHARP CRACK. IT BOUNCES OFF HIGH INTO THE AIR. THE WINO DOESN'T MOVE. HE'S HAVING SICKENING DREAMS. NOW THE FIRST BOY TAKES OUT HIS PENIS AND PISSES ON THE WINO'S HEAD. EVERYBODY LAUGHS. THE WINOS HEAD IS STEAMING FROM THE HOT PISS. THE LITTLE BOY TAKES A CAN OF LIGHTER FLUID FROM HIS POCKET AND SQUIRTS IT ON THE WINO. EVERYBODY FLICKS MATCHES. HE'S A PILE OF MEAT COVERED IN SHORT BLUE FLAMES. HE DOESN'T NOTICE ANYTHING. THE FLAMES HAVEN'T BURNT THROUGH HIS CLOTHES TO HIS SKIN YET. THE CHILDREN PANIC. THEY'RE SCREAMING HYSTERICALLY. THEY'RE SCARED THEY'LL GET CAUGHT AND THEIR PARENTS WILL

PUNISH THEM. THE FIRST LITTLE BOY TRIES TO PISS ON THE WINO, TO PUT OUT THE FIRE, BUT HE CAN'T PISS ANYMORE, SO HE RUNS AWAY. WHEN HE'S GONE I GO INTO THE SCHOOLYARD AND PISS ON THE WINO. NO-ONE CAN SEE ME. IT'S DARK NOW, AND MOST OF THE STREET LIGHTS ARE BROKEN OUT. I GET DOWN ON MY KNEES AND LOOK AT HIM. HE'S A FILTHY DOG, WORSE THAN ME. HE SMELLS. I LIKE HIS SMELL, BECAUSE IT'S SWEET, LIKE MINE. HE'S MUMBLING INCOHERENTLY. HIS WORDS ARE A PART OF HIS SICKENING DREAM. THE ONLY WORDS I CAN MAKE OUT ARE, "PLEASE" AND, "THANK YOU".

I STAND UP AND KICK HIM IN THE BALLS. I WANT TO SEE IF HE'LL REACT. HE MOVES A LITTLE, BUT DOESN'T SEEM TO FEEL ANY PAIN. I FEEL WARM IN MY CROTCH. I LOOK AT HIS FACE. IT'S THICK WITH OLD ACNE SCARS, SMEARED WITH FILTH. HIS TEETH HAVE ROTTED OUT OF HIS MOUTH. HIS LEFT EYE IS COATED WITH A THIN YELLOW SKIN, THE PUPIL VISIBLE UNDERNEATH. BUT THE MAIN THING I NOTICE MAKES ME SHAKE, I FEEL SO GOOD: IF HIS DISFIGUREMENTS WERE CURED OR ERASED HE'D LOOK EXACTLY LIKE MR. SMOTHER. I'M IN A DREAM. I LOVE HIM. I FEEL SICK. I'M SPINNING. I REALISE I'VE THROWN UP. IT LANDED BESIDE HIS HEAD. I BEND DOWN AND LICK AWAY ANYTHING THAT SPLASHED IN HIS FACE. I FEEL BETTER. I TRY TO PUT MYSELF INTO HIS MIND. I WANT TO SMELL HIS DREAMS. I HAVE TO BE OBEDIENT. HE DESERVES OBEDIENCE.

I GRAB HOLD OF HIS ARM AND PULL HIM UP. HIS ARM IS STRONG UNDER HIS OVERCOAT. I FEEL HAPPY. I SLAP HIM IN THE FACE, TRYING TO WAKE HIM UP. I DON'T WANT HIM TO MISS ANYTHING. HE LOOKS AT ME INDIFFERENTLY, THEN GOES BACK TO HIS DREAMS. BUT HE SEEMS CONSCIOUS ENOUGH TO WALK. AS I LEAD HIM AWAY I WHISPER INTO HIS EAR THAT I'M SORRY FOR BOTHERING HIM, THAT I'LL MAKE HIM FEEL GOOD AGAIN. WE STOP TO REST AT THE FENCE. HE LEANS AGAINST IT, HALF CONSCIOUS. I STICK MY TONGUE IN HIS EAR, CAREFULLY CLEANING OUT ALL THE STALE WAX THAT'S ACCUMULATED IN THERE FOR MONTHS. HE DOESN'T SEEM TO FEEL ME DOING THIS, BUT I DON'T CARE. I SWIRL IT AROUND IN MY MOUTH UNTIL IT BECOMES LIQUID, SPIT IT BACK INTO HIS EAR, THEN SUCK IT OUT AGAIN, TAKING IT THROUGH THE CRACKS BETWEEN MY TEETH. WHEN I'M DONE WITH BOTH EARS I SWALLOW EVERYTHING. I DON'T FEEL SICK AT ALL. I LIKE IT. I'M THINKING ABOUT MR. SMOTHER. IT WOULD PLEASE HIM TO KNOW I'M DOING THIS. I DESERVE TO BE HATED BY HIM. IT FEELS GOOD.

I LEAD HIM DOWN THE STREET, PRETENDING WE'RE TWO DRUNKS HELPING EACH OTHER WALK. I BURY MY HEAD IN HIS SHOULDER AS WE GO, HIDING MY FACE. IT'S DARK, NO-ONE CAN RECOGNISE ME. ALL THEY'LL BE ABLE TO SAY IS THAT THEY SAW HIM WALKING WITH A FAT MAN.

WE COME TO AN ABANDONED BUILDING. I LEAD HIM ACROSS THE VACANT LOT IN FRONT OF THE BUILDING. IT'S PITCH BLACK HERE. MY SMELL SEEMS STRONGER. HIS SMELL IS MIXING WITH MINE. I LIKE THE NEW SMELL. IT'S SUFFOCATING. I LAY HIM DOWN AGAINST THE WALL. HE SAYS "THANK YOU", LOOKING UP AT ME. HE REPULSES ME.

I KICK THE PLYWOOD THAT'S NAILED OVER THE WINDOW I WANT TO GO IN. I CAN'T SEE ANYTHING. I LIGHT A MATCH AND HOLD IT INSIDE THE WINDOW. THE ROOM IS PILED WITH DEBRIS, OLD FURNITURE, ROTTING GARBAGE. IN THE CENTRE OF THE ROOM THERE'S A WIDE HOLE, WHERE THE FLOOR HAS CAVED IN. IF WE FALL IN THE HOLE WE'LL BREAK OUR ARMS AND LEGS, AND BE EATEN BY RATS. AS THEY RIP AT ME THEY'LL EJACULATE, AND SO WILL I. IF WE KEEP TO THE SIDES OF THE ROOM, MOVING ALONG THE WALLS, WE WON'T FALL IN. THERE ARE SOME STAIRS ACROSS THE ROOM, IN THE FAR CORNER. I WANT TO TAKE HIM UP THERE. IT WILL BE PRIVATE. I CLIMB THROUGH THE WINDOW INTO THE BUILDING. I CUT MY ARM ON AN OLD NAIL. IT DOESN'T HURT. I CAN SMELL MY BLOOD. IT'S SWEETER, MORE REFINED, THAN THE SMELL OF MY BODY. I PULL HIM IN AFTER ME. I HAVE THE FEELING HE'S HELPING ME, BECAUSE IT'S SO EASY. I FEEL LIGHT. I HOLD A MATCH UP TO HIS FACE. HE'S SMILING. IT MAKES ME SICK. HE'S CRAZED. I DON'T KNOW WHAT TO EXPECT. HIS OPEN MOUTH IS LIKE THE HOLE IN THE FLOOR, AND THE RATS LIVE DOWN IN HIS STOMACH. I SWAY. I ALMOST FALL INTO HIS MOUTH. HE GRUNTS. I SMELL IT AGAINST MY FACE. IT'S THE WORD, "PLEASE". WE WORK OUR WAY ALONG THE WALL. WE FINALLY GET TO THE STAIRS. BY THIS TIME HE'S CONSCIOUS ENOUGH TO MOVE ON HIS OWN. HE WALKS UP THE STAIRS IN FRONT OF ME. HE MOVES SLOWLY, BUT HE'S SURE OF HIMSELF, AS IF HE'S BEEN HERE BEFORE. BY THE MATCHLIGHT HE LOOKS LIKE A DRUGGED GIANT. I'M GLAD TO BE FOLLOWING HIM. I'M BEING PULLED UP THE STAIRS BY HIS SMELL. HE'S CONTROLLING ME.

THE ROOM IS EMPTY EXCEPT FOR A COUCH, AND SOME CANDLES IN THE CENTRE OF THE FLOOR. SOMEONE MUST HAVE STAYED HERE BEFORE THEY BOARDED UP THE BUILDING. I LIGHT THE

CANDLES, THEN I SIT DOWN ON THE COUCH. HE SITS DOWN NEXT TO ME. I'M COVERED IN HIS SHADOW. WE DON'T TALK. HE SEEMS TO BE WAITING FOR SOMETHING. HE LOOKS AT ME LIKE FOOD. HE DISGUSTS ME. HIS SMELL IS STRANGLING ME. I REALISE HE'S WAITING FOR ME TO GIVE HIM SOME ALCOHOL. I HAVE TO DO SOMETHING QUICKLY OR HE'LL GET SUSPICIOUS. HE COULD KILL ME, IN ORDER TO PUNISH ME. I ADMIRE HIM FOR THAT. HE CAN DO ANYTHING HE WANTS. HE SHOUTS AT ME. I DON'T UNDERSTAND WHAT HE'S SAYING. HIS VOICE IS A ROAR. IT STINKS. IT'S ECHOING THROUGH THE ROOM. I'M CHOKING. I TAKE OUT MY POCKET KNIFE AND HOLD IT OPEN IN MY LAP. I'M IN A DAZE. I'VE ALWAYS BEEN HERE WITH HIM, IT'LL NEVER END. HE'S STANDING UP. HE'S READY TO RUN OUT, DOWN THE STAIRS. HE'LL FALL IN THE HOLE. I STAB HIM IN THE THROAT. HE FALLS DOWN IMMEDIATELY, JERKING AROUND THE FLOOR LIKE A FISH, THE BLOOD PUMPING OUT OF HIS NECK. IT'S PUTRID, I'M GAGGING. HE ROLLS OVER ONTO THE CANDLES I LIT, THEN STOPS MOVING. THE ROOM HAS GONE DARK. I FEEL AROUND ON THE FLOOR, REACH UNDER HIM, AND PULL OUT A CANDLE. I LIGHT IT AND HOLD IT IN FRONT OF HIS FACE. HE LOOKS EXACTLY LIKE MR. SMOTHER. I FEEL HAPPY, I START TO CRY. I TOUCH HIS CRUEL EYES. I STICK MY FINGERS IN HIS MOUTH. IT'S WONDERFUL: HIS COOL STRONG TONGUE, THE TONGUE THAT SHAPED THE WORDS THAT MADE ME OBEY. NOW IT'S PERFECT. I FEEL MYSELF GETTING A HARD ON. IT'S WARM, NOT LIKE BEFORE. MY PENIS IS HUGE, HARD, FULL OF BLOOD. I TAKE OFF HIS OVERCOAT AND SHIRT AND THROW THEM TO THE SIDE. I UNDO MY PANTS, LETTING THEM FALL AROUND MY ANKLES, THEN I KNEEL BESIDE HIM. HIS CHEST, AND HIS STOMACH ARE HARD AND STRONG, EXACTLY LIKE MR. SMOTHER. AS I KNEEL BESIDE HIM MY ERECTION HOVERS OVER HIS BODY. I SQUEEZE IT IN MY FIST AS I CUT INTO HIS ABDOMEN. I WAS MADE FOR THIS. I'M HAPPY. AS I'M CUTTING HIS SKIN AND MUSCLE AWAY, THE SMELL OF HIS INTESTINES ROLLS UP INTO MY FACE. IT'S STALE AND SHARP LIKE WINE VOMIT. THE SMELL MAKES ME DRUNK. I KNOW I'M GOING TO COME THIS TIME, BECAUSE I DESERVE TO COME. I'M FALLING FACE FIRST INTO HIS SOFT INTESTINES. MY MOUTH IS OPEN I'M SUCKING HIS GUTS INTO MY MOUTH. I'M EATING MYSELF. I'M PRETENDING THAT MR SMOTHER IS STANDING BEHIND ME WATCHING ME, MAKING SURE I EAT EVERYTHING. I'M EATING SEWAGE. MY STOMACH IS FILLING UP WITH SLIME. I CAN FEEL MYSELF GETTING FATTER AND UGLIER. I'M WORSE THAN I'VE EVER BEEN. MY SMELL IS DISSOLVING ME. I'M BURYING MY HEAD DEEPER IN HIS GUTS. I LOSE THE ABILITY TO DISTINGUISH BETWEEN HIS GUTS AND MY SMELL. I'M COMING INTO MY HAND, THROWING UP INTO HIS GUTS, EATING IT, THROWING UP INTO HIS GUTS, EATING IT AGAIN. I'M DROWNING IN MY OWN SPERM WHILE I DROWN IN HIS GUTS. AFTER I EAT HIS GUTS, I EAT HIS HEART. THEN I CUT OUT HIS TONGUE AND I EAT THAT. I'M LICKING UP MY SPERM. IT'S STILL HOT. IT TASTES LIKE HIS GUTS. I WIPE THE BLOOD OFF MY FACE AND WORK MY WAY DOWN THE STAIRS OUT OF THE BUILDING.

© Michael Gira 1984.

SWANS

Virtually everything about Swans is hard hitting and direct, a confusion of time and sound. The output is usually slowed down and stripped to create an inner tension which demands release. Suitably located in New York's Alphabet City on the lower East side Swans are led by writer and singer Michael Gira. Other members have included Norman Westberg, guitarist and sometime actor (in *The Right Side of my Brain* with Lydia Lunch), and Roli Mosimann, a Swiss percussionist and session man, as well as one half of Wiseblood with Clint Ruin.

In 1984 Swans released their first British LP *Cop*, a harrowing portrait of a man's continuous struggle with sexual repressions and authoritarian forces. 1986 saw the group release two studio albums — *Greed* and *Holy Money* — exorcisms of such constraints; soon after the group put out a documentation of their brutally realistic live shows entitled *Public Castration Is A Good Idea*. Both Michael Gira and group member Jarboe released solo projects in 1987 entitled *Skin*, while Swans released their fifth studio album, *Children Of God*.

How do you expect an audience to react to one your gigs?

M Gira: It depends on the audience. We've played to audiences that were completely the wrong kind of audience to play to, and they give their response. I don't give a fuck. It doesn't matter. They're experiencing the thing as it is. I don't think it's our mission to teach anybody anything. It's something that we've been working at for a long time and believe in, and if people don't accept it, tough. You can't worry about that sort of thing. If you are worried about that kind of thing, you become a pop band, figure out what people like and then do that. You just have to go where your work takes you.

Do you think people from Europe seem to be more inclined to accept something that is different, or have you found that it is equal all round?

M Gira: Yeah, equally unaccepted all round. (laughs) I think that's changing though.

Do you view Swans, and maybe Sonic Youth and Neubauten, as a movement?

M Gira: I don't think so, not a movement, no. They could be loosely lumped together, very loosely. Well Sonic Youth and us have grown simultaneously, but I didn't know about Neubauten until maybe 1983, so maybe it's just a common tendency that's occurring. The New Brutes. (laughs)

How would you say your music differs from that of a 'punk' band?

M Gira: They're stylized and they imitate each other, and they use a genre which exists and operates within its conventions and cliches in order to stimulate a pre-ordained response. We are completely outside that, basically in our own world. We set our own standards, and people have to come to that. It's not as if we stroke their expectations.

What would you think if somebody refers to Swans as a noise band?

M Gira: I would hate that because that applies to random noise in my mind, undisciplined crap. With us everything is worked out and disciplined. Rhythms are paid attention to and require intense concentration, which is why it's bad sometimes and good others. When we're good, it's extreme and really wrenches your stomach.

How would you describe a noise band?

M Gira: There are all these bands around New York, these noodling little artists who get together and improvise in some loft, invite their friends over, play Kazoos through pickups and beat up their guitars. That's a noise band.

Since things are so organised and worked out before a gig, how spontaneous does it become?

M Gira: It's spontaneous in the sense that it's like taking a mantra and beating it into the ground. It's just a series of words and sound that you use, it depends on the context; the psychic trade off between the people in the audience, between the audience and us, and also between us as a band. A lot depends on how much you use it. Many of the rhythms are very simple, and it just takes concentration to get it going; repetition is like that. So that's spontaneity. In the performance, it just happens or it doesn't.

Live, I would like us to be as naked as possible. The performance should be physical. When I see someone performing on stage, I want to see them putting out something to the audience. I want to get something immediate. That's the sign of a good performance to me, when that kind of thing occurs — when the performer loses himself and the audience members lose themselves, that interaction.

There seems to be a lot of anger coming across in the music, just in the way that you sing.

M Gira: I wouldn't describe it as anger.

How would you describe it?

M Gira: Pain.

What are you painful about?

M Gira: Everyone has a certain amount of repressed pain and a need to express their animal part. That's basically what it is. It's not, "I am painful because I lost my job", or something. You just take the cohesive misery of your life and congeal it into what you are doing.

So, what you're getting out is a pain that's not necessarily directed.

M Gira: It's not directed at anybody. What it's basically trying to do is yank out repressions from both myself and other people. It's not intellectual and it isn't fun. Like The Stooges for instance... that emotion is really difficult to describe because it's so non-verbal.

What are the repressions that you're trying to yank out from the audience and yourself?

M Gira: That sounds like a pretentious statement, but we'd like to present an animal alternative to 'civilized' behaviour, negating for a brief interlude the dull nullities of everyday life. When we reach the peak of animal rhythm, that negates everything else around it. Depending on the live situation, we can either be ecstatic or mundane. That's how it should be.

What do you want someone in the audience to feel during a gig?

M Gira: Complete exhaustion hopefully. Drained. Numb. Numb like you just came.

Would you like the person to be assertive and inspired to do something?

M Gira: That's their choice, that would be requiring too much of an audience. I don't think that ever happens anyway, no matter what anybody says. I think an artist can have many intentions and most of them are never transferable. It could be a catharsis. People do get that from us once in a while, we get it, they get it. It's such a difficult thing to achieve, which is another reason why we're uneven live.

What do you think of John Cage? Would you consider what he does to be music?

M Gira: Sure, but I don't really like it. It's so non-physical, so cerebral, his approach. But I don't have any specific aesthetic about what's good and what isn't in other people. That's their business. I don't want to prescribe some way of working for others, that would be horrible. I just don't like Cage's approach because it's not visceral at all. I like visceral things, I like hard things, things that go to an extreme. I saw him once do something that was incredibly boring... but I'm sure he would say that was part of it. I'd rather listen to Howlin' Wolf!

How important is it for you to get across to other people?

M Gira: It's very important to me because I feel a need to do it, because it's my work and I want people to hear it. I want to affect people with it.

Why do you feel that music is the best medium to get your ideas across?

M Gira: Well, it's not necessarily. I write stories, but I like music because of the physicality of it. I like the pure physical sweat involved in what we do.

Do you think it could be strong in another art form?

M Gira: Another art form is a completely different thing. Francis Bacon could not have said what he wanted to say in a symphony. It's not comparable.

How autobiographical is your writing?

M Gira: Not at all. It relates peripherally with ideas and inserts, but they're not stories about my past or anything. They're more idealised situations abstracted from potentials I see in human interaction.

Do you think it's important for a writer to experience things personally before he writes about them?

M Gira: The thing that interests me more, rather than the incidents themselves, is the frame of mind they imply — claustrophobia or being unable to distinguish your body from a chair for instance. The frame of mind that's implied behind the writing or that one might obtain through the writing. Motivations interest me more than the incidents themselves which is why I don't like the specifically gory or immediately violent ones as much anymore, because they can be misconstrued as being sensationalist.

Have you been interpreted that way?

M Gira: Of course, yeah. I mean that's not a motive at all. It's certainly not a motive for Swans and it's not a motive for my writing. I hate that, I think it's such a cheap motive.

Has it affected you to the point where you now try to steer away from something that could be interpreted that way?

M Gira: No, I don't really have any choice in the things that I do. I do what my imagination dictates that I do.

Do you get tired of depicting the real world?

M Gira: I suppose I don't have much else to depict. I mean everything is based on perception from experience, in combinations of that and extrapolations from it. If you read those stories closely, a lot of the events take place in impossible situations, but they are depicted in such a way that they seem credible. I think some of them fail in the sense that they're not credible actually.

Do you look at some of the stories from 'Traps' as being self-debasing?

M Gira: I don't look at them as debasing me personally, but I look at it as people considering their self-denigration as a form of strength and power.

What would you want a reader to feel after they've read 'Traps'?

M Gira: Just to see the potential, just to see that frame of mind in those social interactions.

Are you affected by criticism at all?

M Gira: I'm really indifferent to criticism. I criticise myself a lot, that's enough. That's one thing I'm confident of in myself, in that I'm highly self-critical. So it doesn't matter to me.

How would you define sanity and insanity?

M Gira: I guess my definition of insane would be not being aware of the consequences or motivations of actions on yourself or others. I don't really think there's much difference between the two. Sometimes I think that some things are defined as insane simply because they are performed to a moral standard arbitrarily imposed by others. In other cases it might be that a person is deluding themselves, hence it's not healthy.

How did the name Swans come about?

M Gira: Arbitrarily.

Did it have something to do with a swan being...

M Gira: Phallic?

No, I wasn't going to say that. Why, did that have something to do with it?

M Gira: No, nothing at all. Actually, it was perverse. I thought it was a nice dream-like image to put with that music.

The output of Swans is very physical though, which could be looked at as being 'macho'.

M Gira: We have been misinterpreted that way sometimes and I dislike that, but I don't see anything wrong with a male expressing his physicality. I think the music fits with that kind of brutality. Although it's a much more emotional kind of thing, it's not actually the literal expression of that. I just picture myself in that scene playing, the sweat and stink and the smell of shit and semen. It isn't 'macho' music, it's physical, that doesn't necessarily mean 'macho'. It's not impressing our maleness over women, our ability to be strong men. We happen to be males.

What period or movement has been the most inspirational for you?

M Gira: I don't really respect any movements because they're all self-defeating. They always seem to end up being hypocritical. I don't respect any 'rock' movements, punk, etc. as the rebellious people always end up being office workers or horrible people. They're all business executives and creeps now. There are isolated exceptions of course.

What are some of those?

M Gira: I don't know, just like some of the legendary events of The Stooges for instance, the fact that they were so ugly and vile right at the peak of the flower movement, wearing Nazi uniforms on stage, Iggy wearing a tutu, and playing three songs in one set that lasted twenty minutes, getting booed off stage, I love that aspect... so violent in the midst of all that prettiness. I respect that; I don't know what else... not much.

Are your lyrics very important, or is it the sound and emotion of your voice being used as another instrument?

M Gira: The lyrics are very important. I repeat words over and over, but that's used to hammer in something. They're the central attitude behind the music. The lyrics are very repetitive. They're painful and abstract. They're not a portrait of something, they're more like blocks of concrete. At times we use the foot pedal, bring in chunks of sound, so it's like building things with blocks — which is basically how the whole sound is built. It's not built melodically.

Why aren't Swans played on commercial radio?

M Gira: We're not played on radio because we're not what is commonly defined as commercial music, i.e. we're not easy to take and we're not inoffensive. Also, our music isn't catchy, nor is it fashionable. I don't really care about commercial radio or changing it at all. It's not an issue which concerns me. I'd rather have people come to me because they like what I do, as opposed to beating on their doors trying to get their attention and approval. I have no beef with so-called commercial radio. I don't care about it.

What would happen if a Swans record charted?

M Gira: I suppose we would make money.

Would you consider that an artistic failure?

M Gira: We don't set out to screw ourselves. We do what we need to do. The work develops honestly.

You have signed with the British label K422. Why did you choose to do that rather than choosing a label in The United States?

M Gira: There haven't been any labels there that would have been interested in this kind of thing. Also, there's this thing that occurs when you're on a British label and you get some attention in England; The United States picks up on it because it's foreign, so I suppose that will occur.

Do you think that the music of Swans will be relevant in thirty years?

M Gira: I don't know. I hope not. It would be horrible. It wouldn't be relevant to then. It exists now.

Do you think it will be remembered at all?

M Gira: Oh yeah, I think it's pretty important. A lot of things that have been important have never had mass acceptance.

What is so important about it?

M Gira: The way that it gets to the point, how it's effective on its own terms... especially how it sets its own terms. There's a real necessity right now for music that is hard, brutal and primal, gets to a point and exposes things — raw and clear. It has to be done right now.

Cling to Dreamtime

Thousands of Dollars

CABARET VOLTAIRE

In 1973, Stephen Mallinder, Richard Kirk and Chris Watson began experimenting with various sounds and compiling tapes of them in Watson's loft. Later the trio began buying second-hand instruments and incorporated these as additional sound sources. In one of their first performances in 1975, the group was attacked and physically forced to stop, with Mal suffering a chipped bone in his back. Still, Cabaret Voltaire — as they now called themselves — continued to antagonize people with their own breed of experimentation, which included the incorporation of their various interests — including German music, the writings of William S. Burroughs, Dadaism and military history amongst others.

In 1978, Rough Trade offered Cabaret Voltaire a non-contractual recording agreement and released their first LP, which was recorded in the group's own studio, Western Works, which had been set up to further their research. They stayed with Rough Trade for 5 years, but also released material on the Industrial label and Les Disques Du Crepuscule. In 1981 Chris Watson left the group to pursue other interests, and the group entered a transitional phase. Although Rough Trade released two of their albums in 1982, Kirk and Mallinder were reconsidering their approach and position. Dissatisfied with their easy Rough Trade cult status, they entered a new alliance with Some Bizarre and saw their next album *The Crackdown* (distributed through Virgin) double the sales of its predecessor and allow them access to video production facilities they had previously been denied by lack of funds. In addition to their own videos they released (through their own company Doublevision) videos by 23 Skidoo, Throbbing Gristle and The Residents. Having experimented with film and video since their early days, the group has worked with director Pete Care, doing the soundtrack to his film *Johnny YesNo*, while Care directed several tracks on The Cabs' *Gasoline in Your Eye* including the single *Sensoria*, which gained them the highly coveted award of Los Angeles Times Video of the Year. They have also had the rare privilege of exhibiting their videos at New York's Museum of Modern Art.

1986 saw Cabaret Voltaire leave Virgin and Some Bizzare to sign a new recording agreement with EMI. In 1987, they released their first album on EMI entitled *Code*.

What do you see as the main motive of Cabaret Voltaire?

Mal: It's quite vague. It's a non-specific motive or entity I guess. It's an exercise, not purely experimental, but just in self knowledge and the whole process of control. Using things that are available to you and concentrating on both the music and the visual side. It's more a course of exploration really. A lot of people go into the same areas with similar reasons but with a specific end in mind. For us it's more a case of making sure we don't blinker ourselves.

Do you find that music is the best medium for you to use?

Mal: We always like to use music because of its lack of snobbery. I mean there is snobbery in the music business, but if you're talking about arts in general, there's a lot more of the basic sort of working class culture in music than say with the visual arts. We never tried to be snobbish at all about it, we never said, "We should appeal to a left wing audience or an arty kind of audience". We tried to cross those barriers and gradually eat away at people's consciousness.

With video I'm interested more in its abuse at the moment. I mean I'm getting very tired of how video is actually supplementing the imagination — which I find quite sad. Because music, for all its faults, did mean a certain amount of effort on people's parts. But the amount of effort has diminished because people are now having the actual imagery laid on a plate for them — their whole concept of a record is now being determined by the video and how good the video is.

What would you attribute some of the changes in your music to?

Mal: It's just development and progression. I don't think we particularly lost any of the initial things that we set out doing, they're still there. You develop, you grow, you progress and you're aware of changing circumstances. I mean the worst thing is to not be aware of the changes around you. One of the best ways to effect change is to travel and to meet people, putting things into a different context. On superficial levels the change of the climate around you; socially, politically, economically and musically as well. It gives you a permanently questioning, searching, non-acceptance of situations. I find that really healthy. It's just masturbation if you stay at one point and flog that one thing to death. You never progress for yourself and you don't get any more out of it.

Why was the early period of Cabaret Voltaire so aggressive?

Mal: It's just in the nature of what we do, we don't try to strike the subtleties and basics of music. Subtleties are there, but not in the basic format. It's just natural.

R Kirk: It's almost an anecdote to most of the commercial bland music, just so much of that stuff that you hear all the time. It was like that when we first started making music, and it hasn't changed so much. So I think while there's something like that to react against, we'll do it.

How important are singles to your relationship with a record company?

Mal: We've never seen it particularly like that. They're not records that are preconceived and actually designed to extend a relationship with a record company. It's just a record and if the record company support us in it, that's OK. But we don't actually do it to please them or do it to be commercial or to remain with them. I think to a lot of people there's a craft in making a hit single. We're not craftsmen in that sense, we work off a gut feeling so therefore if it hits a nerve then it works. But we can't actually sit down and try to craft a single.

What particular market do you think your records sell in?

Mal: I don't know, it's hard to say with us, because we cut across markets. There's the dancefloor market, and there's actually a fringe market or an 'arty' market — and we cut across all of those. I think we can appeal to a teenage popular audience but I think it's hard for us to say which are the best areas. I think the enigma of us has gone slightly because we've been around for such a long time. We could have gone for The Residents sort of anonymous figures, but I think it would have backfired a long time ago.

There is still a certain ridiculous mystique about a lot of groups and we probably fall into that category. But on the other hand, you've got to be aware of the fact that daytime radio is one of the things that enables you to get across to people — but we don't design anything for that. The dancefloor is also a very important thing which has been proven over the last few years. You can get in the charts via the dancefloor. And that appeals to us more because it works on a lot of the principles that we use anyway.

R Kirk: I'm sure a lot of people who potentially would be interested in the music that we do now don't even know of the existence of us because we don't get much radio play and we don't do many TV appearances. A lot of people don't read the NME and Sounds and things like that so they don't even read about us. I think that has changed a little bit because the singles get played in the clubs a lot.

How would you react to a hit single?

Mal: I don't know, I have no idea actually. If we did have any commercial success I don't think it would particularly affect us because if anything was successful, it would sell on itself — not on us. I think we'll always remain quite anonymous and in the background. It would be quite good if we did have something commercially successful because I think it would be on our own terms and it wouldn't be pure hype. I don't think you could hype us. You could push us, but you know ....

R Kirk: People would pick up on it on a novelty level more than anything else. I always thought that might happen with 'Yashar' because it was fairly accessible but it didn't have a voice on it as such. It seemed to me the sort of thing a DJ might consider to be fairly wacky, not knowing anything about our past history.

Mal: There's no point in bringing out records if you don't want to sell them. You make records for yourself, but the more people that buy them the better. If we had a record that went really high in the charts that would be fine. But if I made a record that I didn't like that got to number five then I probably would say differently. But I don't think I'd bring out a record that I wasn't happy with.

Do you think your motives for making records have changed in any way?

Mal: No, and I don't think the aggression has changed either. In the earlier stages, people's notions of what music was were entirely different to those now. It's natural, because people eat away at it gradually. Like with Laurie Anderson or whoever, there is a certain amount of acceptability. Maybe the actual instruments and technology have changed, and therefore it's not as crude as it was, but the aggression is now channelled into areas using the instrumentation and technology that people can identify with.

Musically, how close did you feel TG was to Cabaret Voltaire?

Mal: Well it's difficult because at that time when we initially made contact there was only

Cabaret Voltaire and Throbbing Gristle to our knowledge who were actually doing anything remotely similar. So we actually became friends between us all and from there on it became very difficult to see any divisions or dividing lines between us. But we certainly had an affinity with what they were doing. Some of the basic ideas were very close, they manifested themselves in different ways, but that was because different personalities were thinking through the ideas.

In the end product there were a lot of similarities, but in the background I think those similarities tended to end. I think Gen is one of those people who does preconceive, he does work to a plan, works to a format to get a required reaction — a required result. He thinks very much and conceptualises to quite a large extent, whereas we tend not to. So therefore, the spirit of what we did varied with theirs.

Have you come to any conclusion on the number 23?

Mal: I find it quite funny and quite interesting. People can be, not brain washed, but psychologically tripped. You mention a number to someone and they automatically notice it, that could be number 22 — I mean, I don't know, there are coincidental things in it. I agree certain things like that do exist, I'm not knocking that, but also I get a bit wary of the 23 club with hundreds of people over England sitting down on the number 23.

R Kirk: Mind you, that gig in Derby, the best one we played, was on the 23rd and some of the others I remember have been as well. If someone like Burroughs, who is pretty sussed as a bloke, thinks there's something in it, I tend to think it's worth checking out at least, because he does seem to be a mine of information.

Mal: Yeah, but it's a very crude analysis of numerology to go, "Oh number 23, everybody watch out for it". It does have a significance in numerology but that's almost to discount any other factors. If you actually work on combinations of numbers, intriguing things like that come out, it's not purely that.

Musically who have you listened to and admired?

Mal: Quite a lot of people. I don't think I've ever had any specific heroes. A lot of it goes back to the early seventies when Eno started using tape recorders. It gave us a certain interest. When you start, you struggle, but once it starts rolling it builds. There were a few sparks like early Roxy Music, and even David Bowie around that time, as well as our earlier influences, which were soul and black music.

What have some of your influences outside music been?

Mal: It's just a whole mish-mash. From being interested in Dada, Duchamp, and getting interested in other things, Man Ray, fifties things, certain photographers. There's no one thing that pops out of my head, but there must be certain factors, certain leanings.

R Kirk: Some of the things that Fellini's done and some of Fritz Lang's films... I've got most of Bunuel's films on videotape now, I like most of that stuff. It's not as if I take it as any kind of gospel, but it's quite a large influence. And I think the way that the music was formulated was just by unexplainable things, just chance elements and things like that. And that's still happening a lot in the music that we're doing. I mean we'll just run a tape of something in with a track and then maybe dub parts of it in at random.

What do you find with music that you can't express with film?

R Kirk: More instinct I think. It's quick, you get feedback from it, it's an instantaneous thing. I also think music is a lot more primal. The whole point with film is that the viewer gets it all. It's very hard for people like us to actually sit down and premeditate things, and with films it's very much a craft, it's not immediate. Whereas with sound you can actually do something that is very immediate and very primitive on the input side. And although visually you can get something very primitive or very crude out of it on the output side, on the input side you tend to be very distanced from it.

How would you judge feedback from an audience as to whether something works or not?

Mal: It varies a lot in what you're doing. I mean it doesn't matter what reaction you get in a lot of ways, because if you get an aggressive reaction or a different reaction, you interpret it how you want. You know, if they don't react it is because they didn't get most of it. Or, if they do react, then it was effective. So you win either way. Nowadays, it's like an ego thing in the reverse way. You almost expect a reaction because you expect your audience to be as educated as you are. Whereas before we felt we were a lot in the dark and the ego side wasn't. The reaction of the ego side was like, "It doesn't make any difference, we're more clever than them anyway". (laughs)

Do you find there has been a big difference in the acceptance you have received from people over the years?

Mal: I think you meet more in the middle, we try not to make our music more and more obscure as we go on. So we move slightly more towards people, and the way trends change in music means that people move more towards us as well, so it's a dual thing.

Were you surprised seeing people dance to Cabaret Voltaire?

R Kirk: Well, when we went to Europe, people always used to dance because they somehow took it for what it was and didn't think about it too much.

Mal: It's a bit annoying because we actually suffered from what the audience was. People used to say, "You get an arty, intellectual audience, they've all got long faces and long macs and just stand there." Now that's not strictly our fault because half those people who were like that have totally changed anyway. The hypocrisy is on the audience's part because half those fuckers who had long macs and Kafka books are probably Paul McCartney and Wham! fans now.

What's a long mac?

R Kirk: It's similar to a Big Mac. Ah, terrible. (laughs)

Mal: No, a lot of that is The Bunnymen — they were the ones.

Is it like a trench coat?

Mal: Yeah, and all the audiences were sort of like that — the northern sort of flop cut and long mac.

University students?

Mal: Yeah, that sort of thing.

R Kirk: Polytechnic students actually.

Mal: Serious sort of people who used to come to the gigs.

Some people have said that your music tends to get repetitive and monotonous after a while...

R Kirk: They're the ones with the long macs on obviously!

Mal: Like it sounds the same all the way through?

R Kirk: But it always did! (laughs) To me it was like the big thing — the repetition.

Mal: We only ever had one idea. (laughs)

R Kirk: And I don't remember what that was.

Mal: But it usually works like that. Again you can twist it either way you want. An album can sound the same all the way through. Some people say, "That's boring", others say, "Oh, that group has got a distinctive sound, they've developed it, it's got uniformity". But I mean a lot of disco music is repetitious, reggae is the same. It varies within a few beats and stuff like that.

R Kirk: On the other hand, a lot of the things that I listen to and like are repetitious. I just like the concept of it.

What is it that interests you in repetition?

R Kirk: The hypnotic element of it. The whole point with repetition is that it gives you a single thread in which to bounce things around. If we can keep some continuity then it allows us that manoeuvrability. Also it creates the hypnotic element where you can actually draw people in.

Once you draw them in, are you interested in hitting them any harder than that?

Mal: Maybe that's one of the few things that people can say; "Once people are drawn in, then there's not actually anything that does hit them" — which I think is fair comment. There are certain things that go through what we do which people can relate to. That's why a lot of people tend to use rhythm which is something which can draw people in and act as a thread throughout it. It's the same with the image in that sense; we try not to use purely abstract things. You ought to use solid images that people can relate to in some way so you can draw people in.

With the visual elements and the music of Cabaret Voltaire, a feeling of paranoia seems to be created during a gig. Is that contrived?

Mal: It's not contrived, it's an aspect of what we do. In one way I'm quite pleased that actually happens, because for us to perform, one of the important things is to create an entire environment. And one of the ways of creating a closed environment does involve an aspect of paranoia, an aspect of almost claustrophobia.

Would you find that the best music is projected from insecurity and paranoia?

Mal: Yeah, I think so. Being in a state of paranoia is a very healthy state to be in. It gives you a permanently questioning and searching non-acceptance of situations.

It seems that some of your music doesn't cry out for social change as much as some other bands do, you seem to do it more indirectly.

R Kirk: We probably do it in a more subconscious way. The choice of some of the subject matter for our videos and tapes that we've used have been political — but not in a direct way. It's difficult to explain, but we wouldn't use any old rubbish. We're not random in that extreme, and I don't think it works to be.

Mal: It's alright to say, "Oh, yeah, we're only a band, we're not going to change the world" — that's obviously true — you're not going to change the world. Frankie Goes To Hollywood proved that, they just ended up with a load of dickheads with Relax on their T shirts. But the whole point is that if you've got no sort of desire to change anything, then it's a waste of time. And I think we felt we were going to change something, however small.

Do you still feel that?

R Kirk: I think we have done to be quite honest. Not us alone, but us alongside other people have actually helped change people's conceptions. Like with different sounds that you find on a pop record today — things that we toyed around with — people would never have dreamed of using those things outside of avant-garde music. I mean we were using drum machines ten years ago and about eighty percent of things now in the charts use a drum machine. And I'm sure on a small scale that lots of people like us and TG must have had some effect, no matter how subliminal.

Mal: I mean it's not being conceited but I still think people like us are the reason that people are quite open to accepting chart and dance records that use found voices. I'm not saying if we hadn't done it, nothing would have happened — somebody else would have done it. But I still feel we helped actually change things like that within music.

What is it that interests you about the American voice?

Mal: We live and breathe like an American culture in England. It's just throwing it back in another context. Also, the notion of the BBC type voice isn't contemporary. The American voice has had a more contemporary image.

On 'War Of Nerves' we hear about a rat eating away at somebody's face...

Mal: That's a guy called Frank Turpel who was an American CIA torturer and told everybody what he was up to and then disappeared off the face of the earth. It was taken off a documentary about him.

Do you find it interesting that both of you wouldn't classify yourselves as musicians, even after making so many albums?

Mal: People say we play synthesizers in tune — but I still don't know any notes or chords, it's just what sounds good. There's so much snobbery about being able to play things and it doesn't make any difference whether you can play it properly or not. I mean the point is that it's what people hear in the end that's important, and if it works and sounds right, then that's good enough. I can admire certain people's techniques and things like that, but then again, it's not a case of how cleverly you play, it's the basics.

R Kirk: I mean it's quite interesting to me that a lot of electro is almost stripped of any music, all you're getting is rhythm. In the things that we started doing about 1973 with just tape loops, there wasn't any music involved. It was just creating interesting rhythms more than anything else. And I think with programmable drum computers, it's almost an art in itself to be able to do something like that and go one better than the last record. The wilder and more out on a limb some of those drum programmes become, the more it appeals to people.

In thirty years time what would you like people to remember about Cabaret Voltaire?

Mal: That we made interesting records I suppose. Or interesting videos, that would be enough for me. It would be quite nice if we still got a bit of respect, not, "Oh, those wankers", you know? (laughs) I think it would be quite nice to be viewed with a bit of respect after all that time.

TEST DEPT.

Below the Thames River in South East London lies New Cross. Railway scrapyards litter the community, not far from the deserted dockland. Its atmosphere is one of oppression, while its inhabitants mirror the area's decline. It is no surprise that in 1981 a group called Test Department arose within this industrial waste, often using its remnants to create something aurally compelling. Making drums out of metal barrels and a variety of sounds from discarded springs and coils, Test Department construct musical rhythms which contain rigorously and painfully worked out sounds and textures. The group began performing before live audiences — not in usual venues, but beneath deserted railway arches. The environment suited the groups sound; hard, aggressive and powerful.

In 1984, the National Union of Miners decided to go on strike to protest the pit closure programme, which had been implemented by Ian Macgregor of the National Coal Board and supported by the Conservative government, led by Margaret Thatcher. The autumn of the same year saw the six man Test Department show their support for the beleaguered miners by undertaking an extensive tour throughout England and Scotland with a Welsh miner's choir, with all proceeds going to the miners' effort. 1985 saw the group tour extensively behind the iron curtain. In 1986, Test Department released their second LP *The Unacceptable Face Of Freedom* and formed an umbrella organisation called The Ministry of Power for live events and the release of their records.

Why did Test Dept. begin making music?

TD: Basically there was this huge vacuum, there was nothing which had any energy or any sort of violence in it really. Nothing that was confronting anyone or taking any risks. And we thought it was necessary to do something which was urgent, and some of it gradually affected people and made them feel something.

Is there any particular feeling that you'd like people to come out with after a gig or after listening to your records?

TD: It affects different people in different ways. One of the nicest ways is when they've written to us and said that they came to our gig feeling really shitty and they had a terrible year, and they found it such a powerful force, it really uplifted them — a recharging. And they just went away feeling that they could do things for themselves. A feeling of hope and strength. So many things get thrown at people everyday and our music uses the same sort of tactics, but to such an extent that it mixes you up and then you begin to put them into place.

One gets a feeling of energy from Test Dept., but that energy seems to be pointing in a dark direction...

TD: Obviously a lot of people are afraid to deal with something that intense only because it can uncover parts in people that are not normally uncovered, not even to themselves. The things we're dealing with, say manipulation by the media, are dark areas. No-one knows what goes on before they see the nice packaged product and the nice glossy advert that pleases their eyes. But all the things behind it are just a great, dark mess. And when you reach the darkness it makes you feel a response to something that can be heavy, but it's once you begin to realise what it's doing that you see that. It provides such an extreme summing up of all those things. So it doesn't have to be dark, but it's not light because it's not dealing in fantasy. It doesn't give you room to lay back and say, "Ah, this is wonderful". It's saying, "You've got a problem, you're faced with problems on a mass scale".

The image of the band seems very hard and very physical. Do you think that's misleading to a lot of people, that a lot of people might be scared away?

TD: We certainly don't wrap things in a very clear-cut way. It's expanding a bit now, there are some very soft elements within it and it has tender parts. Music is sound, and if it's working in its most efficient way, it is connecting with different parts of the body. So it has to be hard and physical if it is to be used to its maximum effect.

It also depends on the degree to which you as a listener open yourself up. We've found, through our experience, that the strangest people from many different age groups have responded to it when they've been opened to it. I mean it's the question of what music should be doing. Most music is syrup. It creates a nice, glossy, sticky film over people. We're not saying that we know everything — we're discovering for ourselves, we're opening ourselves up. For us it's an inside progression, and people should see it and accept it in that sort of mind.

Do you think the work of Test Dept. and Neubauten are closely related?

TD: With Neubauten, I feel the sources and the areas they've come from have come together in a brilliant way. And us exploiting it the way we do, and them their way, adds to something stronger. There's no question of a cancelling out or sharing of ideas, but they're just from... I mean a different planet, a different continent, a different attitude and a different language.

Are you interested in getting something into the charts?

TD: Possibilities and combinations come up a lot of the time but ultimately the attitude that people go into that with, the idea of reaching a mass audience more often than not, eventually will come down to making money. And at this point in time, if we did that it wouldn't be for the right reasons, so we're not doing it. There may be a time when we decide to do that. At this moment, it wouldn't be true to what we're doing. The fucking stuff should be in the charts anyway. It would be in the charts if the people who actually run the radio stations in this country had the courage to stand up and actually play music that people don't expect to hear. Because people want to hear anything, an audience is open, but the dictation of taste comes from A&R men and the people who programme the radio stations. In order to have a chart record you have to cynically exploit the formula.

Are you bothered by criticism you get from other musicians who are trying to do something similar?

TD: It's when you see things commercially that you begin to get paranoid about what you have to do. And the people that you're dealing with and the mentality that you're dealing with is pitted against that. There is a common front and a common mentality which, if combined in some way, would be so much stronger, but the people are so fiercely individual about what they are doing and still a touch paranoid. Even on this level, little tinges of competitiveness come in, and one-upmanship. It's a very petty paranoia which ought to be overcome because it's damaging to the ultimate effects of the music.

Are you spiritually involved?

TD: Maybe spiritual is the wrong word. When you really begin to play and when we're working hard, a slight but immense feeling takes over. You can't really describe it, it's not particularly spiritual or ritualistic or whatever. I mean you can go through periods where you play and you just black-out and carry on playing and will not realise the amount of time that has gone by. We'll be totally immersed with it to the point that you don't even have to think, it just comes. It's nothing that you need to rehearse or study for years and years before you ascend to that level. It's in everybody and it's just when you discipline and channel yourself that you find that. And it's the equivalent of the spiritual level, but in a very intuitive way.

What else have you listened to in the past where you've found that true?

TD: The Russian composers around the time of the revolution. We used to play Shostakovich prior to the set. One of the first tape intros that we involved was a Shostakovich piece that ran for about ten minutes, this incredibly slow build up, and then it would reach a certain peak when we'd begin to distort it and it would begin to twist and change. Then we'd actually intercut that with machine noise — and that noise would begin to take over. So it was a transition from classical into us. We've ended with Albernini before, when you just take people down with that classical, almost church-like feel to the music — incredibly sombre and uplifting. But we find new pieces for each performance.

Why do you feel it's more important to play in a natural environment that in a club?

TD: It's more important for the general feel, the atmosphere and for the people who see it. They can take away so much more. What's the point of feeding the commercial industry, the one that just shifts people in week after week, just becoming another part of it. It doesn't matter what you do on the night, people still go with the same expectations and they're going to get something a little more offbeat. So fucking what? They just crawl off more pissed at the end and they've had another night out. They don't even remember in six months time. The people who remember are the ones for whom you've done something really special and years later they're still going to have that with them as being a valid experience.

Do you find that you're preaching to the converted by doing that?

TD: I think it's the other way round. If you're just going to play ordinary clubs, then you're just playing to people who you should expect to play to. They're the people who are going to go to those clubs, unless you're a complete surprise. For instance we're going to go over to New York and play the Kool Jazz Festival on the last night in Irving Plaza along with a Nigerian Chorl Player! (laughs)

It surprises me that a band like Test Dept. would be invited.

TD: Exactly, it's brilliant. So that is a situation where the audience don't have a clue as to what they are going to get. That is where the whole thing becomes worthwhile, because there we're dealing with a completely unknown audience. When you're dealing with clubs in Britain, you're dealing with bullshit, you're dealing with small cliques of people who go there week after week. It's not a question of converted or unconverted. In Glasgow, we played in the Scottish National Orchestra's hall which used to be a church. And when everyone came in, they had to sit in church pews and couldn't drink or smoke. They had to sit and wait for two hours for it. It was brilliant, and that was against expectation. So because of that, people were made to behave in a different way.

How do you want your music to be regarded?

TD: It should be something that anyone can listen to and appreciate — in a way that someone like Shostakovich is. That was pretty strange for its time, but there's a feeling of strength that carries people with it. Just with its immensity, and solid base of emotion. The problem with pop music is that it only has that little bit of soul, but it's just a three minute catch line that's gone in two weeks. In addition, Shostakovich was dealing with the state of the Russian nation, he was dealing with the soul of a nation. That's the key, that it's something within all of us, it's not something high up and far away that you've got to look to find.

Do you feel that it has become necessary with a performance to include a visual accompaniment such as film or slides, especially since people have now become accustomed to video?

TD: It's more a hangover from the sixties and the seventies when people would go and see bands and would take it for granted that you should stare at a group of people on stage and their huge light show — it has become very passive. That wasn't the original intention, but it has become a huge monster. But that's pointless because there is not very much to look at. The actual possibilities of having films shown in a context different from those in a cinema are huge. Most people can break away from usual experiences of seeing films, which are now very much in the stale, narrative or documentary tradition with voice-overs. Live, there is so much possibility of combining film directly with music and also in much more exciting context than being glued to a seat in a cinema. You can use the scale of the place that you're playing in and the scale of the sound. It's much more immediate and spontaneous.

How do most bands in the charts, and that have promos appearing on MTV, use video?

TD: It's completely superficial. It's just an advertising medium to sell their product. It's as simple as that. We prefer to treat film very directly, in a very raw way and with raw sound, and forget about all the traditions of Hollywood and documentary — to just get back to some of the original intentions when people first started using film at the turn of the century. We go for confrontation and pushing things to the limit.

What are some of your reasons for meshing live music with pre-recorded audio tape?

TD: We've always used tapes, but it was quite a primitive way of using them. Now we use live tape mixing. Four tracks of different things that, depending on the way that we're actually playing and the speed, can be adapted by the tape operator. Before it was fixed — whereas now it can actually depend on the spontaneity of the band. And on those tapes, we can use any sound we want really.

On a basic piece, the progression of it depends on where you will manipulate the listener to go. A tape is often used underneath to create an atmosphere so something will be really unnerving for you and you don't know why. So we'll take sounds or sentences that, out of context, have a really unnerving quality. You can't hear it straight away consciously, but it goes in.

What would you be interested in getting across to people underneath the surface?

TD: It's really about the information you impart. A particular piece like 'Total State Machine' has bits coined off World Radio that will suddenly fly in and fly out, but it's tied in with the impact of that song and what it's dealing with, state radio and state information. That particular song has to do with the efficiency of the state. A person might not know the reference, yet that reference when it was made was done with that mentality. We're criticising, documenting and laying open to the public information of dubious character.

What would you like to get across to people after they've seen you perform live?

TD: We've made a few references to Shostakovich, dealing with the fascination of the period that, as regards to the twentieth century, was the one period of biggest change for a mass amount of people. Imagery and art of that time was all geared towards that incredible social change, the complete overthrowing of a past system in every way. You don't attempt to operate that way on a political level, but on a level of what we're actually doing — trying to encapsulate change. To actually give you a certain sense of power within the system, to manipulate yourself instead of being in the marketplace as one of the mass.

Individuality in other words?

TD: Well no, because it's a collective. It's very difficult. Maybe putting your individual conscience into what you do, whether you work with other people or not, but not for selfish reasons. Hopefully to give them some fire to change what you want. The easiest thing within any political system is to be given a false sense of security. Britain, as far as democracies go, is not that bad on a world level, but there's still a fuck of a lot of dirt that gets filtered through the press. We know that through the way we've looked at the system in operation and we've tried to divorce ourselves from it and build up our own strength. All you can do is provoke, with the same degree of distrust, understanding or deception, that dirt of what is evil and dark. That's what fascinates us, that's what we're trying to understand and come to terms with. And you just try to understand what you can do in the areas that you work, against all that... shit.

What do you consider that 'shit' to be?

TD: The total manipulation of everybody — in Britain cynically for money and nothing else. The God in Britain now is efficiency. It's efficiency that dictates whether you will go onto the scrap heap or progress. And the loss in freedom, as in the choice to work or say what you want to say, is the strongest erosion at the moment. That's what concerns us most just now. Three examples that you've seen lately are GCHQ, the treatment of the miners and the Falklands. Make no mistake, the Conservatives are in control and the only thing you can continue to do is stir. It's not only the choice to do or say what you want that's being taken away, it's the choice to think that's being taken away. Because people don't even think about how they're being controlled and manipulated. And they are to a greater and greater extent all the time — which is where the need to be direct comes in, the degree to which you really need to stir anger beyond an aggressive emotion. But what we give to you, as with the media and what we present, is Test Dept. as a propagandised commodity. You're uncovering the stone, the beetles, the dirt and the filth, and then you peer in. All that we are involved in doing is taking the active part of lifting the stone away so that you get a slightly clearer view of the things that frighten you.

What's your biggest criticism of the British political system?

TD: A couple of years ago we had particular political ideas and it was very easy to talk about the system and criticisms of that. You now have got a government that are eroding things so fast that you'll probably end up voting for the party you never thought you'd vote for. It's really becoming desperate. The irony is that we are a product of the Conservative government in England, and that is the reason why some people find what we do attractive. They've seen what the Conservative government has done to this country and we have become increasingly relevant through that. If there had been a socialist government it would have been a completely different story.

How closely did the beliefs of Test Dept. relate to the miner's strike in Britain?

TD: Basically our ideas manifested themselves in the strike, but it's also all the other things that grew out of the strike — like the way this country has been run and the measures which are being taken by the state as a force against the general public. Their term is "the enemy within" which has lead to an increase in police powers, the courts backing up the police and the whole state system being used against individuals.

You've got a system which is the army, the police, the top lawyers through to Saatchi and Saatchi and they've got it completely working for themselves! The implications are quite frightening. It's never been used in that way before, not in such a concentrated effort. And if that is the beginning of how things are going in this country, where does it end? Especially since there is a landslide in the government, the Trade Union laws that they're shifting in — like them basic withdrawal of the right to picket — are all greatly in the government's favour.

One of the keys of the strike in Nottinghamshire was the term 'police state' which arose. Right at the beginning of the strike, a lot of the miners went from Kent and came down from Yorkshire into Nottinghamshire where they wanted to persuade working Nottinghamshire miners, by speaking on the picket line that it was their duty to go out on strike because they couldn't look at it just for themselves. The miners were actually having a lot of success in the first few weeks. The Government obviously saw this and knew this was happening, and it was at that moment that a siege was put around Nottinghamshire so that the police wouldn't actually let anybody in. So the actual right to go and speak was taken away, and that is when the first clashes happened. That's when people who would never ordinarily be stirred up, angry or violent in that way found themselves stopped and being told to go back home. Their freedom of movement was taken away.

But it wasn't a strike dealing merely with wages and jobs. A lot of miners said that since they'd been away from the pits, it was the first time that they realised what a shitty job it was, but it was all they had basically. They wanted to keep the things that were important in their lives and their communities. They were fighting for their self-respect and their dignity; not just being made redundant from their jobs, but being made redundant as human beings. Hundreds and thousands of people just being pushed under the doors and being quietly forgotten about and feeling totally helpless. What sort of principle is that to run a country on? Either you efficiently produce something for sale or you're just cabbage. That's not the way this country should be going. What sort of society do we want to see and how are people valued? Are they just valued for work or are they valued as human beings?

A lot of the miners viewed it as the last spearhead against management and control of their destinies. If this union gets fucked over — which is the strongest union — then there is very little organized opposition to the policies that are being implemented. The Labour Party, as such, sold themselves down the line to gain votes. Everything became tactical, the major politicians were scared to confront and reveal the truth because it would lose them votes. It became a television and media orientated communication battle, where they only presented the information that wasn't going to alienate a large sector of the population.

How would Mrs Thatcher view the differences between the Solidarity movement in Poland and the Miner's strike in Britain?

TD: They go through incredible twists of logic. In this country, they use the scare tactic of the hard left; "Militant Tendency", sounds like a disease. They can support Solidarity by saying that it's the Commies that are against them. And here they can put down the unions because they say that the Commies are behind them too. Therefore the "hard left" are the Commies no matter where they are! (laughs) And it's just a total twist of logic because the unions are performing the same functions in both countries, standing up for their own work force. In fact, in the early 80's the British government were openly supporting Solidarity, praising them and waving their flag. It was front page news — they had extended newscasts devoted to the Poland issue every day, and now that's suddenly forgotten and buried.

But they can play on so many factors that influence and sway public opinion against them. When the strike first began, the Government stated that they weren't interested in involvement in industrial affairs. And less than a year later, they were actually preventing the Coal Board from opening negotiations. They wanted to see them NUM destroyed. They didn't want to see any negotiations where there could have been some sort of settlement which would have given the miners — not victory — but some sort of strength which they could go away with. The government just wanted to see their faces rubbed in the shit.

And can you believe the position of them just sitting there fat and contented watching a trickle back to work as if people were trickling back to work on some great principle? They were going back to work because they had been out on strike for eleven months and literally could not handle having no money. That's what "starve back to work" means. It meant that those people were completely desperate. The Government just sat there waiting until they felt that enough had gone back to work so that they could crush the union. And that is founded on such sick principles. It's such a sick mind that can sit back and let that happen. And it's because those people are so fucking rich and live so far above it that they can look down on this little world and it doesn't affect them. It doesn't affect them emotionally at all. They don't know the meaning of hardship. They never will.

But their tactics are amazing. With the riots that were happening in Britain in 1981, the Government immediately put a blanket on that information so it wasn't publicised, so no-one knew what was happening outside their own little community. So in that isolation, it seems that you're up against so much with no allies. It seems futile. And that's what they were doing to the miners as well. And until the government has actually made it so bad for everyone, it's very hard to think of anything direct happening or a confrontation all over the country.

Basically, all costs that are mounting up one day are going to hit home; the Falklands and how much money they're pumping to keep that going, buying all the American missile systems and the cost of the miner's strike. Plus, they've had to sell all the national assets like British Airways and British Telecom just to keep it afloat so that it doesn't completely collapse. And where is the money going to come from? By that stage, you end up not having a job, you can't work and you end up being conscripted into the army or into youth training schemes at the age of sixteen. Otherwise, you're denied any sort of livelihood. They could just send you off to fight wars — and you're not even fighting for your country because other people own it anyway!

LAST
FEW
DAYS

SONIC YOUTH — BAD MOON RISING LP — LYRICS:

side one:

1. BRAVE MEN RUN (in my family)

[7 SONGS]

SEVEN DAYS AND SEVEN NIGHTS / I DREAMT A SAILORS DREAM OF SEA / SEVEN DAYS AND SEVEN NIGHTS
I DREAMT A SAILORS DREAM OF ME / SEVEN DAYS AND SEVEN NIGHTS /THE WORLD WAS MADE AND LOST
BRAVE MEN RUN / IN MY FAMILY / BRAVE MEN RUN / INTO THE SETTING SUN / BRAVE MEN RUN / INTO
CAPTIVITY / BRAVE MEN RUN /IN MY FAMILY   ~(lyrics: Kim Gordon)

SOCIETY IS A HOLE

SOCIETY IS A HOLE IT MAKES ME LIE TO MY FRIENDS
IT'S RUNNING DOWN MY STREET WITH WHITE POWER SNEAKERS ON THE
BEAUTIFUL BEAT OF BLACK FEET - SOCIETY IS A HOLE IT BEATS MY
FRIENDS BIG HEADS MY FRIENDS HAVE BIG HEADS - I CAN UNDERSTAND IT
BUT I DON'T RECOMMEND IT - YOU GOT BIG BIG HAIR AND EVERYBODY IS
SCARED - SOCIETY IS A HOLE IT MAKES ME LIE TO MY FRIENDS
THE ASSAULT OF HOLY NOISE - THERE'S A SLAP IN MY FACE
MY FRIENDS ARE GIRLS WRAPPED IN BOYS - WE'RE LIVING IN PIECES
I WANT TO LIVE IN PEACE - SOCIETY IS A HOLE   lyrics: Thurston Moore

WHO NEEDS YOU

"I LOVE HER ALL THE TIME"

"I LOVE HER ALL THE TIME"

SHE COMES INTO MY MIND TWISTING THRU MY NERVES - I DON'T
UNDERSTAND A WORD SHE SAYS - SHE'S ON MY SIDE
I LOVE HER ALL THE TIME

I love her all the time   lyrics: Thurston Moore
I love her all the time
I love her all the time
I love her all the time
I love her all the time
I love her all the time
I love her all the time

AMPS SET THUR. — VI-7.1/V2-7/M-8/T-7/B-5/T-7/HM-9/EM-6/
B-7/R-10 on & off

She brought new meaning to the phrase "DRIVING A HARD BARGAIN"!

ALONE? WHY?

side two:

BAD MOON RISING   KILL YR. IDOLS

4. GHOST BITCH

Slowly pour the liquid down/for miles & miles it flows along/rose colored neon lighted/swirl around turn around/
feel the touch of my hand/swirl around swirl around/fellow shadows black & blue/all around all around/
locking arms side by side/crouch down before the fire's light/you're the first day of my life..
I had no belief before/until I had this dream last night/I still remember their savage cries/
so serious in their rite/faces painted in joyous fright/in the dawns early light/
oh say did you see/the color of my eternity/and the sweat on my skin/our founding fathers
laid right down/+ Indian ghosts from long ago/they gave birth to my bastard kin
America it is called/a sensation of eternity/locking arms side by side/
crouch down before the fire's light/you're the first day of my life
~(lyrics: Kim Gordon)

I'M INSANE

LOVE STARVED BACKWOOD TEASER FARM GIRL HOT EYED BRIDE
STONE COLD BLONDE A QUIVERING MENACE ATOMIC WALLOP WHOLESALE MURDER
WE WANT OUT WE FISH AT NIGHT SEX IN HEAVEN TOUGH TOWN A CRUEL TOUCH
SAILORS LEAVE SIRENS SCREAMING LAP OF LUXURY A SHOW OF VIOLENCE
TAKE OFF YOUR MASK LAY OFF MY BROTHER KISS MY FIST STOP AT NOTHING
A STEAMING SWAMP A TROUBLED HEART THE SKY IS RED I CAN'T STOPP RUNNING +
HER BABY STARES THE SECRETS THERE SO HELP ME GOD I'LL SING AT YOUR FUNERAL
THE STUBBORN AIR THE KILLER MOB A RED BONE WOMAN A DOUBLE CROSS
BIG FAKE BITTER LOVE UNDERBELLY FREEZING JUNGLE
ONE STEP MORE HE'LL STIR YOUR SENSES SCRATCH YOUR SURFACE AND NAIL YOUR HEAD
MURDERED ANGELS BODIES IN BEDLAM A WOMAN SCORNED YOU CAN'T HANG ME
TIED TO MY JOB A BLAST SCENE ALIBI TIED TO A TREE IN A BLIND ALLEY
NOTHING BEFORE A BIG FEAR DON'T GET CAUGHT BY HER FATHER'S FRIENDS
SWAMP GIRL FADED THE TIGER'S WIFE A FRENZIED LOVE HOT CLIMATE
TWISTED PASSIONS FLESH PARADE DEAD AHEAD A WORLD SO WIDE
BIG RIVER LOVE CAMP THE HOUSEBOY AND HILL GIRL THE AGONY COLUMN
DON'T CROWD ME IT'S TIME FOR CRIME STRANGE BREED RIVER GIRL'S MISERY INDEX
INSIDE MY HEAD MY DOG'S A BEAR SHE WAS SIGNIFICANT I'M INSANE
— lyrics - THURSTON MOORE

FERLIN HUSKY SWAMP GIRL COLOR

BOYD RICE

For years, Boyd Rice has been creating environments consisting of noise — tapes, digital delays and sequencers spewed out at maximum volume, which most people seek shelter and comfort from, rather than seeing what effect it has on them. On record, Rice has done this in several ways. *Pagan Muzak*, a seven inch single packaged in a twelve inch sleeve, was designed to be played at any speed. Consisting of seventeen lock grooves, each containing a different noise, the record — like its predecessor — had several holes drilled into it creating a multi axis which allows the listener to achieve endless playback possibilities and makes him an active participant. Operating at times as Non, Boyd's live performances have gained varied response with some people finding it torturous, others finding it soothing. At times Rice doesn't even appear on stage, but controls his noise output from a dressing room leaving spectators to watch a scarecrow of himself on stage. Aurally, Rice has collaborated with Current 93 and Coil as Sickness Of Snakes, and has released *Easy Listening For The Hard Of Hearing*, an album recorded with Frank Tovey. Rice has also acted as associate editor to *Incredibly Strange Films*, a RE Search guide encompassing exploitation, oddities, super obscurities, and "Some of the wildest movies ever made".

During a performance by Non, a massive wall of sound is achieved. What are some of the reasons for creating such an atmosphere?

Boyd Rice: There are a lot of reasons, yet it's not so clear as to be limited to a small number of specific motives. Firstly, when I began to do this, I was aware of precisely what functions ordinary music wasn't fulfilling for me and I knew at the same time things that ordinary music inflicted upon people that I didn't want inflicted on me. It seemed to me that no matter what music presented itself as being, or what image was presented along with the music, it was all very similar in its effect, and very strongly tied to the same ideas, values and beliefs that comprise the human mind and thus the human world. So I wanted to create a form of stimulus that would bypass the mind, a form not rooted in the mind that would hopefully give rise to an experience more primal in nature. I wanted to do something directed toward the organism as a whole. By organism, I mean the body and brain as a whole. And I make a distinction between the brain and the mind. My feeling is that the mind is composed of ideas, beliefs and values, all of which have been inserted into people's brains in order to help them understand and interpret the world. But, in fact, those things are the very factors which prevent them from ever being able to see what's really going on. They keep people from ever having any sort of direct experience of things.

Let me ask you: What is belief good for? If something is actual, there's really no need to believe in it. You only have to believe something if it isn't true, because if it were, belief wouldn't be necessary. Is it necessary to believe in breathing or fucking or eating or dying? Of course not. It's just like; if laws were real, they wouldn't need to be enforced, because if laws were real, it would be impossible to break them.

Do you feel that an audience has ever come to terms with what you are personally trying to do with your performances? Do you think that has expanded their ideas of what music was, and did you want that?

Boyd Rice: Not really, but that's not my primary concern either. I wanted to do exactly what it was I wanted to do, whether an audience would ever be able to completely come to terms with it or not. Because it's easy, very easy, to express a whole range of things in such a way as to make an audience understand them. It's far more of a challenge to do things exactly as you think they should be done and not care who understands and who doesn't. To tell the truth, it's not actually any challenge for me to do things this way because it simply would not occur to me to do them in any other way.

Actually, quite a few people have approached me and said things about what I'm doing that came extremely close to aspects of the music that I supposedly never talk about, and the fact that people were aware of certain effects the sound had on them with no prior knowledge of such possibilities shows me that it has certain characteristics that are there for anyone who is able to allow themselves to experience it completely.

This is a difficult question because, to begin with, I don't really have any narrowly defined idea of what I'm trying to do or what I'm doing. It's a lot more vague than that. I know that people react positively and use what I do in a lot of different ways. I don't think I'd honestly expect people to sense much of what's there, because it's simply not made to correspond to people's facilities for interpretation. I think that coming to terms with it takes place at a level beyond understanding, and that only by going beyond understanding will you tune into the finer points, although it's not necessary to be aware of the subtleties to just enjoy it and have fun with it. I think what I do can be very fun, I mean it is fun. Fun is a very central thing for me, and I know it's there in the things I do — though I'm not sure how much people

NON

pick up on it; because fun means a lot more and different things to me than it does to most people.

What do you consider music to be, if anything? Do you consider most of your things to be music?

Boyd Rice: Anything can be anything if you want it to be. Music can be a toy, or a tool, or a human parasite, depending on the music itself and the attitude of the listener. So music could be anything and I suppose anything could be considered music. I made plans for a concert in 1975 called Hazard Music, and it consisted of a box of bullets dumped out on a barbecue grill (over hot coals) in the centre of a room with chairs for the audience placed around the perimeter of the room in a circle. Between the spectators and the ammo would be large sheets of glass, so when a bullet heats up and fires, a person would hear the glass shattering about a split second after they heard the blast, and know whether or not the projectable was heading in their direction (though it wouldn't give them time to run, just maybe time to know it was coming). So anyway that was a concert. Maybe the audio portion of it was extremely minimal, but I'm sure the New York Philharmonic would be hard pressed to match the emotional impact! So, as far as I'm concerned, music can exist far beyond rhythm and melody, the important part of it is the response it causes in the listener, not the means used to get that response.

I suppose I feel that pretty strongly, though I'm not interested in arguing the boundaries of music or pushing back its horizons. Because basically I don't feel as though what I'm doing is music or has much in common with music. I'm not a musician and my motivations aren't particularly musical. I can't read music and I can't play any instruments. It would be easy to relate what I do to music, since they involve both sound and some degree of structuring, although that would be misleading, a bit like saying a church is the same as a mortuary since both are built of brick or marble. Actually, that's not too good an analogy since a church is much closer in spirit to a mortuary than what I do is to music.

Do you feel that your product has a similar effect on people live as it would on record?

Boyd Rice: The effect is intensified live and can be taken further than on record, just due to the fact that through sheer volume the sound can become a physical presence. In some cases, the sound has been so loud that audience members claimed they could no longer hear it, they could only feel it. Of course, records and performances are two distinctly different types of situations, and each has their own peculiar advantages and disadvantages. It seems to me that they shouldn't be viewed so much as being closely inter-related, and that people should approach each with an eye towards taking advantage of the possibilities unique to the form and exploiting that as much as possible. I always found it funny that some bands weren't able to reproduce what they had on their albums or that bands couldn't capture on vinyl the energy of their live sound. It's because the two situations involve completely different sets of circumstances. Even people's attitudes towards the two are different, and some things that work on record wouldn't translate to live performance at all, and vice versa. I've tried to make the most of whatever extra capacities each category possesses. I know that both areas can be explored a lot further and taken far beyond where they're at now — and I've got plans to do just that. Lots of plans.

Why did you release a record of live performances?

Boyd Rice: I decided to put out an album of live performances because that's an area I've been dealing with for quite a few years and it seemed natural to put out some sort of document of it. 'Pagan Muzak' was an album that most people had a very difficult time coming to terms with, due mostly to the fact that nothing similar had ever been done, so people didn't know how to react to it or what to think. Most people refused to believe it was an album. So I figured it was about time to release an album where the tracks all had titles and so forth, so at least it would have the superficial appearance of just a normal record.

Do you experiment with certain high and low frequencies in order to create a physical reaction on people within the audience?

Boyd Rice: Of course. I've always used a lot of high and low frequencies. Before I worked with sound, I'd intuitively felt that certain sounds seemed to correspond to various mental and physical states, and I felt that by approximating those sounds, it would be possible to induce those states. And I was correct.

Are you still experimenting with the instrumentation and methods that you used on 'Physical Evidence'?

Boyd Rice: That's hard to say, because I used a wide variety of methods to produce the various things on that record and it reflects only some of the techniques I've used. Mainly I've used tapes in conjunction with some devices I invented and built that are basically devices to structure pure sound into rhythms. So in that way, the tape recorders aren't used as playback machines, but rather as a sound source. In this way, I'm able to structure sounds that ordinarily you wouldn't be able to get. With the sounds I like, you can't just go into the store and get something over the counter that's going to give you those sounds. I've also used tape delays and digital delays in conjunction with my ordinary set-up, so I could make a sound on sound rhythm that would keep going and then play along with it at the same time and get a lot of layers and levels of sound. I've used that same approach with different objects and with my voice — hitting trash bins with a small sledgehammer and so on.

Of course, now there are a lot of bands that bang on pieces of metal, but that I did a long time ago, just like Z'ev, who's been doing metal percussion since I first met him in 1976 or so. That's a long time. And I don't feel that Z'ev has ever gotten the credit he deserves. Most people don't really remember what the whole atmosphere was like, but back then anything using a synthesizer was looked upon by the general music or rock audience as being radical and avant-garde. Today most of the songs in the top forty use synths and they're used in commercials and TV themes, they're everywhere. And for years I've been telling people that someday noise would be assimilated into mainstream pop music, and it's already starting to happen. I don't necessarily think it's of any great importance that noise elements are being incorporated into mainstream music, but it just goes to show how people deny themselves access to vast areas of experience, then all of a sudden are willing to accept something they never did before. And when they're used to it, they wonder why they never looked upon it as just an ordinary thing. Like when I first began doing noise, people hated me, they felt that what I wanted to do was just be as obnoxious or disagreeable as possible, that I wanted to torture an audience and make them miserable. And I would tell them that there was nothing horrible about noise at all, that what I was doing wasn't done out of animosity or meant to be violent or aggressive. I was simply doing what interested me, and if others were interested or affected by it, that's fine. But if they allowed themselves to be tortured by it, that's their problem, and further, it serves them right to suffer.

Do you feel that some of the music that you do lacks an inner feeling or 'soul'?

Boyd Rice: Definitely not. I feel it lacks the superficial trappings and emotional cliches that pass for feeling in most music. It's a common mistake for people to say that what I do is cold and emotionless, when in fact it doesn't lack emotion, it only lacks the cartoonish emotional cliches most people are used to. There's a whole range of emotions that seem to exist beyond the grasp of a lot of people, and that's too bad. But the world isn't as shallow and one dimensional as some would have us believe.

Why is correct playback possible at maximum volume only with some of your experiments, like those with tape loops?

Boyd Rice: Because at certain levels of volume you cease to think, and when you can no longer think about it, you're forced (allowed) to experience it. As long as people use the intellect and try and interpret and understand what they see, everything they view is tainted by what they think. What they believe and the values they've accumulated will get in the way of them having a true experience of whatever is at hand. So in order to get them, you've got to override the mind.

You seem to have managed to create quite a low profile for Boyd Rice and Non. What have been the reasons for that?

Boyd Rice: Mainly just the fact that I enjoy living my life. My priorities vary widely with most people's. The things that excite me are the things that other people either ignore or don't care about, or don't even notice. So I've always got enough pleasure close at hand, and at the same time, I've always tried to pursue whatever it is that excites me most. This means that I'm nearly always extremely happy and always up to something. Now for most people, I think that performing or making records probably fulfils a very primary, very large place in their life. But for me, I'm always at the point of doing whatever interests me the most, so in other words, I don't do what I do for the same reasons most people do. And as a result, many times my 'career' is put on the back burner in favour of some interesting pursuit or adventure. And when I do music, I do what I most desire to do, not what I think other people will like to hear, or not what I feel will make me money, or not what I'm told people will expect of me.

It's odd, but in a way I feel that I've done consistently what every band says they'd like to

do but never actually do. Because bands will say publicly that they are only doing commercial stuff until they gain an audience, then once they're accepted, they'll do what they're really interested in. But when they allow their audience to dictate the nature of what they do, it's easy to forget your original, genuine impetus. To think that you can do what you want by doing something that you don't want to do is confusing to say the least. Compromise will only get you less of what you want, not more. And less than all is not enough. I've gone to great lengths to ensure that I never have to do anything less that what I choose to do. It's not always easy, but it's always worth it. I've lived in cemeteries, in caves and abandoned houses. I've stolen in order to eat and I've lived off food from the garbage bins, but to me, none of that is any sort of hardship. It's a hardship to live your life when you're not doing what you want, that's the only hardship. The rest is fun. I enjoy living in caves and all the rest. It's an adventure.

What drives you to express your interests in the musical field? Why do you feel that is the best way for you to express yourself?

Boyd Rice: Because sound has a greater capacity for overwhelming the senses. It has a greater capacity for affecting the senses and overriding the mind. Sound can take possession of a listener in a way that no other stimuli can. Plus, sound can be more a form of experience, as opposed to most forms, which are generally 'about something'. (i.e forms that tell stories or promote certain ideas or beliefs etc.)

Do you feel that music, art or literature can be too educated at times, that people look into it too much rather than responding to an initial feeling?

Boyd Rice: Definitely. As far as I am concerned, the intellect is a disease. It imposes values where none exist. Values don't exist in the world, they exist in the mind and are purely imaginary. They're completely fictional and to project them onto actual things or situations can only result in fictionalising the world and your experience of it.

ONE DAY, I STOPPED HATING.
I CEASED ALL MEANINGLESS ACTIVITY.
I COMPLETED THE CIRCLE.
I SET MY SIGHTS STRAIGHT.
LIKE AN ARROW I FLEW.
I STOPPED ACTING.
I GOT TIRED OF PLAYING WITH YOU.
RANDOM VIOLENCE AND DESTRUCTION
BECAME MY REASON FOR LIVING, MY OUT,
MY EXCUSE. WHAT IS YOUR EXCUSE? DESTRUCTION.
WITHOUT HATE, WITHOUT FEAR.
WITHOUT JUDGEMENT. I AM NO BETTER
THAN YOU. NO ONE KNOWS THIS BETTER THAN
I DO. I JUST GOT TIRED OF PLAYING
PARLOUR GAMES.

I AM THE INCINERATOR MAN. A DISCIPLE OF THE SUN.
I'M YOUR MAN. I DON'T WANT TO WASTE YOUR TIME.
I DON'T WANT TO TAKE YOU JUST ANYWHERE, I WANT TO
TAKE YOU NOWHERE. I'VE GOT A MAGIC TOUCH. BLOW
OUT THE CANDLES ON YOUR BIRTHDAY CAKE, GET IN
THE CAR, WE ARE GONNA FLAME BROTHER.

DRAWINGS S. AMOEBA

JOEY ★ ARSHOLE

WORDS VAL DENHAM

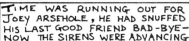

TIME WAS RUNNING OUT FOR JOEY ARSEHOLE, HE HAD SNUFFED HIS LAST GOOD FRIEND BAD-BYE — NOW THE SIRENS WERE ADVANCING

THERE'S ONLY ONE PLACE TO HIDE THIS BIG MUTHA AND THATS CLEAN UP MY ENORMOUS ARSEHOLE!

GUN SHOTS, MOIDER, COMPLAINTS, NOISES? PERHAPS YOU'D — LIKE TO LOOK FOR THE BODY — FRIENDS

TWO HOURS LATER...

OKAY JOEY, YOU WIN — IT LOOKS LIKE YET ANOTHER HOAX CALL

OKAY WHEN THESE TWO QUEENS MAKE AN EXIT, I VISIT THE JOHN!

VERY LUCKY JOEY BOY MAYBE A LITTLE TOO LUCKY THIS TIME? MAYBE YOUR BUDDY IN YOUR BUM WASN'T QUITE AS DEAD AS — YOU IMAGINED....

HE'S ALIVE AND HE'S TEARING ME APART FROM THE INSIDE!

ONLY ONE THING TO DO NOW JOEY BOY, ONLY ONE THING

PHUT!

MISSED!

POOR OLD JOEY BOY HE LIVED BY THE ARSE AND HE DIED BY THE ARSE, AS FATHER KNOX SAID "A LOUD NOISE AT ONE END AND NO SENSE OF RESPONSIBILITY AT THE OTHER" WELL THAT WAS JOEY BOY.

THE END

METANOIA
THEME FOR "CAPTURED MUSIC"

The urge to capture and preserve pieces of our experience has run through much of man's development. From the earliest creative efforts, right through to current developments in communication and entertainment technology, attempts have been made to snatch moments from time and hold them in a state which might enable another to experience the event for themselves. In other words, a vain attempt to make experience repeatable.

Recent work in Egypt and Japan reveals the existence of possible primitive forays into the recording of sound. At the present time, no conclusive evidence as to the function of the 'supposed' equipment has emerged, but it is clear that at least an awareness of the possibility existed.

Coincidentally, the first 'recordings' both visual and aural that did not rely on the direct intervention of the human hand (painting, sketching, transcription of music, etc.) arrived just before the turn of the century. It is impossible to re-experience the impact these inventions must have had at first hand, paradoxically, the reason for their invention. So from the outset, their original purpose was lost.

If it is thought on reading these words that this is not the case, it should be remembered that most people are aware on any exposure to any media (which may be viewed as a conglomeration of such devices for recording and then disseminating experience, events and information) that the whole picture is not present. Most people on reading a newspaper, watching the News on television are apt to disbelieve what they hear or see at least once in the course of a sitting.

This is not to condemn the devices out of hand. It is not the fault of the builder when a drunkard smashes a brick into someone's head.

Dating from the early 1930's (and possibly before this), when French radio broadcast Musique Concrete manufactured from live manipulation of wax discs, and soon after, when Varese started to introduce some of the first tape-recorded machine sounds into the orchestra ("Deserts", etc.), realisation has gradually dawned as to the other possibilities of the recording of events — in this case, events in the sound world (although the rest of the theory holds true for the visual image also).

In other words, the realisation came that 'snapshots' of the world, i.e., representations lifelike enough to jolt the memory, could be altered, juxtaposed with others, repeated endlessly, and subjected to as many perversions as the operator of the tape recorder desired. It offered the unnerving feeling of playing a kind of lesser God, manipulating common, everyday sounds into the mould the whim of the creator happened to alight upon.

And with a few, very few exceptions, this is the way that it has remained. Recent developments enable theft by 'sampling' another's composition, which in turn may well have been sampled from something else, and so on ad infinitum. The initial results of this process must have been very disturbing. Again, we cannot now recapture this effect, due to a familiar process — namely, assimilation. What was regarded as daring, provocative, ground-braking, now occupies the supermarket shelves, the most conservative of broadcasting networks, and finally, even brings forth tired glances and yawning from the very people it originated from. Because it no longer belongs to them.

But the point is, surely, that it never belonged to them in the first place! The sounds were not theirs — they attempted, and still are attempting, to plait with fog, to cage the sky. Unfortunately, they have mistaken the act of pointing with the object being pointed at.

At this point, it is our contention to suggest that the reason why this has happened is the concentration on the 'Entertainment' factor, or rather, Aesthetics over meaning, function and content.

Indeed we would go further and state that our work addresses the problem by treating the raw material as fragments from life, to be treated with respect as this deserves. Although not the experience itself, a well-made sound recording of place (or person or thing) nevertheless contains a fragment of the 'soul' of that place (or person or thing). By examination of auditory phenomenae, psychological and physiological use of certain frequencies, careful testing and construction of 'situations', 'environments', 'programmes', which might be any number of tactics in combination, an artificially induced 'place' can be created which can, under the right circumstances, produce true communication between people on three levels of human perception head, heart and hands, (or if you prefer, Body, mind and spirit).

We see this as infinitely worthy of our support, judging by the almost complete lack of others investigating this, to us, quite crucially important area. The possibilities afforded by such a chance to speak directly to one another are breathtaking.

In this way, we are returning experience to itself, returning machines back to their rightful place as servants, and hopefully, people back to each other instead of the present tendency for people to compartmentalise and separate one another.

So, our position we prefer to state as being concerned with research into sound and to a lesser extent, visual material etc., in order that communication may be made between people, rather than the present system of reciprocal vampirism. This may of course include the study of music, and has in the past, during out fruitful examinations of the ritual, religious and other ancient forms of encoding information in search of just such a form of 'direct', 'experiential' communication as above. As we have stated before and elsewhere, we have forgotten, almost wilfully in some cases, these important and extremely efficient methods.

Our problem, then, is to make these methods both new and old available for utilisation by all, in fact, to positively encourage their assimilation (but not their dilution or corruption).

Rather the reverse for all the efforts noted hitherto.

But what makes some of these previous efforts so interesting is their accidental and unwitting use of just these devices. The framework has been miraculously constructed in the name of entertainment, and this is all it carried. Rather like getting an African elephant to carry a golf-ball on its back whilst you walk alongside it through the jungle.

As with ourselves, it is the same with all we create; our capabilities are so under-used that it now takes more and more people to accomplish less and less. We are devoting our precious time (although it does not seem to be such to many) to the creation of ideas, objects and processes that pass directly into our refuse system. We try and try to escape the one thing that can be truly called our own — ourselves. We create diversion beyond enumeration — it screams at us every second along streets, in our houses, and most dangerous of all, inside our minds.

Although we are only beginning to take the first steps along a long road, we believe that the processes offered by research into areas of our work and those connected with it make possible contact with ourselves and our environment. The truth may be painful, but at least it is the truth.

So the 'capturing' of sound does not imply that we can or should create 'another' world which we can then inhabit, leaving behind the wreckage of the present one. By the intelligent use of this tool (and tool it should remain), a mirror can be cast up apart from communicating with symbols open to many different interpretations, one that brings us HERE, to come to NOW. Because this is where we are; and by dealing with this, we form the basis of where we might go. At present it lamentably seems as if we are trying to run before we can walk. The fact of the 'forgotten' knowledge only makes our position more criminal.

And if we do not address ourselves to this question, namely that of how better to speak and communicate with others, so that real creation may occur on this planet as the result of effort and intention, objective will, then all we will be doing is making desperate sign language from the funeral pyre.

Third draft completed New Year's Day

© 1987 The Hafler Trio

THE HAFLER TRIO

I n 1981, Christopher Watson decided to leave Cabaret Voltaire to work as a sound recordist with Tyne Tees Television in Newcastle. Watson joined up with Andrew McKenzie and then Dr Edward Moolenbeek as The Hafler Trio, a sound research group with whom Moolenbeek had been involved for some years but which had been defunct since 1975. On hearing a twelve minute broadcast on Welsh radio, Moolenbeek wrote to McKenzie and Watson suggesting "areas of mutual interest", notably his liaison with Robol Sound Recordings in Sweden, a research organisation that had been set up by the late Robert Spridgeon to carry on his lifetime's work into the perception and utilisation of sound.

Watson had first become interested in sound recording whilst a member of a chapter of Hell's Angels, enthused by the psychological effect caused by the 'beating' and 'phasing' of motorbike engines revving up. His main interest since has been in the field of natural history recordings. McKenzie — the most frequently seen face of The Hafler Trio — had released his first record at the age of fourteen and was involved in the setting up of a now well-known sound magazine. His contact with many religions and schools of philosophy would bring an authority to the work of The Hafler Trio gained through direct experience.

Part of Moolenbeek's intention in contacting McKenzie and Watson was to make available information and equipment that had resulted from his past association with Spridgeon — work that had often been subject to censorship and denial. The first LP "BANG" — An Open Letter, made full use of Robol's facilities, referring the listener to "the limitations of silence" and "the non-medical use of microphones" — subject matter that was to ensure that The Hafler Trio's work would be received with both admiration and scepticism.

With subsequent material on the Belgian-based label L.A.Y.L.A.H., the group concentrated more upon their own research into sound and visual media — *Alternation, Perception and Resistance, Seven Hours Sleep* being widely acclaimed everywhere but in Britain. In early 1986, The Hafler Trio presented a series of 'lectures' in Europe titled *Three Ways of Saying Nothing* (made available on LP by Charrm). This was followed by *The Sea Org*, an 'introductory' guide released by Touch that included examples of Moolenbeek's 'Sound Painting' — a technique whereby selected frequencies are directed at carrier materials to give an optical definition to various research patterns.

The group does not restrict itself to commercially available recordings — work has been undertaken on behalf of medical specialists, geologists and meteorologists amongst others. Present projects with Touch include *A Thirsty Fish* and *Ignotum Per Ignotius*, the latter to be the outcome of many years of study into alchemical processes.

PAINTING BY STEPHEN STAPLETON

When Cabaret Voltaire started, what were you trying to do?

CW: Upset people basically. In any way possible. To infuriate them, to annoy them generally and to stimulate people. It was such a low period and we just felt forced to actually go and provoke people as much as possible.

Was there anything in particular that you wanted them to do?

CW: Just get off their arses basically and do something for themselves and listen to what we were doing. It was a very aggressive time, sort of the pre-punk era really, which we were helped by enormously. There was a lot of sympathy between us and a lot of the early punk groups, if not in style and content, then in feeling behind it — to stimulate people as much as possible — which was the prime intention of Cabaret Voltaire initially.

Did you set out to do it just through music?

CW: No. Recorded sound was a very immediate thing which was easy to achieve and relatively easy to get out to people. But, although we had very limited facilities then, we also used film and literature to a certain extent. We published one or two things, but we concentrated more and more on sound because it was a way we all felt comfortable in working. We were also stimulated by a number of things around us, not necessarily music but the general environment. We thought it would be nice to involve some things that we were interested in.

Did you find what you started to do at the beginning was direct enough?

CW: Yeah. We could go out and confront people a bit. That was direct enough, it was very direct and very physical at times.

Did you find it worked better live, or as well on record?

CW: Well, we didn't actually release a record for about four years. And the reaction between what we put out as a recorded piece as opposed to live was different. We used the two in totally different contexts really. Live performance was more of a basic stimulus because of the very basic facilities we had. And the techniques that we were employing were perhaps more subtle applications in a controlled environment — of a small recording studio, and it allowed us to experiment both ways.

Since you didn't have any records out, did you find that your output was confined to the Sheffield area where you were working?

CW: It was, but it was also the start of the rise in this country of the fanzine which rapidly spread across the whole country. A distribution of non-commercial publications which helped a lot and gave a lot of feel to the whole thing. Through that we discovered other people and we were able to communicate ourselves through the printed word, which was quite exciting. I mean it was a discovery for us, it was not a new discovery, but it was something that we were able to use.

What was your function in the band?

CW: At that stage we were all interested in virtually the same thing, and so there were no strictly defined roles. It was a corporate purpose — "We the final product". We just got together and did it basically, by the best means we could.

What instrumentation were you using?

CW: Tape recorders and various bits of home-made, borrowed and stolen equipment that we sort of scraped together. But initially it was through tape recorders as it was an interesting medium to work in, and still is. I mean that's as relevant today in what Andrew and myself are doing with The Hafler Trio as it was ten years ago. More so, to a greater extent, because we now have better facilities, we realise more what we want to do and put a far stricter control over it. We were quite naive obviously in the early days.

Did you view yourselves more as musicians or artists?

CW: Neither. It was just something that we had to do. We never set out to be a group, or film-makers, or experimentalists, and we certainly weren't interested in being musicians. By definition we were; I mean I don't know how much you know about the original Cabaret Voltaire, in the early period of the group going back to the Dada roots of it. In Zurich in the early part of this century, there were a group of artists who got together around the time of the First World War with a specific hatred of the established art forms of the time. They formed themselves into groups who had various functions. And one of the groups of people, which varied in numbers at different times, used to have a small room at the back of a cafe in Zurich which they used for their various forms of performance art and putting on things in a very anti-establishment way. They called themselves The Cabaret Voltaire. And we found a certain sympathy with a lot of their initial ideas and an affinity with their techniques. So strongly, in fact, that we used the name. It was as much of a tribute as a term of reference for us.

When did you decide to use a more structured approach in terms of songs?

CW: It was something that we found ourselves moving towards as we refined and honed down the initial experiments. We found that we were sufficiently interested to pursue it when the thing started to sell records and we realised we could communicate to a large number of people. It was just a case of growing up and refining some of the ideas we had. And some of them actually turned out in conventional song structures, although we used non-musical techniques and instruments to achieve that result.

Why did you decide to leave Cabaret Voltaire?

CW: Ah, it's a difficult question. There are a lot of reasons, some of which are very personal and not really relevant to decisions that are made. But I wanted to do something else, I wanted to broaden what I was doing in recorded sound. The framework of Cabaret Voltaire was becoming more and more refined to a particular area and I wanted to explore areas outside of that. Eventually I decided after a lot of heart searching that the best way I could do it would be to leave. And that's one of the reasons, but I mean there were a lot of... it was very... I mean I still don't know if I made the right decision or whatever. I still argue about it within myself and think about it a lot, but I felt at the time I had to do it.

When you left did you think that Cabaret Voltaire were going into a more song-orientated direction?

CW: I didn't feel as if we were going in any particular direction. I saw other things which interested me and it wouldn't have been right at the time to try and move the whole group towards them. At that time they were just ideas and I didn't know if they would work or not, but I felt a strong desire and compulsion to explore them. So the direction that they were going was irrelevant really. I mean I enjoyed what I was doing at the time with them — largely so. There was never any true direction to Cabaret Voltaire, it was very much the possibilities of exploring various avenues. It just so happened there were one or two avenues I wanted to go further up.

Have you talked about working with Richard and Mal again in Cabaret Voltaire?

CW: No, we haven't, no, but I would — that's something that I did express. I mean I have no argument with them at all and so — yes I would. I mean obviously things would have to be sorted out, but I wouldn't rule out the possibility at all.

Did you refer to some of the earlier things that you did with tape recorders as "music" or was it something else that you termed it?

CW: I mean yes and no. I don't think it would benefit or be detrimental to give it the term "music". Call it what you will really, I wasn't interested in defining it as anything at the time. It was irrelevant if it was music or not to me, and still is. They're other people's definitions and pigeonholes which they will apply no matter what you say.

Do you have a definition yourself of what music is?

CW: Organised sound... I mean I don't really know, what's music to me is not music to somebody else. It's a definition, it depends on which part of the world you're in and what you are doing at the time. I wouldn't know what it needs.

You mention organised sound. Would you consider the noise of the car that just drove by to be music or would it have to be put together in a composition?

CW: I wouldn't know if it was music or not, but it is set in a composition. The sounds surrounding us at the moment of the car going past, whether they're deliberate, random, or organised — exist, and that's all they need to do really. It could well be music, yeah. If it is interesting to you, then yes.

With Cabaret Voltaire how did you want an audience to react or view you when you played live?

CW: That changed depending on the situation we were in and the actual time slot we were in. It gradually evolved in that we were trying to interest people in different aspects of the sounds. It also varied from performance to performance. I mean sometimes we used films and created a soundtrack to a film as we were actually playing. So at that point we obviously wanted people to listen and watch. Other times we wanted to physically move people, actually try and make them dance.

Why did you decide to use tape recorders instead of conventional instruments?

CW: That goes back to the very early days when it was just tape recorders. It was such a powerful instrument to me and it was the instrument I learned on. It's such an immensely powerful and creative instrument. And it was one of the ones that I knew best, and I'm still exploring the possibilities and the influences it has. So it was a conventional instrument to me. I mean I have dabbled with playing a keyboard, but only in a very crude sense. I was simply interested in the sounds that it could generate, more so than using it as an instrument.

Something I've certainly, with Andrew, got more interested in the use of in the past two or three years is the actual manipulation of live recordings. But at that time I was very interested in actually taking set pieces off the TV and manipulating them in a very traditional sense, in the Burroughs cut-up sense almost, to reveal various hidden sides of things and to reveal the pure aspects of things. So, found sound played an important part. I think the emphasis has changed now, I'm more interested in live, natural sounds and the ambiences associated with those — acoustics in particular.

How important is it for you to have your music heard by other people?

CW: Well, that's one of the primary functions, to actually make it available to as wide a cross section as possible. It's vital to the survival of it. Again, with particular regard to The Hafler Trio, a lot of the results of what we do depends on feedback from people, and we use that as an intrinsic part of the recordings as well. But it has always been important. There's no point in making records unless people are going to hear them.

How important is something like radio airplay to get that across?

CW: Well, obviously very important, but there are so many forms. It comes in the form of a national radio station, local stations, independent ones and pirate ones — which are the most interesting because of the attraction of anything that's of a clandestine nature. I think radio is a grossly overlooked medium in general and is abused so much simply for music. I think principally it takes more imagination to listen to the radio than it does to watch TV. I'm certainly interested in what the imagination does to recorded sound and how people perceive it and construct their own images to go along with the radio pictures. I find it more stimulating generally than television in that respect.

What effects can frequencies have on a person?

CW: They have an effect every second of your life. Different frequencies used in combination with each other have a variety of effects; the basic level of use for suppression — sonic cannons and actual use in physical aggression — to creating quite pleasant effects on people. I mean there are obvious examples of usage of different frequencies just to create an effect. Like in Vietnam, the use of loudspeakers and things, a sort of general, physical control. Through the power of broadcasting as well.

Andrew McKenzie enters

Are all these consciously heard by a person?

CW: Well, no, that's the point of some of them. You can feel sound just as much as you can hear it. There's a girl who has just joined one of the London orchestras as a timpani player who is stone deaf. There was a London radio programme on which she described the effect of how she can actually play. She feels the different frequencies through different parts of her body. The high frequencies actually resonate through the bones of the lower forearms, the lower frequencies resonate in the legs and the tibia and fibula. She's using the whole body as an acoustic receptacle, as an acoustic lens.

Andrew: It's part of what we are concerned with now, it's a perfect illustration of the way that sound can be used and the way that sound is all around everybody. And there's no escaping from it. It's not something you dissect in a laboratory because it's part of you.

CW: It's affecting us now, it's affecting the reactions you make to certain things. Again, back to the car.

Chris Watson exits

Could you explain the relationship between The Hafler Trio and Robol Sound Recordings?

Andrew: Well, Chris and I re-met about six months after he left Cabaret Voltaire. I had actually met him a long time ago when Cabaret Voltaire was still a relatively obscure group. When Chris left Sheffield he was out of the habit of recording stuff but it was still something that he wanted to do. So we started mucking about and doing experiments but not with the idea of releasing it at all. We eventually did two radio programmes which subsequently went to quite a number of countries all over the world.

Through this we came into contact with Dr. Edward Moolenbeek — the third member of The Hafler Trio. He's a professor of acoustics who writes papers and gives lectures, and is basically a complete 'no compromise' person which attracted us immediately. He said that he had heard some of the stuff that we were doing and said, "You might be interested in these..." and sent us over photocopies of some fragments of Spridgeon's work. It was amazing. Somebody had been doing the same sort of things that we do, but thirty or forty years ago. And Robol, through Edward, provided equipment and encouragement and it grew from there.

We are phasing out being involved with Robol because they are asking us to do things that would take up too much time. It wouldn't be worth our while to cut down our field research to the point where it became too specialised. Robol is a non-profit making organisation, but they do research for the Swedish government which is an area best left to them — as there's too much pressure from the party sponsoring the research for there to be necessary objectivity. But it has been quite good, a very fluid situation. They've never leaned on us and we've never really demanded anything from them. We've always been fairly independent of them. They've supplied things and we've publicly acknowledged that we are grateful to them.

Who was Robert Spridgeon?

Andrew: I haven't read all the things that he's done or know all that much about the man himself because his writings are so hard to get hold of. But he was a crucial figure in the field of sound research who did mainly theoretical explorations in the area. He always insisted that sound should have a practical application and never be taken passively.

People are always influenced by sound, but in very subtle ways. Spridgeon recognised that it was possible to measure and control these influences and that many other cultures had recognised this in the past. But he would be provocative in a very obvious way. He'd turn up to do a lecture and then slag off all the people who came to it just for coming. But he would still give them the germ of his ideas, so at the end there would be a handful of people who were genuinely interested. He was a very forthright person who didn't suffer fools gladly. He enjoyed being called an elitist. So we have been influenced by him, used ideas that we've come into contact with and developed them from there. We've gone into the practical aspects of the things that would've been impossible in Spridgeon's lifetime.

He died in 1963, but his son — also called Robert, still runs Robol. We still have sporadic contact with him but I can't help feeling sometimes that his approach to the whole idea is a little different to what his father would have wanted. He seems a little too ready to take on projects and think about their implications later.

What is Edward Moolenbeek's relationship with the group?

Andrew: He comes over to England every now and then and we work on things together. Also, he sends us a lot of things by post that he's found. So he is an integral part of the unit. Vital. We hope to be able to use his considerable artistic powers in the near future.

What have been the most interesting projects in research that you've worked on recently?

Andrew: Probably the most interesting is a recent development in audio processing which involves a very sophisticated form of equalisation expansion and harmonic / temporal placement. This machine can give you any acoustic you like merely by telling it the co-ordinates of the room. So you can have the acoustics of the Taj Mahal inside a matchbox or wineglass. It's a completely new dimension. But the revolutionary part of it comes with the output — which is ambisonic. Inside this is a special circuitry extra to the ambisonic which gives height information. The human brain is incapable of perceiving height, so this is a very clever perceptual illusion. If you have a noise coming from above you, you must turn your head upwards to 'read' where it is coming from, but this machine will actually give you this information. Of course, this is very much in its infancy, but I think we're only the fourth people to use it in this country. If that gets into a lot of recording studios, you'll actually hear a giant leap in terms of the way people approach thinking about sound. It means that you don't have to think about how it sounds, you can actually control it. You don't have to get a studio with a live area and a dead area.

Also, we have been working on some recording linked with public application which should see the light of day very soon. They concern something called 'feedback loop impression traits'. These make use of the seven second delay between experience and memory. A sound is generated and followed by 'physical' noise — not necessarily very loud mind you — which travels through the nervous system and coincides with the previous information. Therefore, this can lead to information being intelligible only at the specific point in time and no other. There is no gap between thinking about and 'understanding' — in the fullest sense of the word.

Another aspect of this is the negative and positive aspects of temporary threshold shift utilisation. In this, you make the listener temporarily deaf to one or more of the frequencies depending on playback volume and speaker elasticity and position. The positive effect means that the frequencies are retained after they stop on the recording, thereby being superimposed over the proceeding and subsequent sounds. This effect varies with the variable I mentioned before so that different listeners receive different information entirely.

What are some of the differences between sound and acoustics?

Andrew: Acoustics are the whole effect of sound, whereas sound can be in any acoustic. Acoustics are the study of environmental factors as well, whereas sound is what comes out of the instrument, synthesizer, processor or whatever.

Would you consider your first record "'Bang" — an open letter', to be a "music" record?

Andrew: We are far more interested in dealing with the mind's aspect of things rather than just the entertainment value. You can be entertained by information in the same way that you can be entertained by anything else, the entertainment is like a side issue. We are far more interested in providing information that they can perhaps pick up on and use for entertainment purposes or scientific purposes or whatever. It's a much wider field than just putting on a record and being able to dance to it.

The difference between us and experimental musicians is that we can actually take that record and tell you exactly why each and every single sound was in such an order and how it was treated. Whereas somebody who is an experimental musician might say, "Well, it was complete chance, it was a nice coincidence". With us, coincidence comes into it a lot but we actually use it, edit it and take out all the uninteresting bits. It's not a stream of consciousness thing, it's a very controlled product.

Some of the things happening within 'experimental music' are involved in the same sort of areas. Stockhausen dabbled in some of the areas we've done, but we investigate it as a pure phenomenon — not a side issue. We're not trying to make a round point in terms of political, social or ideological issues. We're more interested in pure ideas; actually making somebody get off their arse and say, "My God, this record I've been listening to for ages and ages can be used", or, "There's a practical aspect to sound and I'll be much more careful what I listen to in the future", or, "Ultra-sound might not be a good idea", or, "Sticking my head in a bin and getting deaf might not be a good idea". I would hope people would be much more selective.

Why is that?

Andrew: Because there is so much sound. It's continual bombardment. In restaurants, in stores, however inconsequential it might seem at the time, sound is actually having some influence on what we are doing. And it's a question of saying, "I'm actually going to listen to it now, I'm not going to sit and accept everything that people throw at me", which is much more of a direct continuation of what Cabaret Voltaire was about in the early days anyway. It was just basically to get underneath people's skin and make them think, even if it was just for a second.

Have you studied the use of subliminals very much?

Andrew: We did go into that in a very technical way and actually tried to see if it would work, but it's not as effective as people might think. A lot of the sting has been taken out of their usage because you can now go and buy subliminal cassettes for stopping smoking or something like that. People know that the sound is going to influence them but they don't know that everything else is doing it as well. Subliminals are much more effective when presented with an image, the linking of sound with image. The image can distract from the sound, so the sound goes in, or it can be the other way round. You can show a really gripping film sequence and have a subliminal soundtrack which nobody will notice at the time, or you can have very dramatic music and very opaque visuals.

Do people actually recall and remember subliminal messages?

Andrew: It's not as specific as people think. It's very powerful, but not in a direct sense. You can encourage people to do things, but you can't bring them to the pool and make them drink. You can't say, "You will buy an ice cream" — that won't work. But you can say, "Perhaps it would be a good idea if you went and bought some ice cream". You can insinuate in much the same way as most of the media does anyway. They did try something a long time ago in America where every fourteenth frame was a single frame of, "You will buy an ice cream", and at the interval quite a few people did actually buy ice cream. But the reason we abandoned it was because basically there was not much creative use for it other than for stopping smoking and that kind of thing.

Is there any way to gauge how well subliminals have worked?

Andrew: You can do various experiments and that is why it comes back to feedback — just seeing and checking people's reactions which can be an interesting little project to do. But you actually create subliminals unconsciously which is probably a more interesting area. They are very hard to define because you have no control at the time with what's happening.

Have you done much experimentation with ultra-sound?

Andrew: Ultra-sound is a very well researched field. It's something that hasn't progressed to the stage where it could actually be encoded properly on to a record, so there's no immediate danger of anyone putting out a record that can kill people, for instance. The French developed a sound cannon in the 1930's which was an ultra-sound cannon, literally a tank with a bloody great big speaker on it. But they found they couldn't direct the ultra-sound. The frequency that's most dangerous to life is 7 Hertz, and the man who first found out about this died finding out about it. He was in the studio and generated 7 Hertz and it literally curdled his insides.

The dangerous thing about increasing public transport and reliance on any kind of motor appliance is they generate ultra-sound at very low levels which is why people get travel sick — it curdles their insides to a very slight degree. Obviously it's not a constant tone, as a bus or car speeds up and down it varies the level. Travel sickness is the thin end of the wedge. It could conceivably, with a country that were prepared to put enough money into it, turn into a formidable weapon. But they're not really interested in that, they're more interested in jamming signals that you get on shortwave radio — like 'The Woodpecker' that the Russians are generating at the moment. It's really loud because it's such a strong signal. That's where all the energy of the military response is going at the moment — micro-sounds as weapons. There are thousands of radio waves just flying around and it's only now that people are realising that these can actually hurt people.

Do you think people will start using them in negative ways?

Andrew: It's inevitable. Whatever anybody comes up with, there will always be people that will use things in negative ways. You can't have one without the other really. It's a known fact that you can cure cancer with ultra-sound, but the people in power are just using it for harmful purposes. If you cured cancer, all the nursing homes would go out of business overnight. If somebody is doing something, you have to see who that benefits. If somebody is letting old people die in nursing homes, to whose use is that? Obviously it generates a lot of money, so why not keep the patients there.? Like the old thing about vitamin C curing colds, I mean it's complete rubbish. It's vitamin A that does it. But they're not going to say that because they want people to have colds so they will keep buying vitamin C and other cold medicines.

How does The Hafler Trio relate with most music groups?

Andrew: I would like to think that we are in some way quite different to most of the other people in groups because we are not really interested in the sort of things that most other people are interested in. Most of their influences lie in very musical fields even though most of the people would probably deny it. Whereas we are involved in sound — which only includes a little bit of music. I think that there is a wider application and a greater fortune in that kind of research.

Do you have a set of standards for what music should contain?

Andrew: My definition of music is just organised sound. The word music has just been used so many times that no-one really knows what it means anymore anyway. Sound and music were originally used for ritual purposes — it had a function. And that's what we are trying to get back to. The fact of actually using sound and doing something with it, rather than just sitting back and going, "This is really cosmic man, pass the joint", and just accepting it. So that you can actually do something with it. People tend to be subjecting their lives to music, whereas they should be subjecting music to their lives. It's very depressing once you get into it that people can't see the wider aspect of it.

Why can't they?

Andrew: Because it requires effort. People are very lazy. I think intrinsically people have been trained to be lazy. They can sit in front of the television and vegetate all afternoon if they want to, as many people now do. When television first came out, it was a really amazing thing that somebody had a television, somehow it was more special and somehow people were far more alive to the possibilities of it. Whereas now there's this complete barrage of information on all levels. And it's a big step to say, "Right, well I'm not going to listen to all that, I'm actually going to pursue this". Or, "This is interesting, this isn't". Rather than just watching the music channel and saying, "That was a good video, that wasn't".

Do you feel The Hafler Trio is responsible for the interpretation that other people might have of your work?

Andrew: A very interesting question because when we finally decided to release some material to the general public, Chris was worried about this — and this was one of the areas that depressed him during his time with Cabaret Voltaire — control over the product. So we decided to look at this problem with an eye to solving it to our advantage. We did the necessary research and found, or should I say realised, that there are a lot of parameters which can be controlled, if only the effort is made to use this at the outset. The fact that playback situations are inevitably different from one another is one very good example. This is called the acoustic reflex. This name is given to the total time taken for a sound generated to return to it's original point in space by means of reflection from whatever surfaces are in the room. We make use of this in certain experiments by treating the sounds with override analogue directors, so that depending on the type of room and the relation of the speakers, each person can hear almost a totally different recording due to the delicately balanced phase relationships of the sounds which cancel various elements out at different points. This, of course, makes something like installation or soundtrack work so appealing as the variables can be controlled to a much larger extent and many more interesting effects unique to that situation can be created. All these reasons make it possible and absolutely necessary for us to collect as much information about the place, situation etc. of playback as possible. So the uses and interpretations can be narrowed down to such an extent that what is put out always contains an 'x' you wish to have communicated —you can depend on that, but the shades of meaning end up being altered to suit each individual recipient. We have not as yet in all our work and research encountered any completely wrong interpretation of our work.

DIAMANDA GALAS

For the past decade, Diamanda Galas has been living the life of a recluse, working and training to develop her voice so that it can mesmerise listeners of all musical inclinations. A former immunologist and researcher in Neuro-chemistry at the Scripps Research Centre in La Jolla, California, American born Galas has also received multiple degrees from the University of California. In 1982, she released her first record, *Litanies of Satan*, the beginning of a gut-wrenching attack on the public aided and abetted through the use of multi-microphones and electronics.

Galas is just as comfortable performing with London's Test Department as she is with the New York Philharmonic or John Zorn. She has often performed works of Shoenberg, Verdi and Xennakis, as well as her own compositions, striving to execute them with her body, blood and an infinite number of voices and shrieks, giving birth to emotions otherwise incapable of expression. 1986 and 1987 saw the releases of Galas' mass trilogy *Masque of the Red Death*, whose first performance was in June 1986 at the Osweg Shipyard in Linz, Austria.

"What sympathy in death discloses we who fester here are very much alive and watch unmanned compassion fly to safer zones". From *Masque of the Red Death*.

How did you begin working?

D Galas: Persons from the Living Theatre suggested that I should perform in a couple of mental institutions in San Diego. I did this and followed it up with performances in art galleries and other venues suggested to me by enemies of the art world.

How did you first come to Europe?

D Galas: In 1979 my work reached the ears of Yugoslavian composer Vinko Globakar. He had been searching for a few years for a singer with a large vocal range who would sing what everyone else said was impossible. One prerequisite was that the singer be able to begin every evening singing like a lyric soprano and finish screaming like an animal. The work also involved the production of multi-phonics and other more extreme vocal techniques at specific pitches, and a great deal of improvisation, all of which had to be memorised and performed on many consecutive nights at the Festival Avignon. The work was based upon a true story published by Amnesty International about a Turkish woman who was arrested for espionage and tortured to death. We toured this work in France, Italy, Mexico and the US between 1979 and 1982.

Why do you sing in so many languages?

D Galas: It would not occur to me to do otherwise. My relationship with the world is not founded by a territorial domain which is geographic. Although I presently compose in five languages, I have performed in ten different languages during my work with European composers.

How do you compose?

D Galas: Alone.

How do you refer to your work?

D Galas: My name alone should suffice since there seem not to be other persons sharing this endeavour.

Who do you think comprises your audience?

D Galas: I have footlights to temporarily spare me from that information. After shows I ask my crew much as you might inquire of a policeman the death toll after a terrible accident.

What do you think about while on stage?

D Galas: The stage is a place of confession, isn't it? Angels, devils, hell, the unfortunate postponement of revenge, heaven, or a murmur of the firing squad as contact with deceitful ex-beloved is made. But do not be confused. One is only worthy of a confession who is equal to the task. Heat may mould the blade, but only cold precision brings it home.

What is the difference between your offstage and on stage persona?

D Galas: The offstage is more violent; alternatively, I would say that between assumes only two characters. Among is a better word. This form is tenanted at once by many people; if I were to select one of them over the others she would be strangled to death.

Where do you live?

D Galas: Hotels in London, Berlin, Linz and San Francisco. I do not anticipate a change in this moving back and forth. By now it has become indispensable to my system of thought and work.

Do you believe in God and the Devil?

D Galas: The Greek Orthodox, Agnostic or Atheist may recognise in the plague the certainty of the Devil, but no hope in God. God (as divine mercy or salvation) fails to materialise, and the Devil (as the improvident or impersonal force of nature) remains king.

The man who goes to his death alone (without God) but rejects the powerlessness or bitterness of the beaten man, and instead transforms the terror of his passing into compassion and fraternity, assumes the paradox of Saint, and is the master of death. (Respectful reference has been made to the playwright Philip-Dimitri Galas (1954 — 1986) as I interpret his coverage during the last year of his life. But I do not know what he knew).

How open is your work for interpretation?

D Galas: If I imagine it to be closed to interpretation, that would not alter anything, would it? As well, any answers I may supply to any questions about my work can only hope, at best, to not confuse honest interpretation.

What kind of performers do you like?

D Galas: Boxers, opera singers, circus performers, Greek and Arabic singers, and certain men in dangerous professions.

What do you think of performance art?

D Galas: When I do think of it I imagine it to be a conspiracy by greedy West Village psychiatrists to promote self-reverential studies by otherwise unprolific art debutantes living in New York lofts with too much wall space.

What are your impressions of naked pricks in art?

D Galas: In general, male artists should leave that endeavour to more gifted boys in the Marine Corps who want to raise a few bucks over the weekend. The sight of anything less can be quite unpleasant to any woman of good taste.

What men do you most admire?

D Galas: Those who know best how to serve.

You have alluded to Aids as the current manifestation of the plague in 'Masque of the Red Death' …

D Galas: Much of my current work is composed for the dying of this disease, the dead, and the people they have left behind. I do not, however, choose my subjects for their effect. I feel, rather, that they have chosen me as a mirror and I say this without pretension.

Is there a 'Divine Punishment'?

D Galas: Naturally there is no divine punishment. What is intentionally misapprehended as God's judgement is nothing more than an unfortunate set of chance operations, germ warfare, or both. What I document is the process of slow death in a hostile environment.

What do you mean by 'conceptual death glee club' which you've made reference to in interviews?

D Galas: All hippie mystical metaphors become impotent in the face of the nightmare made flesh. At this point the little celestial poet may be seen searching for safer symbols with which to intentionally alienate himself from a society which he may despise but which should, in my opinion, despise him even more.

Listen man,
It will soon be time
To guard a man until the Angels come
Let's not chat about despair
Death's not fancy feelings
If you are a man (and not a coward)
You'll clasp the hands of him denied my mercy
Until his breast becomes your own.

DETACHED INCIDENT   SIGIL
HE BEGAN BY BREAKING THINGS   HE BROKE THE GLASS
ON HIS TABLE NIGHT. HE WALKED INTO IT CRAZILY
AND IT SHATTERED. "WELL IT IS POSSIBLE THAT THE
'CONFUSION' IS NOT LTD TO MYSELF" HIS FIFTH
PERSONALITY SHOUTED FROM THE BOTTOM OF HIS
HEAD FUCK." THEN HE DRESSED HIMSELF WITH THE
GREATEST **CAVTION** DENYING THE ROMAN
CONCEPT OF TIME   THE JULIAN CALENDER. "WELL
THAT IS NOT MY PROBLEM. IT IS THAT/OF THE
CLOCKMAKER CELESTIAL OR WHATEVER. A FOREIGN
GENTLE MAN TALKING STRANGE POLITICS THAT
VERY FEW HAVE HEARD. "I CANT ARGUE, WITH YOU
YU HAVE ANSWERS TO QUESTION, I HAVENT EVEN
THOUGHT OF. AS SAND BECOMES SILICON, SILICON
BECOMES SAND. A HIGHLANDER IN DOUBTS.
PRIVATE IDENTITY VERSUS CORPORATE IDENTITY.
SATURATION OVERLOAD NO IMMUNITY. CORPORATE
MASKS. A TAP DRIPPING IN THE DISTANCE AS THE
GODDESS OF THE VOID APPEARS BAPHOMET
WAS NOT HER SUN. COMPUTER VIRUS. CRISIS
MANAGEMENT IMAGE INSEMINATION. NO ALIBI
FOR THIS NEW-EROTIC BORE SCARCITY
AUTONOMIA ACTION DIRECTE. ESCAPE ROUTES CLD
THIS IS STRANGER GO MUCH STRANGER
THAN LOVES. "TROUBLE IS OF COURSE MY JOB AND
ITS A SERVICEMANS JOB TO BE READY FOR
EVERYTHING" BAPTISMS OF FIRE SILHOUETTES

AGAINST THE WALL, ESTABLISHING A SENSE OF TRUST PERSONAL HYGIENE AND SOLEMN DREAMS. HE NO LONGER HAS THE BLESSING OF THE FRIENDS OR COMPATRIATS NOR THE POST AIDS MYSTICISM TO SUSTAIN THEM. A VICTIM OF A JOYRIDE, SLAUGHTERED BY DAY TO DAY FANTASIES A NAMELESS AND PLACELESS WAR IS HAPPENING NO ONE KNOWS WHY, THE WAR INFORMS AN AIR OF DELICIOUS UNCERTAINTY. SEXUAL INSOLENCE. **THE FIRST TASTE OF HOPE IS FEAR**. THE FIRST MANIFESTATION OF THE NEW IS TERROR. I SEEK TO CURE THAT WHICH IS DEEP INSIDE.

FAREWELL UNTIL WE MEET
AGAIN IN DREAMS

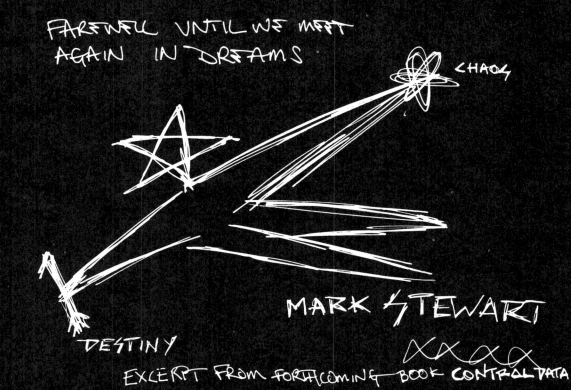

CHAOS

DESTINY

MARK STEWART

EXCERPT FROM FORTHCOMING BOOK **CONTROL DATA**

TRAPS

When I look at myself in the mirror the heat comes to my face. I'm convinced time has slipped and I've just left the mirror: Now it's someone else standing there pretending to be me. When I shut my eyes they invade my body, so I have to keep them open. I don't own my body. Yesterday I went through the phone book at random, picking out men's names that seemed interesting, calling them up and inviting them to come over and fuck me. Finally one accepted. When he arrived at my door I opened it but left the chain attached. He could see me in my nightgown. His body matched his voice, which had been rough and crude on the telephone. He was large and hairy. His face was dark, pitted. His hands were huge: I wanted him to choke me to death. I let him in. I undressed, lying flat on my stomach on the floor, hoping he'd see how vulnerable I was and kill me. Instead he kissed the back of my neck softly, then gently fucked me. I tried to squirm, to become violent, so he'd get angry with me and hurt me, but instead he reacted by losing his erection and apologising. I stood up, looking down at him as if he were a useless, retarded child, and told him to leave. I went to the mirror, massaged my breasts, pulled the nipples up to my mouth, and sucked them for hours. I lost myself, I forgot where I was, I lost control of my body. I don't know who I am. I want to be obliterated. I want to be sucked into my cunt.

ANOTHER TRAP

I'm a small thing, plotting suicide, sucking my toes. I'm locked up in this piss soaked public bathroom. They're having a good laugh about me outside. I can hear them slurping their beer, burping, farting, cracking jokes about me, imitating my voice. I'm naked in here. The smell of my body overpowers the smell of their shit and piss. I smell like misery. It's private, I know it's strength. I usually keep it under my clothes. Right now I'm letting it come out and make me drunk. I love the way I smell. They could easily break the door open. They'd find me in here on the floor, a retarded infant. I'm better than they are. Their jokes feed me. They don't know what I'm doing. I wish they'd break the door down. I think if they saw me in here like this they'd be ruined.

DAVID TIBET

Recurring themes in the work of Current 93 include religion, magic, history and ritual. Through tape loops and minimal instrumentation, the group conjures up images of beauty and horror simultaneously. Whereas the melody carried throughout is often as soothing as a chant, the interaction between electronic effects and David Tibet's possessed cry — feeds the listener various visions. These might include a peek inside the catacombs where spirits, once surreptitious, have now plotted for an out and out attack on the other side, or a journey into the mind of a little girl — becoming closer to the outside world which will eventually enlighten her or take away her inherent innocence. Throughout their records, one thing remains constant: The atmospheres created by Current 93 transform and breed many responses, allowing themselves to be interpreted to varying degrees.

What is the significance behind the title Current 93?

Tibet: When I was still in PTV, Fritz from 23 Skidoo, Geoff Rushton and myself recorded three tracks. We were thinking of a name and at that time I was still very interested in Crowley which was a major input in my outlook. And the 93rd Current was a technical name of Crowley's for Thelema. I liked the idea because it implied something at the same time as being anonymous. When I lost interest in Crowley — very rapidly, I did think of changing the name. But on the other hand I thought, "The name isn't that important anyway and people know it, and if I change the name, people might not buy the new record because they don't know who it's by". (laughs)

What made you lose interest in Crowley?

Tibet: I think it's just the passage of time really. I got my first Crowley book when I was twelve. From then on I started collecting Crowley and after a while I assimilated it all. I used to be interested in ceremonial magic but eventually I realised it's just a rehearsal of reality and there's something ludicrous if you think about it objectively: a lot of people dressing up in robes, waving swords and wands.

You just lose interest because they get so involved in complexity for the sake of it, and after all the years of studying it and reading it and perhaps trying to put it into practice, you realise that you're not left with very much — apart from what turns out to be ego. Crowley obviously had a lot of valid things to say and was an interesting man. His dictum, "Do what thou will...", I still agree with because it's a mystical, anarchistic doctrine. But you find you're just running around in circles which seems to be common with a lot of people that get into Crowley and are interested in him for good reasons.

There's also a danger that bands use people as images. You get the impression that they're saying, "Well we don't have any ideas, but we're interested in Manson, Crowley, Jim Jones, Hitler, whoever it is, so even though we're not very good, because we're interested in this, we must be fucking weird". But it's escaping the fact that there's no content there and it's just gratuitous image posturing. Which is why 'Lashtal' was Crowlean, it admitted it on the sleeve notes — and it had a specific aim. But 'Nature Unveiled' has very little to do with Crowley on it.

What was the idea and motivation behind 'Nature Unveiled'?

Tibet: On the first side, 'Maldoror Is Dead' the main influence lyrically and atmospherically was Maldoror by Lautreamont, which is my favourite book. In terms of darkness and humour, it just seems to encapsulate everything; it doesn't take itself too seriously but at the same time it has got this intense terror or complete hopelessness that permeates — atmospheres that I like to wallow in I suppose. With the actual lyrics, a friend of mine had died unpleasantly, and I was very cut up about that. And it was a situation where I was so broken that I started writing the lyrics to it. Not because I write poetry in extreme emotional situations — I think that's a pretentious reaction like, "Alas, alas, I must go write a poem". But I was laid desolate and I just wrote 'Maldoror Is Dead' and then fitted it into the Crowley loop which is, "Um, Um, Um," which is Crowley chanting and playing a drum in funereal fashion. And everything else was added on to it. The chants and vocal effects were just other ways of expressing the mood that I had at that time, which was the most depressing period of my life.

The other side, 'The Mystical Body of Christ in Chorazaim', was meant to be an apocalyptic mass but not in any structured sense. I've always liked the idea of a piece of music that, when the world is being destroyed, would be playing on huge speakers all over the world and it would just collapse to this final fanfare. That was my interpretation of what I would like the music to sound like if I had the choice when we all die. But at that period, it was very much the mood that I was going through, it was really depressive and depressing. So it was a reaction to that really.

What is Chorazaim?

Tibet: Just as Jesus was born in Bethlehem and raised up in Jerusalem, so the medieval Christian scholars believed that the Anti-Christ would be born in Chorazaim and brought up in Bethzaida, which is based upon a passage in the gospels where Christ says, "Woe to thee Chorazaim, woe to thee Bethzaida", and then goes on. That was partly because of the fact that I was really interested in conspiracy theories and general plots of that sort — apocalypticism and the Anti-Christ legend. There's a book I've got about Anti-Christ in the middle ages which is my favourite after Maldoror. I just love the complexity of it and the desperation it conveys, that there's no hope — Anti-Christ is coming.

Do you place a lot of importance on the lyrics or are they used more or less as an additional sound?

Tibet: I think it works in a dual way. The lyrics are important, but again not because I feel I'm saying something that people should take notice of. They're important to me because, if you read books like 'The Torture Garden' by Mirbeao, or 'Sodom' by De Sade, or 'Heart of Darkness' by Conrad, there are bits of those books that you read and you just get a chill all down your spine because it fits in with the moment so brilliantly. I mean the lyrics that I do are the sort of things that I would like to feel send that sort of thing up myself, not necessarily in other people because it's a personal thing. For the listener, the important thing to do is to listen to the tone of the voice. Whereas for me it's listening to the actual lyrics. But in between the two there's a sort of, not chemical reaction — that sounds very pretentious, but an expression that I put into the lyrics that changes hopefully into the mood that I want to get across. So you might not hear the lyric, but you'll hear the mood that I'm trying to imply.

What do you think are the best listening conditions for 'Nature Unveiled'?

Tibet: In my experience, I found that it's music you should listen to at about two in the morning when you're completely pissed off, in complete blackness, and it will have a quite unpleasant affect on you — and certainly change your attitude. I think if you're doing something else, it really depends on your sensitivity or what sort of person you are. Either you'll just carry on doing the washing up and say, "What's this pile of shit?", or it'll depress you and you'll think, "I can't listen to that", and take it off. Obviously people are going to do with it whatever they want — from playing it in the toilet to giving it to their granny. It's ambient in the sense of formal ambience, not like Eno tinkering away, but with a strong atmosphere.

Do you think the frightened feeling that one might get acts positively or negatively?

Tibet: My relationship with that is so prominent in my mind that I can't really think what effect it would have on other people. Just from experience some people have said, "Oh please take it off, I don't like it, I'm feeling uneasy", — things like that. Comments usually along the lines of the exorcist thing or sounds of a black mass or something like that — which is good. It's a summoning, but it's not a summoning in the sense that, "This record is really weird and will summon up demons". It's just a summoning up of atmospheres that people would normally prefer to lay dormant. I really dislike groups that say things like that, so I want to clarify that I'm not saying it's going to summon up latent whatevers from anybody that listens to it. I'm just saying for me it draws up things which I'd forgotten about and which I'd rather forget about.

Do you experiment with frequencies at all on 'Nature Unveiled', or is it possible to do that on a record?

Tibet: On 'Lashtal', the synthesizer buzz is at the correct frequency noted in The Grimoires to raise up Malkunofath. So that's an obvious frequency. On 'Nature Unveiled', frequencies are used but not in a theoretical way. We haven't decided that you start shitting yourself at minus fifteen kilohertz or whatever, mainly because the technology is not there to do it properly. There are slowed down subliminals on it, but not in a sense where we're trying to get subliminals into people's minds. It was more playing around with the tape recorder and just putting down phrases that I liked which had an atmosphere to them and seeing if it increased the atmosphere.

What are some ways to disguise a subliminal?

Tibet: For example, putting it fairly up in the mix, not massively prominent but noticeable, and then slowing it down until it's just a one second phrase lasting about twenty seconds or something like that. Another method is just putting it so low down in the mix that you're not aware you hear it. Obviously you do hear it, whether your conscious hears it as well or whether it just dissipates through your system nobody is sure about. I think that subliminals are interesting, but a lot has been made of them and I still hold that if you're searching for a specific atmosphere, you don't need subliminals at all to do it, there are much better ways. It might not sound as impressive or arty but it's a lot more practical.

What exactly is a Tibetan thighbone?

Tibet: It's a ritual instrument used by Tibetan Shamanists. If you talk to people who don't know much about it, they'll say it's a black magical rite for raising demons, which it is in a sense, but then Buddhism isn't that way inclined. There's a rite where you sit in a graveyard, you're meant to sit on a corpse cross legged and blow this thigh bone and this summons up the demons. So what it basically means is that you're sitting in a graveyard, you're shit scared and you're blowing something that is made out of a thigh bone. It's a way of bringing all your fears to the surface. You're stealing terror that they had and becoming stronger and cleansing yourself. They always had to be made from either the thigh bone of a very young virgin who'd been raped or killed, or the murderer. The idea is that you're trying to summon out the worst parts of you. The actual instrument that you're using had to be the closest you could possibly get to evil, which is the little virgin girl, the purity destroyed, or the murderer. Obviously for Buddhists, those are the two extremes of horror they could comprehend.

I first used the instrument when I met Gen and we were formulating the ideas of PTV. They were almost impossible to get hold of and we liked the sound and the whole image of it, the mystique and the atmosphere behind them. And we thought it would be interesting to use them as a centrepiece of the new group, which I felt worked very well. I mean we only used it on the first LP and once on the second and it was more of a statement — it's an interesting instrument and it's symbolic of something.

What are some of your thoughts on religion?

Tibet: Religion; it's just a pile of shit, isn't it? Any organised form of philosophy or thought is garbage, it's just another excuse for moulding people, cloning people. That having been said, religion has also produced some remarkable works of art, architecture, statues and music. I do love the imagery of it, and I think all religions have had certain beneficial effects. But in the end, I believe that those effects would have come about without the invention of organised religion anyway. Basically it's more of an excuse for oppression and telling people what to do. "If you don't believe this, you'll go to hell", and so on. It's depressing really because people have taken this garbage for so long, I keep thinking that they must wake up one day. But alas, that means you're forgetting just how stupid and sheep-like people are.

What about people that go to the other extreme, for instance Satanists?

Tibet: Well, Satan is the opposite of God. You can't worship Satan unless you're a Christian, because unless you're a Christian, you don't believe in Satan anyway. So Satanists are just childish people.

Do you believe that Satan is a force?

Tibet: There's certainly a force that people define as Satan or Uriman, or whatever name they've got for it. I've never been keen on this dualistic thinking. People assume that there are two powers, good and evil, in constant combat. Most people would say that God is the superior power. But in that case, why did he create something to fight against him which is inferior to him anyway and that he could destroy? The devil has been fought ever since Zoanastrianism. There's obviously power, but as far as I'm concerned, it's all the same sort of power anyway because you have to look at the old cliches, like, "One man's meat is another man's poison", "What's bad for you makes me stronger". There's a force obviously and it's a force to be respectful towards. You never know. But Satanism is such tedious garbage. If you look at people who are Satanists, the leaders like Anton Lavey, for example, who wear plastic horns on their heads (pause); he's quite a witty writer and I'm quite aware that he's a con-artist, and he knows it, and is just ripping off arseholes. But Satanism, goats... like really scary... fucking terrified. (laughs)

Can somebody start off within the ying of organised religion and then come to a knowledge of his own God or whatever, even though it might be the same God that the organised church believes in?

Tibet: I certainly think it's possible. I think that people that progress from organised religion and eventually come to that knowledge say, "They've progressed through Christianity and eventually came to a complete Spiritual understanding that Jesus is the saviour". They have what the magicians call "The conversation of their Holy Guardian Angel". They come to that rapport where you're dissolved in the godhead. It's certainly possible to do it through organised religion, but I feel that if you've got that within you anyway, going through the organised religion is just going to slow you down. In the end you get to that knowledge which everyone gets to, but you get to it despite all the dogma and shit you've been fed. And you get that a lot quicker because your imagination and freedom of thought isn't crushed down by the weight of centuries of useless tomes in Latin and arsehole priests wittering about things they know absolutely nothing about. Religion is garbage, pure and simple, but I don't think religion is an evil. There are different forms of religion and it would be very easy to argue — and correctly I believe — that Christianity is a far greater evil than Buddhism because the more dogmatic the religion — and you'll always find the most dogmatic religions are monotheistic religions, Christianity, Judaism, Mohammedanism — the more evil they are the more convinced they are correct. And the more keen they are on slaughtering everybody that doesn't agree with that.

With a school like Buddhism it's Mahayana, the greater vehicle, the lesser vehicle.

They're dogmatic but there's far greater scope within a religion like Buddhism or Hinduism for people to evolve their own little sects with complete freedom. Whereas if you're a sect within Christianity, you always end up being something like "The Church of the Latter Day Knowledge of Poison Handling Snakes of the Lord" (laughs). If you're a little sect within Christianity, the chances are very high, Jim Jones for example, that you're a complete nutcase, whereas within Buddhism or Hinduism, there's scope for people to take their own identity with them and go and find their particular pathway to Godhead... How very pompous of me... And furthermore, courses are available from the David Tibet Self-Knowledge Foundation, with wonderful badges — only ten dollars for a lesson. (laughs)

Is there any sort of message which Current 93 manifests through its music?

Tibet: The only message, if there is a message behind it, is a purely anarchistic one, just fuck everything. I'm not interested in dogmas or morals. There's one passage that sums up everything that the Current manifests: "The sound of the bell of Gionshyn echoes the impermanence of all things. The hue of the flowers of the teak tree declares that they who flourish must be brought low. Yea, the proud ones are but for the moment, like an evening dream in Springtime. The mighty are destroyed at the last, they are dust before the wind".

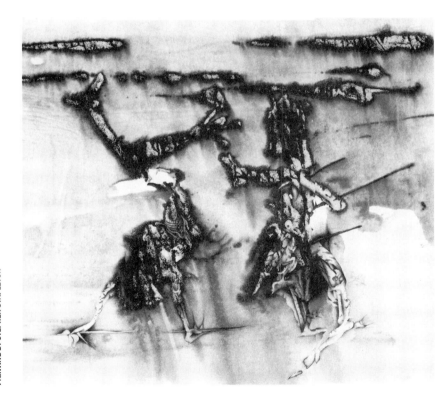

PAINTING BY STEPHEN STAPLETON

Westway, London W12, January 1977

CHRIS & COSEY

Chris Carter and Cosey Fanni Tutti were one half of Throbbing Gristle, who officially began at the *Prostitution* exhibition at London's I.C.A. in October 1976. The show included nude photographs (many of Cosey herself), displays of used tampons, a striptease by Fanni Tutti and the first performance of Throbbing Gristle — much of which was financed out of a million pound grant from the government to the Arts Council. The fact that the money had been spent on such subject matter upset several M.P.'s, but as TG explained, "We are presenting information. Without people, information is dead. People give it life." And thus began the information war of TG, which its members had been fighting in various forms over the years. When the group disbanded, Chris Carter and Cosey Fanni Tutti continued working together. In addition to varios releases as Chris and Cosey, they also formed CTI (Creative Technology Institute) and their own label, Conspiracy International.

In addition to recorded projects, Cosey has performed at the Georges Bataille festival *Violent Silence* in London in 1984. She has, at times, appeared unclothed in numerous men's magazines, as well as being photographed by the renowned Bill Brandt. In 1985, Chris Carter released his second solo LP having previously released *A Space Between* as an industrial cassette. In addition, CTI released its second video *European Rendezvous* through Doublevision. The group released their eighth album *Take Five* in 1987. They have collaborated on numerous records, including the twelve inch *Sweet Surprise* with Dave Stewart and Annie Lennox of Eurythmics. Chris and Cosey currently live and record in a refurbished schoolhouse in Norfolk.

What exactly is CTI?

Chris: It's developing, it keeps changing. Originally it was meant to be like a workshop of ideas, an umbrella name we could use for different projects that we had in mind. To be a production company almost, because as CTI, we'd work in video, on record, in film and with other people. If it's a CTI thing, it usually means that it's more than just Chris and Cosey. That's why 'Songs of Love and Lust' was a Chris and Cosey album, and then the next album, 'Elemental 7', was a CTI album — because it had John Lacey on it as well.

So other than music, film and video, is there anything else that CTI is involved with?

Chris: Just research generally that we're all working on — the people that are involved with CTI. Hopefully when we have accumulated so much material, we can publish the results. We do actually have a lot of output, but people that follow us in one particular way don't often see all the output that we've got. I mean we do a lot of things, it's an international thing, it's a working business. It's not centralized — it's more of a co-operation.

Whatever happened to the independent bands?

Cosey: I think what happened was that people sold out and went to the majors a bit too early, and the majors made money out of the new sales that had been found and restructured. And they just put up barriers again.

Chris: For the first couple of years it was like ten steps forward and then the next couple of years it was like five steps back again, so it has gone slightly backwards.

Cosey: We've broken a lot of ground, but most of the groups in the English charts now have sold it down the middle. It's not sour grapes, but as far as I'm concerned I wouldn't want to be commercial in that way at all because I love my own time too much and I don't want someone else telling me that I've got to go here or there. But I'm not worried about that. All that bothers me is the situation of the independents at the moment. They're not being as helpful as they could with the people that have got a market waiting for them. And there are people that are interested in our kind of music, and Coil's and Gen's, and yet they don't want to get out to those people, 'cause after all they're in it to make money. As much as they say, "Oh no man, it isn't", they do actually have to make money at the end of the day to keep it viable.

Another thing that bothers me is when you've put a lot of work into it and you think, "Oh, that's great", you're really pleased with it and you want to get it to as many people as possible. You don't want it to be in the charts, but you do want it to be with people who want to hear it and who'll enjoy it. And when you deliver it and ask a week later, "How's it all going?", and they say, "What was it?" and they don't even know what it's called, you begin to wonder what the hell you've bothered for.

Why wouldn't you want something to go into the charts?

Cosey: Because of the pressure, I couldn't take it. Seeing what happened to Annie and Dave of Eurythmics, I mean they were prepared for it as they were quite successful with The Tourists, but they're tax exiles now. They can only be in England for so many days a year, and that to me is like some kind of sentence. It's not success to me, it's like a thing hanging over your head. Once you've got so much success and so much money, you're no longer your own person, I don't care what you say.

What would be the best way to get across to a large group of people if it's not through a major label?

Chris: The way that we tried to do it in the beginning. Start your own label up or go to a very,

very good independent label and try to keep some integrity. It makes it ten times harder to do it, it really does, but if you've got it inside you and you want to do it that much, you should do it that way. It's the only way to do it.

Does it cost much to put out your own records?

Cosey: You can do it all quite cheaply, I mean nothing's cheap in that respect, but we've got our own studio that we've built up over the years. We've bought equipment when we've had royalties coming in, instead of buying clothes and things like that. So we set it up because we knew that music would be an ongoing thing for us and we'd always want a studio to record in. That's our way of avoiding studio costs and avoiding working in a studio that's not very sympathetic to our kind of sound. So that part of it money-wise is taken care of. The only other costs are the sleeves, the pressing and the cutting. But the worst cost is the studio time.

Chris: We're having trouble getting records released, I mean I feel sorry for the people who are just starting out. I feel like they have no hope at all. And there seems to be a much bigger chasm growing between pop music and the underground. A few years ago there was a cross-over point which was quite healthy. Now it's either very pop and very mainstream or it's completely the opposite. And at the moment record companies, even the independent record companies, only want stuff that's going to sell records. Like when we started as TG, although it seemed hard at the time, looking back on it, it was probably quite easy because there was a market for that sort of thing and it hadn't been there before. Whereas now, the market has already been there, been swallowed up and now there is nothing. There's no way for people getting music like that out anymore. Even if you start your own company, it still has to go through one of the majors or independents to get out.

What are some of the problems that you have encountered in putting out your own records?

Chris: It's the administration that we hate doing. One of the reasons why TG split up as well, apart from Gen and Cosey, was that we'd turned into like record moguls, and that's all we were doing. We weren't producing any music at all, we were just constantly in the office.

Cosey: Doing mail order and our tax forms and all that, it was crazy.

Chris: I mean it's already like that a bit now, even with CTI. It would be nice if someone offered us a deal just to take that away from us. We know that we could let someone else do it — we hoped Rough Trade would. And they did it for a while but they just didn't follow it through and we ended up doing a lot of it ourselves.

Looking back, what were the reasons that TG split up?

Chris: I don't even have to look back, 'cause I know, I knew at the time, I mean...

Cosey: TG split up because me and Gen split up.

Chris: It sort of divided us into two camps, there was Gen and Sleazy, me and Cosey.

What would you say were the biggest differences between TG and CTI?

Cosey: Well, TG was a group and I wouldn't say we were really a group. But it's difficult to say. CTI is more easy going than TG. I mean TG started off as a joke in the beginning. We were quite serious about breaking down the 'rock and roll' thing, but it was tongue in cheek at the same time because we knew we were giving them a load of rubbish soundwise just to get them out of their expectation of music. So it started as a joke and people took us seriously, you know? Then we actually started marketing ourselves. Abba had their own label and everything, "let's market ourselves like Abba...", "Let's use a symbol that people can look at and say, oh, TG". The best colours are red, white and black, the Nazi thing is so strong that people look at it straight away — you don't ignore it — so we picked up on that. Then we picked a symbol that would be easy to copy and easy to recognize and that's how the flash came about. That worked and then we did the military uniforms and people copied that. So it was really little games that we were playing but not in an adolescent way, not at all. It was just really interesting research for us, how far we could push it. And we pushed it as far as we wanted to.

After a while how serious did you become about making the music?

Chris: It got very disciplined in that sense. The singles were quite carefully worked out and some of the LP tracks we did were as well. But they were more like experiments just to see if we could do it. It wasn't anything we could do all the time.

What were the reasons for doing the more melodic tracks?

Chris: Just to get a particular sound that we wanted, rather than just jam. Personally I've always done a few things like that, even with some of the TG tracks. And the ones that Cosey did and even some of the things Gen did were quite melodic and low key.

Cosey: It was just an idea that would come to us and we'd say, "Let's try to do it a little bit more like Bucks Fizz, or something 'romantic' for a change". And that's how it would turn out.

Is your recording process in the studio similar now as it was then?

Cosey: It's exactly the same, but we're a lot more competent at recording now. We get a lot more clarity and we go for a lot higher quality. Also, we don't compromise half as much as we used to with TG because with TG there were four people, and to all agree on one thing was quite difficult and we would give in on certain things. Usually the rough element was Gen, and Sleazy always did the tapes and everything, including a lot of voices that we used to mix way down which would be classified as subliminal I suppose. They were almost conversations, interesting stuff.

Our side of TG was the softer part. But a lot of the things that TG did, the ones that were hard and industrial, were all born out of gigs. They were all born out of the hostile reception that we had to try and fight against on stage. So it was like a battle — a sound battle, trying to win people over. We used to have to win our audience's attention and the only way we could do it was with violent and aggressive music. We couldn't shout at them or physically abuse them 'cause it would have just ended up in a brawl. The only way that you can do it is with sound.

Did you find once people had heard about Throbbing Gristle that you didn't get that type of reaction?

Cosey: Oh yeah, it was horrible. That happened at The Lyceum, the last London gig we did. We had a lot of groupie types there, people just coming because it was TG, they didn't even know what TG were, they just had to be there. So they came along with their TG uniforms and little badges and we did choral music and church type music for half an hour.

Chris: But all the TG fans realised what we were doing, they were in on the joke almost, laughing their heads off and watching these other people scratching their heads thinking that they should be liking this. But the live gigs that CTI did were very much like TG, but it's just because we were half of TG anyway, it's something that we couldn't get rid of.

Are you trying to get something across with CTI like you were with Throbbing Gristle?

Cosey: I want to get across how we feel at the time we do the music, and just hope that people who listen to it enjoy it as much as we do. I think the kind of music we do in our sphere is like the classical music of the eighties because we're using the instruments of the eighties in an intuitive way. We're going for emotional feelings out of the senses we get, like they do in overtures. They're very emotional and they build up and they let you down, and that's the kind of structures I like in our music. The ones that evoke feelings.

Do you know what you're going to do before you go into the studio?

Chris: No, very often we don't. It's usually worked out in the studio, sort of as soon as we open the door. That's it, we go in with a blank page and just start dabbling and very often we use the first take.

Are the words written in the studio as well?

Chris: The words are written as we do the music. We can tell whether it needs words or not. It's like sketching. Cosey writes down little phrases and we have a little green book that has loads of little phrases written in it and we skip through that.

Can you describe your usage of TV voices used in songs, for instance on 'Put Yourself in Los Angeles'?

Chris: It was just fascinating because we did that when we were at Monte's, it was the last few days that we were in America and TG had finished. They have these religious stations and that was from a famous one in San Francisco. I just did loads of tapes of it and placed together different phrases. It just summed up Los Angeles at that time, although it was recorded in San Francisco. We went to Los Angeles and it was all totally crazy, all the TV and everything, and it was just coming at us — it was bananas. And just the fact that he was using that phrase, it seemed to fit really well. And 'Hairy Beary' was from a really inane American kid's programme. I've never seen anything like it in my life.

Cosey: I always find that when I get to America, the first two weeks are great and after that I get scared of the American attitude that... if it's there, then it's recognized as being there, but when it's gone, it's dead. Like the guy that came to pick us up to go to Disneyland said, "Oh right, Disneyland", and then he said, "Oh, my friend OD'd last night as well..." And that was the end of it, in the same sentence, no more — nothing. I thought that just sums it up, just what I've always thought, one minute you could be there, and the next minute you're not and it really didn't matter. LA, in particular, I've found to be like that.

Chris: The media in America I've always found to be completely over the top, radio and TV and all that. But it spills over into real life, they sort of merge and the bits in between I find really fascinating.

Do you like performing live now?

Chris: We hated the bits in between. The actual being on stage was great, but the way we actually toured was very unusual in that we did it all on trains and all our gear was in little flight cases, and although they were small they were incredibly heavy. There were just the three of us, no roadies or anything, bumming around Europe.

Cosey: But unfortunately you'd get there and nobody would be there to meet you, and sometimes we didn't know where we were going.

Chris: Typical Rough Trade organisation. Nobody knew who you were or what was going on and yet when you actually did the gig, it was full up with thousands of people there. We wondered how they had ever known about it. But we had no bad gigs as such, they were all really good. In fact the only sort of downer gig was the London one we did at The Ace because Rough Trade thought The Ace was going to advertise it and The Ace thought Rough Trade was going to advertise it, so nobody advertised it at all.

How spontaneous are your live shows?

Chris: Although we use a lot of backing tapes, we vary them slightly. We would drop half sections of things we're going to do and put in new things. Everything we do on top of the backing tapes is improvised anyway. I think improvisation is the sort of release that we definitely need. Sometimes what you feel like doing one night, you don't feel like doing the next — and it shows. So some nights we do a lot of vocals and other nights we don't. I don't think I could actually think of playing the same tunes every night for a whole tour. Even if I could play properly, I just wouldn't think of doing it.

How much is the voice used as an instrument, another noise, another sound?

Cosey: Quite a lot. When you listen to music sometimes you put in a line yourself. You're not singing the lines, you're singing your own interpretation that you've heard somewhere in it. People pick up on different little lines from records anyway, different parts they've heard and repeated to themselves. I like that 'cause when we listen to something I sometimes say to Chris, "Oh yeah it sounds like this kind of thing", and I voice in something like that. It doesn't have to be a voice as such, just something that comes out from inside you. I like to sing in tune sometimes, but I'm not really bothered by it.

If you don't sing in tune on a song, is that sometimes done for a specific reason?

Cosey: Sometimes I can get in there and I can sing perfectly in tune and we're really surprised. And then another day I can go in and it just doesn't work, there's no way I can hit it. My voice is really weird because my true voice is actually very low, yet women in general sing very high. So my natural instinct is to go high. But it's only every now and again that I can find it and it's a certain pitch in the music that brings it out. And we're not very often in that pitch or that key.

Chris: I mean someone that teaches people how to sing would probably tell Cosey which key she should sing in, but we don't know anything about notes or keys so we don't know which ones to use anyway. And we do manipulate the voice a lot so sometimes it doesn't matter if it's in tune or not. And what happens quite often is that brings out a different kind of melody or different sound which is quite nice.

How would subliminals be used in a recording?

Chris: It varies a lot, it depends why you're using them or what you want to get across — if anything. Sometimes it can just be a train of thought that you want to start off in someone's head, or it could be an actual political message you want to get across. We don't want to say what ours are and we don't want to give anyone ideas of how to listen to them or what tracks they might be on. They're not on all the tracks, but we want to get some feedback from people and see what they think they might be.

Cosey: All we've had is people asking us what they are. We just want people to tell us if they can hear them, and if so — where. If they went through each track on 'Love and Lust' and figured out what was going on and what they felt about it, they would probably come up with them anyway.

Chris: The other thing is to leave your mind open, you shouldn't be listening for them really. It's like when you've got the TV on and you're not really watching — it's suddenly there and you don't know you've seen it until a few minutes later. Subliminals don't work with all people. Some people don't get them, some people do. It can be a constant subliminal that's there all the way through the track and you have to disguise it in some way. There are various ways we've done that, putting things out of phase or just masking. They could be very short, it could be words or it could be sentences. But it's something that we're working on all the time and we're going to keep developing.

Could you summarise your reasons for using subliminals on a record or video?

Cosey: It just adds texture to the whole thing and we forget sometimes that they're actually in there. We usually mix those to the fringes, but it does actually fill out the sound. And you get a thing where you can hear say four things going on, but you can't place what's filling it up. It's just like an atmosphere more than a sound. The thing with subliminals in sound as far as I'm concerned is that you've got a track and there are hidden depths to it and the deepest depth is the subliminal one. So all the time you listen to it, something else is uncovered and you never get tired of listening to it. There's something else coming out each time, and I think that's a really nice thing to do.

Can you use subliminals for dubious means?

Cosey: Definitely, "You will go out and buy our next album even if you don't like it". Yeah you can do a lot.

Chris: I'm not actually convinced you can make people do things against their will, but you can suggest things to people, I'm sure of that. But it depends what state of mind they are in at that particular time.

Cosey: There's the old one of the smell of bacon when you come to the meat counter. They have got those little things — like air freshener — that just give out the aroma to try to make you buy bacon.

Chris: But the Muzak Corporation in America have spent millions of dollars on research into different speeds and tempos of music that they play at different times of the day in supermarkets. In the morning they want to rush you through and in the midday they want to slow you down. So they use different keys and different melodies that they know will effect your pace. And for factories where people are working they use subliminals underneath the music as well. But they've done whole books for radio stations and TV stations on what type of music to use at news time and what type of music to use for children's programmes. Fascinating, it really is.

Did you find that if you used subliminals during a performance that people would respond as expected?

Chris: Sometimes we knew how people would react in advance, particularly with TG. Live, we knew that if we put a certain tone through, people wouldn't hear it but they would feel it. It was the same when we used brilliant white light shining out at the audience as well, just to disorientate people — totally throw them off. We were just using the audience to experiment on for our own purposes really. And we used a lot of mirrors to put people off.

Cosey: So the audience could see themselves as they looked at us, you know? We thought, "It's the music they came to listen to so why the hell do they want to see us doing it?" So we played behind a screen or we put the mirrors so they couldn't see us because the bright light was shining in their faces.

If somebody said that some of the things that TG did weren't music but just a racket and feedback, how would you react?

Chris: Well, some of it was. It was like non-music really, it was meant to be that. People couldn't take the fact that we were a group and we weren't playing music. It was a wall of noise, but it was meant to be that — redefining music. Anything can be music, I don't like giving things labels at all. I was listening to the washing machine the other day and there was this real nice rhythm with this tone that kept coming in and I thought, "God, that would make a really good song". (laughs) And I could imagine writing a song around the sound of a washing machine because it was so regular and melodic.

How would you use a subliminal visually?

Cosey: It's all suggestion, but suggestion is quite powerful really. If you do it repeatedly during whatever you're watching and you flash up an image, or a certain product is spoken of, people go out and recognize it without ever having seen it before. So you could flash up an album sleeve a few times in the video and they subconsciously see it. And then when they go out and see it in a shop they recognize it. It's like Deja Vu, you think you've seen it before or you've seen a certain person before.

How did TG incorporate audio frequencies?

Chris: We used audio frequencies in a live situation, like very high powered low frequency audio signal to make people do things that they wouldn't want to do — making people feel ill and dizzy and stuff. Like four hertz or something, but at incredibly high power — like a thousand watts. It's so low that you don't hear it, you just feel it. And high frequencies as well, we used to use those quite a lot.

What effect do certain visual frequencies have on a person?

Chris: You can bring on epileptic fits and things like that. Different frequencies just trigger it off in different people. And you can make people vomit with certain frequencies.

What goes on in a person's brain to make them react like that?

Chris: It's like a sensor inside your brain that's connected to your visual sense. It can happen to almost anybody. In fact in London, the GLC governed all the discos, and there's one frequency they can't use on their strobes. They have health inspectors coming down regularly to check they don't use that frequency.

Has anybody ever complained that they had been damaged by the experimentation of TG?

Chris: People would often tell us what they felt or what had happened to them, but they never actually said they had been damaged. The two incidents that stick out in my mind was when a guy had an epileptic fit because we were using a strobe, and a woman said she had an instantaneous orgasm, she had no control over it... which she quite liked.

Cosey: "When's the next gig", she said. She shouted for the same track from the audience. "Please play so and so!" (laughs) We were a bit careful about what we did. We used to experiment first in our own studio and then limit it a bit when we did the gigs.

Chris: But when you've got a lot of people in a fairly small club, it varies from person to person. You get things called 'standing waves' when you use infra-sound. You can just move slightly from side to side and you'll be inside, like in phase or out of phase depending on where you stand in the room.

By the end of TG people had started to come for the reasons that you wanted them to. What were some of those reasons?

Chris: To experience something different. Initially, it was like an experiment that we were doing with sound, like using infra-sound and ultra-sound. A lot of people didn't know that at the beginning, but they were coming along to be part of the experiment — for us to give them some infra-sound treatment or whatever even though they knew it might be bad for them and might not be pleasant.

Cosey: The other thing was that we wanted to expel the old rock and roll thing where you went around after a gig and hung about, got pissed and went home. And it was no different the next day than it was the week before. So we wanted people to go out to a gig and experience a totally different sound to what they had heard before, and approach sound in a different way the next time they went out.

Chris: At the time it was new music, it was completely different and it was more of the philosophy behind the sound rather than the sound itself. Although some people liked the fact that it was just noise... Well a lot of people did.

Cosey: It's just that the people that did come to see us by the end of TG came for the reasons we wanted them to and not the other ones. Like LA was absolutely atrocious, I walked off for the first time in how many years... I left them all on stage, I couldn't stand it, it was terrible. But the next gig was great. I mean we weren't talking much at that point at all, and after LA I just said, "Look, we either do San Francisco as a group together or we just get a flight home" — there was just no point. And it was just somewhere else that night. That was the best gig we ever did, the best TG gig. It was great.

Did you know it was going to be the last one?

Cosey: Yeah, and it was the strongest, most magical... You never felt normal, it was like you were projecting. You were on the stage and you felt you were up here looking down. It was great and everybody was coming up there with you. It was really good. You can't describe that kind of feeling to anybody that you get off a gig that's going well like that, 'cause you feel it from the beginning. You start playing and you suddenly feel the strength coming through, you feel everybody with you and you just go up and up and up.

Was there communication between the members of TG during that gig?

Cosey: Oh there definitely was, but it was more telepathic than anything. It wasn't physical.

Are you very spiritually involved?

Cosey: We know a lot about it, but we don't sort of theorize it and talk about it much because I feel it dilutes the power. The more you talk about it the weaker it is, the less power you've got anyway. I just believe that if you think about things strongly enough and positively enough, they happen. If they're meant to happen, they do. And if things don't go right, there's a reason for it.

Would you say that the general philosophy behind Chris and Cosey's music has changed dramatically since Throbbing Gristle?

Chris: The sound has changed and the veneer has changed, but we're still basically half of TG.

Cosey: The approach is still the same, it's just that people that interpreted TG saw it as a big movement coming on — into magic, into fascism. We weren't at all, we were just interested in all those things and weren't frightened to experiment with them. But it wasn't a thing where we said, "You should do this", and "This is the way we are". We don't actually shout about the things we're into, that's the only real difference now. We've done the public exploration of it, we don't need to do it anymore.

Any historical manifesto is a programme collection of movement aims, forms and principles, fundamentally unfinished, infected by itself and left to the time dynamics (e.g. the Communist Manifesto from 1848, the Futurist Manifesto from 1909) which reveals the short-lived and demagogic character of its aims. LAIBACH is the recognition of time universality; our organisational activity is an intense agitation and constant systematic, propagandistic — ideological offensive. In accordance with this, our basic items of programme orientation are constantly discussed and redacted, so that the programme is not a theory based on dogmas; on the contrary, it is subject to regular revisions and redefinitions in a process of continuous treatment and dynamic transformation.

Consequently, any final manifestive version doesn't exist; the basic theses and programme documents are instead formulated and systematized into some groups of interests within which they are concentrated through ten items of convent. These ten items represent the fundamental programme of the LAIBACH KUNST doctrine.

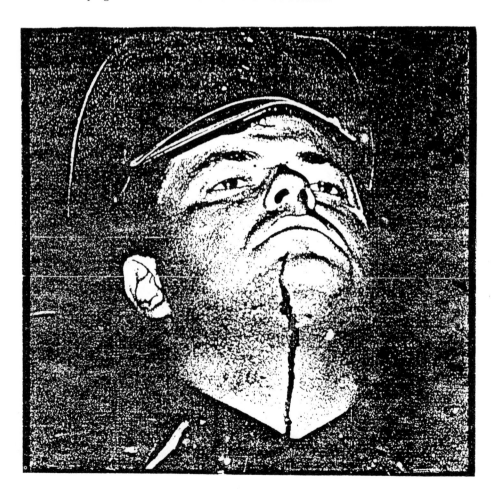

1. ART AND TOTALITARIANISM DON'T EXCLUDE EACH OTHER: TOTALITARIAN REGIMES ABOLISH THE ILLUSION OF THE REVOLUTIONARY INDIVIDUAL'S "ARTISTIC FREEDOM". LAIBACH KUNST IS THE PRINCIPLED CONSCIOUS ABANDONING OF PERSONAL TASTE, FAITH AND REASONING; IT VOLUNTARILY ACCEPTS FREE DEPERSONALISATION AND THE ROLE OF IDEOLOGY.

2. LAIBACH TAKES OVER AN ORGANISATIONAL SYSTEM OF WORK AFTER TOTALITARIAN MODEL OF INDUSTRIAL PRODUCTION (COLLECTIVE SPIRIT AND IDENTIFICATION WITH IDEOLOGY) WHICH MEANS: NOT THE INDIVIDUAL, BUT THE ORGANISATION SPEAKS. OUR WORK IS INDUSTRIAL, OUR LANGUAGE POLITICAL.

3. LAIBACH IN ITS WORK PRIMARILY ANALYSES THE RELATION BETWEEN IDEOLOGY AND CULTURE IN THE LATE PHASE, AS PRESENTED BY ART: RESEARCHING THE FORMATION OF INDIVIDUAL AND MASS SOCIAL CONSCIOUSNESS. IN RELATION TO THIS, LAIBACH BUILDS THE SYSTEM OF PROPAGANDA AND FUNCTIONAL MECHANISM OF INFORMATION AS A SYSTEM OF CONTROL TO BE REALISED THROUGH MASS CULTURE.

4. LAIBACH FUNCTIONS AS A CREATIVE ILLUSION OF THE RIGID INSTITUTIONALISM (IN IDENTIFICATION WITH INSTITUTIONS). A SOCIAL THEATRE OF POPULAR CULTURE WITH AN ENTRAINED PROGRAMME (ONE TRANSMITTER AND A MULTITUDE OF RECEIVERS) IT IS COMMUNICATION WITHOUT COMMUNICATION.

5. OUR MAIN INSPIRATION (IDEALS NOT THROUGH THEIR FORM BUT AS MATERIAL OF THE MANIPULATION ITSELF) IS: INDUSTRIAL NAZI KUNST, TOTALITARIANISM, TAYLORISM, BRUITISM, DISCO...

6. LAIBACH'S MUSICAL (ARTISTIC) APPROACH IS A MOVE INTO THE AREA OF PURE POLITICISATION OF SOUND AS A MEANS OF MANIPULATING THE MASSES.

7. LAIBACH IS THE RECOGNITION OF TIME UNIVERSALITY.

8. HIERARCHICAL PRINCIPLE IS CONNECTED WITH ORGANISATIONAL UNIVERSALITY OF THE GROUP IN ACTION. THE RELATIONS WITHIN THE GROUP ARE IN HARMONY WITH SOCIAL AND INDUSTRIAL FORMS OF PRODUCTION. LAIBACH IS THE MECHANISM CONSTITUTED BY INDIVIDUAL ORGANS, SUBORDINATED TO THE WHOLE: THE MEANINGFUL SYNTHESIS OF INDIVIDUAL POWER.

9. THE TRIUMPH OF ANONYMITY AND SHAPELESSNESS IS DRIVEN TO ABSOLUTUM THROUGH THE TECHNOLOGICAL PROCESS. INDIVIDUALITY IS BEING ABOLISHED. THE MEMBERSHIP IS FLEXIBLE AND ANONYMOUS WHICH FACILITATES CONSTANT INTERNAL REPLENISHMENT AND CONCEALS AN OPTIONAL NUMBER OF SUB-OBJECTS, ACCORDING TO NEEDS.

10. LAIBACH IS AN ORGANISM BORN FROM THE AIMS, LIFE, AND MEANS OF THE INDIVIDUALS WHO KEEP IT — HIGHER THAN ALL OF THEM BY POWER AND DURATION.

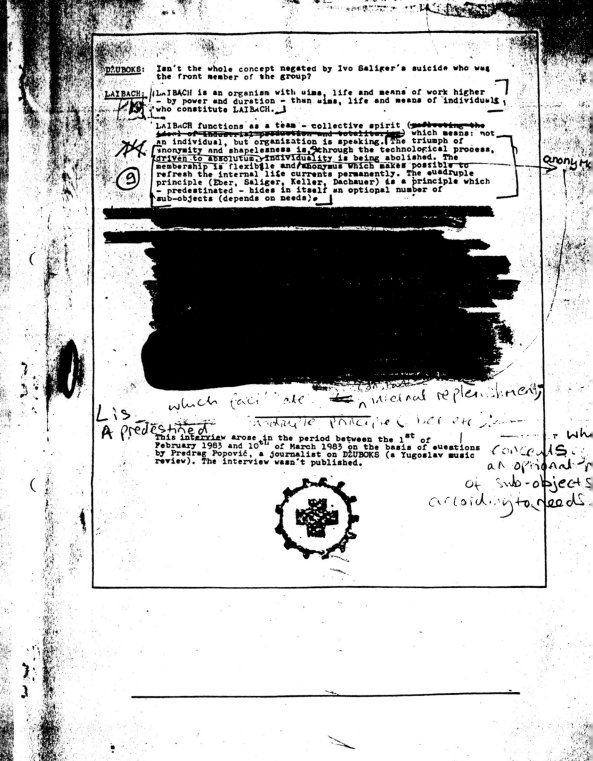

DŽUBOKS: Isn't the whole concept negated by Ivo Saliger's suicide who was the front member of the group?

LAIBACH: LAIBACH is an organism with aims, life and means of work higher - by power and duration - than aims, life and means of individuals who constitute LAIBACH.

LAIBACH functions as a team - collective spirit (~~reflecting the ideal of industrial production and totalitarism~~) which means: not an individual, but organization is speaking. The triumph of anonymity and shapelesness is, through the technological process, driven to absolutum, individuality is being abolished. The membership is flexible and anonymus which makes possible to refresh the internal life currents permanently. The quadruple principle (Eber, Saliger, Keller, Dachauer) is a principle which - predestinated - hides in itself an optional number of sub-objects (depends on needs).

[redacted]

which facilitate ... internal replenishment

L is a predestined quadruple principle (Eber etc.) ... which conceals an optional ... of sub-objects according to needs

This interview arose in the period between the 1st of February 1983 and 10th of March 1983 on the basis of questions by Predrag Popović, a journalist on DŽUBOKS (a Yugoslav music review). The interview wasn't published.

PSYCHIC TV

"I was Elvis Presley before he was."

The D.A. would say, 'Hey man, you were trying for a record career'. I had a record career. I didn't want a record career. I'd just got out of one prison. I didn't want to go into another."

AN HOUR WITH CHARLES MANSON, BROADCAST ON KLX BERKELEY, CALIFORNIA 1983.

In 1974, correspondence began between Monte Cazazza, notorious for his early work within the San Francisco art world, and COUM Transmissions in London. They eventually worked together on numerous projects, including the Gary Gilmore Memorial Card and Monte's eventual recording on Industrial Records. Cazazza also engineered *Mission of Dead Souls* — the last live performance of Throbbing Gristle at Kezar Pavillion, San Francisco. Instrumental in the development of ideas of the Temple Ov Psychic Youth, Monte now heads Psychic TV USA and occasionally plays live with the group.

Hilmar Orn, an Icelandic native, was once a member of the group Peyr, and also worked on various film projects and soundtracks for Icelandic Television. In 1984 he moved to London, where he began working full time with Psychic TV. Collectively and individually the present members of Psychic TV have exhibited their work in film, music and performance festivals all over the world. They have works in many major art museums and collections, and have published countless articles, manifestos and graphic works in numerous publications internationally.

When Psychic TV started, did encouraging a certain physical appearance contradict the idea of people being individuals?

Genesis: (pause) We experimented with people's susceptibilities. We always say in interviews that people don't have to look any particular way. We always stress that it is not, in fact, important. But in one way, if you set up a very particular image, it then gives you far more ways to sidestep — even on your own. All I have to do is grow my hair back and that's a radical move — and that changes the way people interpret the way that I look.

You can draw an analogy with smuggling. If you send somebody through customs in front of you who looks smacked out of their brains and dubious, and you're behind them in a casual suit with a wife and child, the odds are immediately increased that the person who will be pulled first is the guy who looks like he is going to be into drugs. And actually they could be working together. But archetypes can be used. Once you understand that they're used anyway, then you can start to play with them to your own advantage — and also re-educate people as to what's done by other people.

Would you say that the ideas behind the music that you have been doing over the past few years have changed?

Hilmar: No, I think it's just the approach. Basically, all the Psychic TV albums have been really schizophrenic in their diversity, but that's also part of the camouflage. We maintain that if you have a limited set of strategies in your dealings with the world, you're obviously going to have very limited access to the world. If your world view is limited, your chances are limited as well. You can see that the group has been going over the whole spectrum basically. It has been doing classical things, it has been doing tongue in cheek things, rock and roll, teenybop, all sorts of things, and this is basically an exercise at the same time as being a statement that people will grab subconsciously. And now the band has been slowly weeding out a lot of the influences which were peripheral or trivial and finding its own character.

What are the benefits of bringing all the aspects of Psychic TV together?

Hilmar: Well schizophrenia, to quote a good man, is, "a healthy reaction against a neurotic society" — that's one of the first points. Basically, Psychic TV can been seen as a mirror, it's just reflecting the image of what is happening around it. The second thing is coming to terms with this state around you and being able to manipulate your own way through it. The Temple Ov Psychic Youth is trying to link all these aspects together into a co-operative whole. For instance, with a lot of the anti-religious things or political statements and the tongue in cheek statements, we were sort of helping people to realise they shouldn't trust things on surface value. People have slowly begun to grasp the idea, they have come to terms with all these diverse things that are happening in Psychic TV and all these diverse messages being put out. So when they finally come out in one song, they may be a combination of messages of The Pope and John F. Kennedy and social and religious commentaries, while also including a nice sense of humour and a good piece of music. People will be able to interpret that instead of seeing it as a mish-mash of unconnected ideas, and we will be able to do more complicated things soon. I mean we are dangling very tasty carrots in front of people, no doubt about that.

Would you say that you have used video to the advantage that you would like to?

Monte: No, we've just started. This is really just the beginning in a way. I want to be as big as Gulf and Western so that I can give them a run for their goddamn money, I'll tell you that. Mark Pauline said, "We want to compete with football games". We want to get out there so that we can really compete. Personally speaking, in all kinds of events, I think that we can do just as good a job; I think that we have better motives and include more valuable information. And I want the quality of our work to improve and the quality of everybody else's work to improve.

Genesis: We want to be as demanding on the public as we are on ourselves.

Do you see a time when the public will be open for that demand?

Genesis: A percentage of them will. If you can change and mutate the popular culture and some of the more intellectual culture of the planet with no funds and about five or six people, then as the old adage goes, imagine what you could do with one hundred or six hundred. Six hundred is enough to completely change the planet — easily. You just have to work very hard all the time. You don't stop, you just work. And it pays dividends. Most groups, most journalists, most TV and most record companies are very lazy, people are basically lazy. So it makes it easier to succeed in what we're trying to do because the competition is distracted with avoiding work. And I think that's wonderful. I like to see laziness in people I don't respect. It's the old syndrome of people being afraid to take a step forward.

Basically, we're trained not to take risks. We are afraid of what any risk may do to us. We may of course end up with something unexpected and wonderful, but people are being brought up in a very pessimistic state of being. You're basically being put into a hypnotic trance about 150 times a day. There's no difference between an induction of hypnosis and stepping into an elevator with about ten people that you don't know. You block yourself out. If you go on the tube in the rush hour, you see that people have learned to switch themselves off. When I had to commute to work doing that book on art, I used to really watch their faces. And people appear normal, but as you look at their faces, they're quite obviously disturbed and neurotic. They've got all sorts of strange little mannerisms and twitches in their faces and hands which they are totally unconscious of — just the tension and stress of switching off coming out in another way.

Everyone used to say, "Don't you hate the rush hour and commuting"? But I didn't because I was fascinated with the evidence of what was going on. I had a policy — you have to have certain rules. One is you should never run for a tube, never, that is the first step towards disaster because you're then letting the tube control you. And these commuters, if you notice, they fight to get on it, they don't just run, they fight to go into this demented state.

People are trained to ignore their own memory facility. With that thing, "Those who do not remember the past are condemned to repeat it", they do it — everyday. The thing that makes us angry about popular music or groups like Duran Duran or Boy George is that they deliberately exploit all those neurotic states, they actually exist through mental disturbance and through people's fear of what they've not been educated to want. People who have been at school are trained not to want to maximise their potential. Basically kids are told, "Don't expect a job when you leave school... forever". That is a ridiculous state to be in. People are told, "Expect to be a heroin addict, expect to be depressed, expect to be on the dole, count yourself lucky if the dole is not stopped when the government gets bored". These are basically the options given to people now. And that's what they are told every day by someone who is supposedly a substitute authority for mum and dad.

So is your goal to make people realise what is happening to them?

Genesis: Our goal is to simply set up an example that is an alternative. We've been through the same conditioning process. We're not untainted, we are damaged, but we are victims, just like them, expressing what we see. And, if by random chance, luck, social education, or whatever, we've somehow come through, then the best we can do is function in that way and express and speak for people as equal victims. Then they can see what they've been told is patently untrue. You can have fun, you can learn to build this quite impressive cultural machine when you've been given no skills by the system you were born into. None of us were trained as musicians or anything. But we've learned how to rig up videos, and we've learned how to build scaffolding, and we've learned how to make instruments and play them.

And that message in itself is always avoided by most people including "the business", and including other groups. Duran Duran and all those other people have a vested interest in perpetuating the legend that rock groups are somehow special. They actually know that they are not special, they pretend that rock groups are these ultra special beings — not normal humans — and that they are the technicians and the ones that can do pop music and you have to consume it. And the record company pretend that they're the only people that can produce records, or can sell them or can get a group famous or whatever. There are all these people lying to each other, and they all do it for their own ego gratification and their own profit at the expense of the public — the people they should respect. The thing that creates the most anger in me is the total disrespect for their fans, their audience, the people who buy their records. The patronising arrogance of them, when most of them are actually unintelligent, average morons who happen to learn to play the guitar.

Do you see one of the purposes of pop music to be strictly for entertainment, as a throw away, disposable product?

Genesis: It's a purpose that was generated deliberately by people who could see a profit motive in it. There was no initial purpose in it. There is no pop music, as such, in older cultures. The nearest you get is the troubadour idea of passing on popular stories, which are usually symbolic of some moral to remind people of what has happened before — to learn from it. What our culture doesn't tell you is how to learn from the song — it's not connected with the history of the culture particularly, except in the most trivial, superficial way. And the nearest it comes is that Elvis used to wiggle his hips and now George Michael does. That's not very constructive for most people, it doesn't solve how they exist, how they live or how they survive. The question is really, "Can intelligence be put into pop music?", and we think it can.

The big problem that we've all got is that the technology is still expensive. Therefore the people with access to that technology rip off what we're talking about and do a really stupid version of it. You can bet your life groups like Ultravox and Duran Duran would use it to portray Simon LeBon in his sports car, or on a yacht with Duran Duran, or in Vienna with Ultravox. But they would totally emasculate the power of what we're talking about. They would use it in a way that everyone is still using TV. And the groups who would make creative use of it are the ones with the least access. One of our jobs is hopefully, to be the crossover group that gets in quick and establishes ourselves as the theoriticians of new television, however spurious some of our theories might actually be. Then, maybe, we can get some sponsorship and train them up in investing in more radical approaches — for their own research. And that's the only option we've got open at the moment for getting access to that stuff. And we don't want it to end up like a contemporary version of Yes or Roger Waters where you get to be this ungainly technological phenomena which is just a big show biz thing. I mean, Laurie Anderson has become like Pink Floyd really. You know, equipment-mania, and it's so preconceived and choreographed that it's more like going to a West End show, which is OK, but I find it less interesting. I think something just a bit more shambolic, home grown and still street level would work better. It has got to be kept a kind of guerilla warfare - not where the technology impresses.

What keeps ideas, within fields such as video, from progressing at a more rapid pace?

Genesis: Everybody wants to own what they do. "Duran Duran are unique, and it's God given, and that's what makes them brilliant and special" — and it's just bullshit. They're as much a result of their upbringing and their input as everybody else — and the sooner people stop worrying about who thought of it first and whether or not they're brilliant because of that, the better. What is useful? What functions? What seems to make sense? What is helping? That is what matters; and the reduction of that down to the tightest compilation of useful ideas, information and techniques. The sooner that happens, the better — without anyone having to commit themselves to an ongoing, suppressive dogma. You get Duran Duran who use a video screen, and what do they do with it? They have close-ups of them playing the guitar above them playing the guitar, very useful! That's a really worthwhile piece of machinery, isn't it? So what does it do? It just masturbates pubescent girls further, that's all.

But Duran Duran are now using a large video screen which gets out to an audience of twenty thousand people at one of their concerts. Don't they get the idea about the power of TV or video across to those people?

Genesis: No, because it totally emasculates it and reduces it down to tinsel. The Duran Duran programme that was on TV was the worst kind of directionless manipulation, in fact a very distasteful form of masturbation (because I actually hold that there are forms of masturbation which can be positive). If you listen to the music, it was a monotone. I think Boyd Rice is better dance music than they are because what he does is totally physical, and your body can't help but respond — even if you hate it. And that's real dance music, when your body has to respond to the frequencies and pulses.

Monte: The whole thing is trying to get out of that circle that you're already born into. Society is already here before you're born into it. There's no way to say that anything is totally original. Obviously, you're influenced by many things that were here before you're even born. I think the whole idea is to try to escape and get out of that so that you can continue on with other things. And then start to see what your real potential is and what you can accomplish.

It seems that a lot of people think that to attract a mainstream audience Psychic TV must 'sell out' or compromise to a certain extent.

Genesis: I always thought that selling out was when you did something just for money and didn't have any motives or principles left. (laughs) That's what I thought it meant anyway.

I guess it's sort of elitism on the part of long standing Psychic TV or TG followers, when A-Ha or Duran Duran fans become interested in the same groups.

Genesis: I think that's a shame. Why does everyone assume that they know best, or that they're the only ones intelligent enough to understand something important. In my experience over many years, you can never tell who understands. Most mini-cab drivers have a much better understanding of British politics than politicians have of it. And most of the black people that I've talked to have a much better understanding of race than the white, liberal, Socialist Worker Party people. And if you're trying to do something which has a real effect on society, you have to be confident that it has the relevance to all of society — not just the easy, elite few who, for all we know, like us for completely the wrong reasons anyway. They maybe like us because they think that no-one else does. And that's not a very good reason. And I certainly don't think the way we play is in any way a musical compromise to pander to suburban people, and I don't think the content of the videos is pandering to them either. So what is selling out? Doing a concert which actually gets the authorities threatening to take you to court? If it means that suburban people actually have a more open mind and are able to develop and think and change, then I'm happy to have them. I don't care who they are or what intellectual class they're from.

I guess they feel it's a superficial invasion of a long standing trend.

Genesis: But that has always been true. We've always said that ninety percent of an audience that anyone gets you wouldn't bother giving the time of day to. There's no way you can say that I have to like everyone in my audience. I think you have to cast your net as hard as possible in the hope that one out of every five hundred is OK — you expect a great loss rate. And most of the people who tell you that they know what we're doing, don't — even though our motives are clearer than ever. We're doing what we said we were going to do, whereas before we weren't for a lot of reasons — suffice to say that other people held us back. And we may or may not be making a terrible blunder, but at least now we're going to experiment with the idea. I think what we're doing should be in the popular arena. I want to see the character of national television changed. Not all the time, but part of the time. I want to see programmes that you or I would make on television, even if it's only from midnight till two in the morning, so the public can have a choice. That's all we're ever saying — give people the choice.

In terms of religion, are you basically concerned with how the church has become a vehicle for other motives — such as political ones, or the church standing for something which has been developed over the years and now is struggling to maintain.

Genesis: Well, both and more. I'm against all inherited systems of belief and value. If it happens that one of those is the purest form of Christianity i.e., live and be nice to people, then I can just about handle it. The problem is that it's not presented that way, you have to take the whole package, and it immediately becomes dangerous again. I think that certain forms of Buddhism are a lot less obnoxious — although some of their beliefs are still pretty much rooted in their geographical aristocracy. Eastern religions actually suited the aristocracy in the East, and Christian ones the aristocracy in the West. I think the motives behind most mass religions are totally dubious, and obviously aimed at social control and the submission of the masses — so they don't get out of order and demand more than they've been told by God, Allah or whoever. They all have their passive side for the average man. You know, the Buddhist — he will be reincarnated and get better next time, so, "Don't complain now, stay in your place". The Christian — "Once you go to heaven, it will be great. It's God's will that your wife and child starve to death and just because Count so and so has a castle full of food, that's because God willed it that he was a Count". And with Muslims — "Allah willed it that you died". Hindu's the same; and they all have this thing that those without economic and other resources should not complain, because it's God's will. And those with the resources are chosen by God because they, like Mummy and Daddy, know better. And you'll be like them if you die enough times of starvation. It's quite patently bullshit. I don't believe anyone comes back. And I don't believe anyone goes to heaven either.

What happens?

Genesis: You just die. It's like any other animal. (laughs) Speaking from my own experience of being physically declared dead twice; but the Christians would argue that God knew I was going to come back so he didn't let me know what it was like — so there's always a way out. It's possible that the brain is so powerful that we don't know all of its qualities yet, that it could leave some sort of reverberation. Another thing that might be possible is that in every brain there's a certain part of everyone's subconscious mind which is linked completely like a blanket. We all actually join up, in some neurological way, which can explain the moments of telepathy or the amazing things that Aborigines, American Indians and Amazon Indians can do with, or without, peyote. It would certainly explain the things that you get with LSD when you open up certain channels. Most people, even Christian mystics that starve themselves in the desert long enough, get this feeling that there is almost a common mind -and that's what they call God. I think it's probably a biological thing and everyone can be potentially linked with it. But nobody, except for a few Shamans and mystics, have any control of how to travel within it.

You get astral projection as an example — people saying that you can train yourself to do that. If that's true then maybe you can leave a residue in that mass section of the unconscious, which means that somebody could think that they've experienced previous life. It could explain a lot of the phenomena of contact with, supposedly, dead people etc., or even the idea of psychic attack from outside. That would be the way that you could begin to pursue it in a vaguely scientific way. I haven't drawn a conclusion. I always like to think of the nearest functional explanation that I can. At the end of the day, the only thing I'm confident in is that the human brain is the root of everything. And most of what we think of as being odd phenomena are just manifestations of brain activity which we have no control over, no knowledge of, or no language to describe yet. I re-read the introduction to 'The Final Academy' document that I wrote about dreams, and I was really pleased with it because that was saying how people dismissed them now, but once the King of Egypt had a bloke just to interpret his dreams, and Moses became the dream interpreter and got his power that way. And so-called primitive cultures, which are actually incredibly sophisticated — like in New Guinea, or the Aborigines, American Indians and Eskimos — give dreams equal credence with reality. And I think that's important. We are very much dream orientated in everything we do. A long time ago when I had just left school, somebody's mother asked me, "What do you do, and why do you do it?" And I said, "I just take my dreams far more seriously than other people. I daydream, and then try and make the daydreams real". And that's really all I've ever done.

Most of the best art of this century is connected with the unconscious. This is the age of the subconscious mind. And that's why there is a revival of interest in magick. It's an intuitive feeling. The unfortunate thing is that most people try to mimic old magick rooted in the previous era, instead of trying to find a contemporary form of magic that is post-Jungian, post-Freudian and deals with Polaroid cameras, cassette recorders, televisions, and what we know about the brain. The ultimate aim in my whole life is to try, with other people, to collaborate on some kind of manual which is a hypothesis for a contemporary form of neurological magick; a book that updates it all and sweeps away all that confusing mimicry, and says that the idea of magick as practiced by some of the so-called primitive cultures is essential to human survival and development. That a combination of primitive and pagan with technology is the only means of survival and growth. Without it we're doomed. If we don't reconnect with dreams and the unconscious mind, I think that's the end. I think the only path for human evolution now is a magickal one in it's truest sense, based on the whole brain — asleep and awake. And if it doesn't happen, there's nothing left to do — it's the only path left, mistakes and all. Whenever it appears that I am ruthless, it's because I will not tolerate less than an obsession with that. And as soon as people waver, I'm not interested. I don't mind them going off and doing whatever they want, but I can't work with anything less than an obsessive interest in mankind and the search for an expression of hope. (pause)

I would like to take the best people everywhere and put them in one place and blast a very big hole in society's structures — psychological and social. We're not so interested in economic — because that's just a result of psychology anyway. Social conditioning and psychology dictate the rest of the structures basically. That's another mistake that so many people make, they go for the material mechanics instead of thinking that actually what is happening is the basics. With anything — if you pick the right spot and chop away at that one spot, one mega bridge can fall.

What would your reaction be if somebody were to say that the ideas of Psychic TV were brilliant on paper, but the darker nature of the ideas and interests tend to overshadow the original ideas?

Hilmar: I would think that they didn't have enough capabilities of grasping the situation really. It's this thing that people demand beauty and consistency in the sense that they want something that will move them only in the direction they want to be moved in. We want to do something more than that. We want to tear structures down from beneath, which means we have to link in with a lot of fears that people have, and we have to deal with areas which are repressed and forbidden for many people.

Monte: If you're talking about a fully integrated personality which can rationally express aspects of its existence, it has to incorporate all aspects of its existence and integrate them. In the jungle, there are nice flowers, but there are also a lot of really violent things happening. If you try and pretend that they're not happening, either you're going to get destroyed or you'll just ignorantly go about destroying all types of other things because you pretend that you don't have those tendencies in yourself to begin with. You have to admit that you have them in order to be able to control them.

Genesis: The motives for what we do with anything are always the same. The motives are to reveal the nature of things so that people are able to deal with them. And also so they learn how to analyze, choose, and then construct something more positive.

Hilmar: In psychological terms, making the individual whole won't happen until he has finally come to terms with the darker side of his shadow. And if he doesn't do that, if he doesn't recognize that he has instincts which are presently being labelled as basic instincts, animal instincts or whatever, he is always going to project them into his surroundings. He will see his worst qualities in other people — and that will irritate him. He will hate these people because they are, in a way, a manifestation of what he hates in himself and doesn't want to see.

Genesis: We don't say, "This is good, this bad". And when you call it "the darker side", I even question that. Is it darker to pretend that everything is wonderful? Or is it darker to be factual and not be scared of it and still see it optimistically? I think our view is very optimistic and not at all dark. What they're doing is experiencing the residual effects of conditioned morality. They've been trained to think that certain things which might be dealt with or hinted at or implied by what we do are inherently dark or bad, when I would question that. Do they mean sexuality? Is it bad? Of course not! Sexuality is sexuality. What's bad?

Are enough people at a gig open enough to make a judgement like that?

Genesis: How many is enough? We're doing a long term re-education programme, training people to become aware of their subconscious and their irrational responses which is what most people are going through — which is the first stage if you like. Other people who have been once or twice, thought more, read interviews and so on, go into, if you like, another phase which is no longer just emotionally responding and just taking that as truth, but actually thinking, "Why am I responding this way, what does it mean? Am I tricking myself, is what is being presented perfectly reasonable?" There's one basic thing going on at many of our events now; if people are listening intently, then the films and videos are immediately slipping into their subconscious, and vice versa. So, at any given moment, people are absorbing information subconsciously and therefore not even aware of why they're responding or what's happening. And it takes time for those images, ideas, sounds, rhythms and patterns to germinate in the subconscious and come through, and sometimes they can create a minor crisis in somebody. But I think the fact that people even discuss things on that level after one of our concerts is an incredible compliment. We are aiming for a mature, constructive, ongoing discussion about what is really possible; the potential that both the audience and the group can have together. And what that can grow to be and the power that it can unleash, and the fact that it becomes a way of life. You can look at the world differently. You can look at other people differently. And that is what we're trying to do. We are trying to encourage people to ask questions. To try to look at the structures behind things, the way that they behave, the way they respond.

Of course our enemies are going to try to think of anything that they can to discourage that happening because it's the most dangerous thing that can go on in any society — to get people awake, thinking, and saying, "No", or "Why?". Anything as basic as that is much more potent than a bomb. People really wanting to understand the biggest threat that control has. Because control is based on non-thinking backed up by physical violence. That's basically how it works, it's as simple as that. That's why people in the more overtly fascist states start with nurseries — they train kids just to babble dogma as soon as they can talk. And it's not because they want them to say the words, it's because they want them not to think.

At the bottom line, it's about thought and not thought, doing and not doing. And that's why, at the very basic level, we are more political than any of those groups that go around spouting cyclical politics, that actually believe in the sham of the political system. They just give the excuse for law and order and everything else. There is actually always a route around the obvious. And we're trying to find a route around a lot of obvious things simultaneously because there's not enough time to play those games. Hilmar was saying earlier that each age generates its own culture to mirror what's happening, and now it is quite patently television. And any group which is not dealing with the nature of television is basically already redundant.

Would it be possible to get a Psychic TV video on MTV?

Genesis: There will be a way round it, we'll find a way around it which might mean that we get a one hour documentary about our activities on National TV there anyway. It's like in England just recently, National TV has accepted us as we are. The great compliment is that they want to ask us what we think. They don't ask us for promo videos, but they want to hear what we have to say. After they've talked to us, they usually go away at least neutral and often allies because what we say makes sense to them. And they're surprised because they usually come prejudiced against us. And the more people there are working within television coming on to our side who are at least prepared to always listen, then the stronger we're getting. Because at the end of the day, we're better off on national television than in NME every week. We can get twelve million people in an hour on TV. It would take five years if we were in the NME. And it would actually only be about two hundred thousand because it's the same readership anyway.

Do you feel that your audience is beginning to change?

Monte: I hope so. If they're not going to change, we're just gonna have to change them. It's the hard way or the easy way and I don't care which way it is. I think we're getting a more diverse cross-section of people which is what I'm interested in. I'd like to really see a wider cross-section from younger to older. Then I'd feel we were making more progress.

Genesis: What we are dedicated to more than ever now is cultural mobility — to present live events where the public are given a chance to see and hear music, ballet, writing, films and videos. So a ballet audience hears music they'd otherwise ignore, and rock fans hear writing they'd otherwise not read, and so on. In a real sense, education by presentation. It doesn't matter whether the audience like it all, at least their information is being widened and challenged. That has to be a healthy development. Also, it puts a little life back into live events. Most of us feel that going to a gig isn't very exciting anymore. We know what's coming, the moves and the time length. So now Psychic TV are co-ordinating the method to revitalise live events, where you have to be there to experience it — no system of documentation can capture it. A technological and contemporary application of what was tried in the sixties with happenings and mixed media extravaganzas. Our video projections expand and challenge concepts of TV, and television is, in our opinion, the most potent force shaping human social culture, political and economic culture, possibly even affecting evolutionary mutation in the brain. Our name is no mistake. It's a deliberate declaration of intent politically.

I think there has been a turn around. I think people are beginning to listen again. There We don't live in an isolated world. I have never been interested in working on my own because to me that seems to be the old way — and also the dangerous path. You only have to look at somebody like Jim Jones or Charles Manson to see how that kind of thing can end up — given even a marginal amount of charisma or ideas. But it also just seems a very unsatisfactory way of working. If what you're thinking makes any sense, there have to be other people who feel the same. And what you should do is look for those people and develop a network of collaborators, and then just maximise the effect of the work you can get done. I don't have to read all the books that Hilmar has read because he has read them. He can save months of library work in an hour. And I can probably do the same for him in certain areas, and Monte, and so on. I'm sure there are things that you know which we don't know which saves us time. The less time we waste, the more we get done.

I think there has been a turn around. I think people are beginning to listen again. There are more pieces to the pattern, and as Hilmar said, "The organisation has been tightened up a lot", so I think inevitably, that will have its reverberation — like ripples. People will feel that all these changes and reorganisations have been for a purpose — which is to make the whole idea closer to the original concept. And just by watching and observing and listening, they'll see what we say is what we try and do. That as soon as we get access to funds, we spend it on more of what we want to do. And the more funds, help, and support we get, the more we'll get done.

The only thing I'd like to leave behind at the end is just a philosophical manual that was the equivalent of having everything that everyone has done in their lifetime in one place. And you could just take and use whatever was still appropriate. That's the most useful thing that you can leave people — actual ideas that make life have more sense.

incantations.Clic ears.Slowly, the   k.Machines hum.Silence cle   Cut up end

start to spin: th IBM computer tape e vortex is set in motion. tape recorders

throb,guitar aler vortex,ever slowly, t.Vocal incantations. The deprogram.Bass

aster,faster.I aw ly concentrate on ake from my dream and lazi whirl faster; f

e front of the au agitation,hatred, ience.From my dream I see a group near the

chines spin: the t,it has encompass dream continues.In the pa violence.The ma

itement: tonight tatory,even strong it continues, incar boredom,fear,ex

rfect soundtrack.   than before,a p

n.The group are rousing.Flexing   scratching themselves,are   I wake aga

eir intent is fo es to a heartbeat. ussing as the sound chang their muscles.

do I.I notice m re,like how drunk re things.Like who they s they focus,

to sense troubl about limits,   .The people on stage sing they are.I star

ut extreme pain. power begins to   the vortex winds up.Their about horror,ab

near the front: ffect.The vortex   the deprogramming takes ein the grou

p take shape as t to about: ho thin three/four women.They start wists: the gro

nger,disgust.I slowly drawn as   am now fully awake,being yet coherent ye

ds.   the vortex exte

to shout now.The vortex takes hold takes shape uglier,as the   They start

stage.Somewher ex locks - I don't about this time,the vort of the people o

n course,all eve of the women move ts are now inevitable.Tw know when.Held

e: I see that the femininity,carefu y are aggressive in their towards the sta

their demeanour ntrol rigid on the - contrasting with the c ly disordered i

age.Demons are w box is being pris iting to be let out: the people on the s

ove: the Security tries to usher y Guard - a callow youth - open.The first

This is the chanced.His youth,once e: he is surrounded,jostl the girls aside.

frail: the women ddenly the people confuse,and taunt him.S stolid,now seem

ir obsessive aur ir spell falters. ,become very fragile: the on the stage,t

pins to suck me in the women and n: I place my body betwe the vortex hey back off.Th|at it's over.   e vortex recoups.1 hope th boy.Somewhow,

ge shriek.The w|redoubled.^hings omen start to shout again,The people on st

ly: the vortex w|he man at the fror|hirls in a dervish dance.1now happen quick

ks at the women:|n back in their   he throws their aggressic|of the stage loo

ixes them with h|s head with territ|is eyes: his fist bangs hi|face.Purple,he f

ack,whack.Althou|rected: the messa|gh the violence is self-di|force,in time.Wh

en are past noti|the whisky bottle,|cing.One of them finishes| is clear. The wom

stage.One of the|nstantly off the   performers moves: leaps i|hurls it at the

of the women.Th|screws up into a e vortex exults.The noise |stage.Floors one

sound: the women|their anger.1heir parody a tribal dance in |ball,a whorl of

hate:the same a|their exploration|3 the people on stage mask|naturalism masks

e is no sync.Gui|.One of the women |tars tear: a voice screams|with terror.Ther

like wonder to t|: she looks down. |1e very front of the stage|walks with child

unch of wires,de|re flowers.She   licately,as though they we|She picks up a b

me stops.The vor|houlder guitar   1ex is at its centre.Cut s|looks at them.Ti

vortex to whole|t appreciation is hall.Careful modernity,ar|bass arc.Trigger

nimal takes over|man screams insul|t Chaotic,dangerous,real. A |stripped away: a

ker' with incred|particular; a   ble violence to nobody ir|'You fucking wan

ugh the air foll|shoulder.I want   wed by shrieks,behind |my chair flies thro

t have it,feel l|cted.The rest   ke crying,stomach constri|my dream: 1 can'

lotsam as the vo|: hospitals,usele|tex fades,its spell bound|dissolves into f

inations,a sleep| ess night........   arguments,recrim

hree and a half y|a tape of the con|ears later,an era,1 play 6 July 1978.T

record of the|se.Directly,that is|nger,the violence,the ha|cert: there is n

near the vortex|ever happened.when| n the noise.Perhaps it ne|Perhaps you can

it never will hav| e: memories lie.   the tape decays,

Pause.

WHORE

I'm waiting for someone to ride me. I'm on my hands and knees. My naked ass is sticking up in the air in a room of clothed men. Their businessman's shoes are shined and I can see the distorted reflection of my face as I press down to lick. I've put myself in this position because I enjoy the power I acquire through self-denegration. Once these men think I'm no better than meat, I have the advantage. They drain their sperm into my ass one by one. I enjoy the pain I steal from their pleasure in hurting me. After they're finished with me they spit on me, then they dress me and push me out the door. Riding home in the cab I'm drenched in the smell of my asshole and sweat. I enjoy the thought of the cab driver smelling it also. When I'm upstairs safe in my apartment I squat over my frying pan and release their sperm and my shit. I let it simmer over the fire, mixed with wine. As I eat, I play the scene over again in my mind, ingesting each man one by one.

A COWARD

I've wasted myself. I've turned myself into something I can't control. I'm dwarfed, minimised by everything around me. I'm cowering. I'm scared of what is going to happen next. Any unpredicted movement, any sound I haven't anticipated, terrifies me, lessens me. There's a pair of scissors on the desk in front of me. I'm picking them up, opening and closing them, pressing the rings of metal against my bone. I'm sticking my finger into the blades and squeezing as hard as I can. They're dull. They won't cut into me. It doesn't hurt. It throbs, reminding me of the existence of my hand — which disgusts me. I hate my body more than I hate the objects and events that rub up against it. I don't despise the conditions of my life as much as I despise the existence of my flesh.

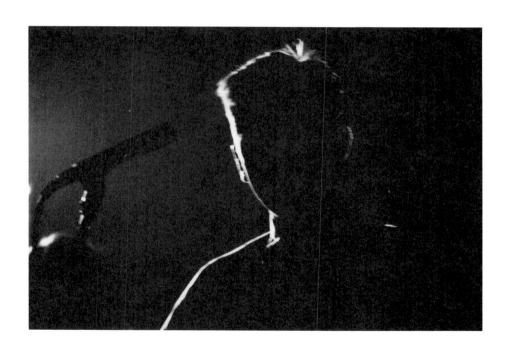

NEW ORDER

New Order played their first concert in July 1980 at Manchester's Beach Club, billed as The No-Names supporting A Certain Ratio. For months afterwards, the group maintained a low profile before coming out early in 1981, playing their first London concert at Heaven nightclub and releasing the single *Ceremony / In A Lonely Place*. A live version of *Ceremony* had already appeared on the final Joy Division LP, *Still*, released after Ian Curtis' death the previous year. Catalyzed like many others by the Sex Pistols' 'Anarchy Tour', Joy Division had begun in Manchester in late 1976 (briefly) as The Stiff Kittens, then Warsaw, with a coarse and aggressive style that fitted the punk movement of that time. In 1978, they signed to Factory Records, by which stage their sound had developed markedly — the two LPs that followed, *Unknown Pleasures* and *Closer* (along with various singles), carried an emotional impact that has rarely been surpassed, though their oblique imagery and fine balance between experimentation and hard rock noise has been widely imitated. Ian Curtis' suicide in May 1980 was a loss made more acute in the light of the mythology rapidly growing around the group at that time.

The three remaining members; Peter Hook, Stephen Morris and Bernard Sumner, auditioned a new singer, but finding no-one suitable recruited a friend, Gillian Gilbert, to play keyboards and guitar. (What's in a name?) — For a time they might have wished they had opted for The Sunshine Valley Dance Band, dogged as New Order were by allegations of flirting with (if never actually condoning) fascism — an accusation that carried over from 'Joy Divisions' being brothels set up by Nazi officers in concentration camps, motivated also by the fashion for occultist imagery prevalent in 1980/81 that was somehow less culpable.

An excellent second single, *Procession*, did little to quieten down speculation; it was not until the group's somewhat algid first LP, *Movement*, that they were finally able to move away from both the musical legacy of Joy Division and the media's auto-da-fe. With *Temptation* and a second LP, *Power, Corruption and Lies*, New Order used programmed drum rhythms reminiscent of Kraftwerk and the feature of New York disco to develop a kind of 'white hip-hop' sound. With *Blue Monday* came an international dance-floor smash that has since become one of the best selling 12" singles of all time. Subsequent LPs, *Low Life* and *Brotherhood* have consolidated New Order's position as the best selling "independent" group in the world, gathering large audiences in Australia, Japan, Europe and America, where in 1984 they signed a licensing deal with the soul label, Qwest.

In spite of their popularity, the group's frequent benefit concerts need little publicity to have their effect.

What are your reasons for staying on Factory when you could choose virtually any other label?

P Hook: The reason at the moment is that it works quite well for us. It gives us the means to further our careers, which usually means money and freedom. So the success that we get from Factory has just always enabled us to go our own way. I mean the only benefits you get from a major that you can't get off Factory is advance money as far as I'm concerned. We don't need it thank God, so we can go our own way. And it's very important for us to stay with Factory anyway because of the people that we work with. We get along very well with them, they help us out and we help them out, so it's a very nice relationship.

The Joy Division records seem to have a searching, atmospheric quality to them, whereas the music that you're doing now seems much cleaner. Would you agree with that?

P Hook: As a generalisation I suppose, yeah, because when you start you do tend to be a bit raw and unbalanced.

Barney: You cannot just carry on and have the same sound, you run out of space to operate.

P Hook: A lot of it is down to experience anyway. The more experienced you get as a musician, the more you ask from recording and the more you ask from writing. It's like growing up as a child. You begin thinking about it more and you want to put more into it. You just grow older, and that's what we've done with our music. I think the technology has just got a lot cleaner anyway, it's just changed a hell of a lot, so it's obvious that nowadays it's going to sound cleaner.

Do you actively try to balance a commercial sound with the kind of artistic integrity you get from doing exactly what you want to do independent of the whole market?

Barney: I think it should be something that people can comprehend. Music is a language, so if you invented your own language no-one would understand it.

P Hook: When we write a song, we don't do it for artistic integrity. We do it because it sounds good. Everything that we do is for that reason — most of the time. And luckily for us it turns out that a lot of people do like it.

It seems the biggest problem with people who do claim to work on a more independent level is getting feedback that is actually divorced of all the NME criticism and innuendo, fashions, "sounds like disco, sounds like electro", or whatever.

P Hook: That's where music has changed in that these independent groups got a lot of attention a while back because they were doing the interesting things. But now, that whole thing has faded out. A lot of people are independent or trying to be independent but are just going under because the independent thing doesn't work anymore. They can't pull it off, which is a real shame because there's a lot of records that have been discarded because the majors have got it all sewn up. There's not that spark of interest.

Barney: I think that everyone has more or less sold out. It's sad, but I thought that would happen anyway.

How would you define 'sell out'?

Barney: Going back on your word or what you said originally when you started out. Completely reversing the original intentions.

Do you think that puts an inordinate amount of stress on a group that is new together and is about to release their first record?

P Hook: The thing about the punk thing when it started was that there was a lot of propaganda about what they did but as soon as it started getting to the position where they could do something about it, they just took the easy way out. I mean it's fine, you do change your mind and I don't know if that's important. People change their minds all the time.

Barney: Yeah, it's not important, but if it's a group that really spouts off about it, I think it's bad. But if it's a group that don't have any strong beliefs, then it's not so bad. It's like The Clash — they release a record, 'I'm So Bored With The USA', and where are they now?

P Hook: What all these bands are doing now is very normal. It's exactly what all the bands they said were shit when they started were doing and they're just doing the same things now. It's like they don't seem to realise that, whereas unfortunately for me, as soon as I see something like that, I realise it straight away and it really irritates me. They might not have the same feelings that way, but it's important to me that we stay as we are instead of changing how they are.

What is the biggest change in music that you've noticed since the early days of Joy Division?

P Hook: I think the only major change in music lately has been money. People now spend ridiculous amounts of money pushing something that they think is going to be a hit. There's a hell of a lot of money about, and money has become really, really important. People can't even consider putting a record out now unless they've spent like thirty thousand on producing it or something like that. That's quite a turn around from how it was. I'm not saying that how it was in the beginning was great, but it's such a complete reversal. It's surprising. It's like they are all playing the game with somebody else writing the rules.

Why do you choose to produce yourselves now?

P Hook: We always had Martin Hannett when we started, apart from our very first record. So when Martin left, we just thought, however misguidedly, that we could do it. (laughs) With Martin Hannett, you would write a song and envision it as the greatest heavy metal song ever heard, and you would think, "This is really mean, this is really meaty", and then Martin would produce it and you would think, "Wow". It was just totally different to how you had imagined it. And sometimes it was disappointing, sometimes it was frustrating, sometimes it was angering, and other times it was really good. And after watching Martin doing it the way he used to do things, I thought it would be really good to try it ourselves. And he taught us a lot about sound and working with it.

Barney: But one of the drawbacks of producing yourself is that it's really hard work. Especially on an LP when you have to please five people, which is really difficult. You've got to compromise on everything. Because when you put something on record, it's there forever, it's not going to change. You don't re-mix everything, we didn't alter the Joy Division ones we didn't like, it's still in that vinyl. Sometimes that is really frustrating.

Would you ever consider re-doing a song, which after it's release you felt could have been done better?

Barney: No, we always said move on to the future. Don't go back on yourself, just keep moving upwards when you're stuck.

P Hook: Martin's attitude was that basically musicians shouldn't be in the studio when he was producing, which I think is really, really bad. Because if you've written a song, it's obviously very important to you, and if you work hard on it like we always do, I think it's very important to see how it turns out. And for someone to say to you, "I'm the producer, you go in there and do whatever you do and come back and I'll give it to you", is completely the wrong attitude,

S T A T E

because you have to live with that whatever they do.

Barney: In a way though, sometimes that's interesting because you can learn off a person that has done it.

P Hook: I mean Martin did teach us a hell of a lot, he taught us to look at music and our songs and our sounds in a totally different way. We had a very narrow vision of them, we'd just turn our amps on and that was it. When we got in the studio, we couldn't understand why the monitors didn't sound like our amps. He taught us to make allowances for certain things like that.

But on 'Unknown Pleasures' when Martin started working on a lot of the sound effects, like doors slamming and opening, did you actually have a hand in the direction of that, or did Martin say, "Here it is, do you like it?"

P Hook: The biggest thing that used to bother Martin was that me and Barney were always on his back. So I can't remember now, but ideas like that used to come from everybody, it wasn't just Martin. He didn't do the whole thing on his own. People used to suggest things, not just the group, Rob and even Chris Nagle. It's really funny how people seem to think in the early days it was all Martin, but it never was just Martin. It's always been a greater input than just him.

I imagine that a lot of the touches that Martin might have added to the sound, like the scrambled voice effects, is the kind of thing that got a lot of people trying to fathom deep hidden meanings.

P Hook: The whole point about the Joy Division thing and the New Order thing is that it was like a soup, everybody made it, and that was the magic of the whole thing. And yet people are very reluctant to credit everybody. They prefer to say, "Ian did this, and Martin did this, and it's the Hannett sound".

Barney: It doesn't matter anyway because it's the songs that matter, not who wrote them.

Because I think the songs come out of the air, they come from nowhere.

P Hook: But I think that people always want an excuse and when you give them something as vague as all of us, they don't like it.

Barney: I think people want a figurehead.

P Hook: That's what happened when we were in Joy Division just before Ian died. Everybody wanted Ian to be the spokesman, and he wouldn't be. People didn't consider talking to us, they just wanted to talk to Ian. And he didn't like it at all. It used to get him really frustrated.

Barney: But people don't really think about it. People think how they've been taught to think.

P Hook: You get it all the time. Like people will say, "How did you write 'Transmission'?" And we say, "Oh I can't remember how we did it". And people would think we were lying. Because you weren't giving them the answer they wanted, they would ask somebody else. I mean people still do it now.

Do you have any kind of desire to lift people's ways of thinking and seeing things?

P Hook: I think it's good to do it by example.

Barney: I do, I think what I liked about 'Blue Monday' was that it has got across to a lot of straight people. It might make people think who don't otherwise think like that, it might just make them a little bit different.

One of the things that is fascinating about Joy Division and New Order is the way that suggestion is used — you never really say what your songs are about.

P Hook: True, the thing is if you don't tell anyone what it's about or what you think it's about, then they're allowed to make up their own minds, so you can't really argue with it.

Do you think that you should take any responsibility, personally or as a group, for what different people might do having heard your music?

P Hook: It's a difficult question because people have always associated Joy Division with suicide, which is like, "I listened to Joy Division until I was so depressed that I topped myself". I can't take any responsibility for that because I used to find Joy Division's music very uplifting. I don't understand why people should associate it with depression and doom and gloom. I think albums like 'Closer' and songs like 'Atmosphere' are really wonderful pieces of music.

Barney: I think it's because some of the songs are sad, and because Ian killed himself, people just put two and two together. Some of them are sad, but some of them are sort of rocky, but because of what happened to Ian, they just channel those songs out and pick up on the sad ones.

Have you been happy with the images that people have associated with Joy Division and New Order songs?

P Hook: I don't know whether I'm happy with it. I find it very interesting. Like Peter Saville is the same as us lot, and I think it's very interesting what he reads into our music. It's good, 'cause he can never commit himself to any kind of sleeve until he hears it. And when he hears it, he gets some absolutely cosmic ideas. I don't know whether he needs it, but he does like to have it. It's like a crutch for him to work on, so it's quite good. It's always interesting how people who like you and who you know interpret the things that you're doing, what images you give to them. We never talk to people that much about it though.

Do you think that a lot of that has to do with the way society creates its own imagery for itself, out of the media and out of something that is just part of a current trend?

Barney: Not really. I think life has become based around the television set, because it's easy and you don't have to think about it. But what people really want is physical sensation. From a horror film you get a physical sensation — you get fear.

Why do you think that people would interpret Nazi references into the imagery of your music?

P Hook: Because it is Nazi imagery. (laughs) I don't know, I think that's very interesting. It's more interesting the more it goes on. It's really funny. But I mean the first sleeve was Germanic if you like, and the name was because there's a certain physical sensation you get from flirting with something like that, which we enjoyed when we started and tried to put it across because we thought it was a very, very strong feeling.

Barney: Well I think Nazism is the biggest thing that has happened to this world in the last half century, and it was interesting at that time when we started out because everyone was spouting about anarchy, so, in a way, you felt you could do whatever you wanted to do, so that's what we did.

What would be some of the reasons for using such imagery?

Barney: Well, why would someone write a book about Nazism? Because it interests them.

P Hook: The whole point about it to me was that if you're trying to put something across, like on a record sleeve, then you try to put that across in as striking and interesting a way as you can so that people will look at it and be impressed by it. We used a lot of that Italian Futurist stuff on the sleeves because we were impressed by the style of what was behind it.

Barney: The interesting thing about Fascism or Nazism was that out of all that hate and all that dominance came art that was brilliant. Like the uniforms they used to wear and the architecture. Out of all that came something that was good. It's interesting, and it's another example that out of all hate comes something really beautiful. It's fascinating. But it doesn't mean we agree with all of their policies. We don't.

P Hook: That imagery had all been used by the Romans before anyway. But because Nazism is nearer, it's looked upon as the influence.

But do you think the way you re-evoke that imagery in a new context, 1970's, 1980's, that you're in danger of encouraging the same thing to happen again unless you're specific about what you're doing?

Barney: No, because it's like — say prohibition. If you hide something away and cover it up, people are going to want it more and it's going to appear better than it is. But if you get it out into the open, it all seems so obvious.

P Hook: It still happens all over the world, even worse than the way Hitler did it anyway.

Did you ever think around 1980/'81 — when you were getting so may allegations about Nazism, that it was all getting too far out of hand?

Barney: No, because we're not Nazis. But it's a fascist thing to stop people doing whatever they want to do, which was happening to us. In a way, it was a test of the anarchy thing, to see whether you could do what you wanted to do. We were being anarchists by using Nazi symbols, but we were a bit too anarchistic for all the anarchists who were around at the time.

Do you experiment with people's perceptions by making both your images and record packaging so ambiguous?

Barney: Well no, we just do things we think are beautiful. We do sleeves that we think look beautiful. We do music we think sounds beautiful or sounds emotional. But a by-product of that is that it affects people in different ways and it's interesting to see how it affects people.

At the moment I'm interested in getting across to very straight people and making them a little less straight. Because I think they are the people, the masses, who are going to bring the world down. And mass thinking is because of television and video, and I believe people are getting dumber and dumber. If you watch TV programmes, everything has to do with sensationalism or a quick thrill. Being in a group I've been in the position where it's fairly easy to get a quick thrill of one sort or another to a greater extent than most people. And I know that it ends up being a real waste of time.

How do you go about getting a straighter audience?

Barney: Be straight but not shallow. Because our music can mean a lot emotionally but it can still sound in general terms so that people can understand. Like you can have a surface image, and if you scratch it, there's something deeper down below.

Why do you feel it is important to play live?

Barney: Because if you just put things on a record, it's like the difference between someone pressing a button here and the missile lands in Europe and kills someone, or me pulling a gun out now and shooting you. Playing live is exciting and frightening at the same time — it's good training as a musician, you have to think a lot quicker and more immediately than when you're in a studio and you can go over things. And because it's a social event. Again, that's one thing I've got against television — it creates weirdos because it locks people inside their houses giving them a perverted view of what is going on in the outside world. Music tends to bring people out more. At least you meet real people and not characters in a TV film or something.

We don't tend to put things down in black and white for people to see and I don't know why that is, it just is. Because really you've got a feeling about what is right and what is wrong, you don't have a policy for making things right or wrong, because nothing is ever that clear cut I don't think. You're not dealing with masses, you're dealing with individuals. You can't take an attitude that will work and convert people, but you can take a fragmented attitude and parts of it might relate to individuals. Because through school and through work I always felt insulted that I was being treated as a type of person and I think that's why we're a bit vague about what we're doing. I think what we're doing is subconscious, it's a very fashionable thing to say, but I feel that my subconscious is much more powerful than my talking to you now.

Do you think that your subconscious is under threat by things like television? How do you react against things like that?

Barney: I'm not trying to react against it. I just sit there and watch it and think it's garbage. Whether that comes out in the music or not, I don't know. I know what goes into it, I don't know what goes out of it. If I knew what went out of it, then it would stop. So I purposely don't think about it. Throughout Joy Division, throughout New Order, I've felt about certain things, and I've felt I've known what is right and wrong, but I'm not trying to express that in music. And I don't know if the music has expressed that, but it has affected people in such a way that it has expressed something. I don't know what it is, but I feel that if I try and understand it, it would be the wrong thing to do. I feel that now is not the right time to try to understand what we've done. I feel that later on will be the right time. You've got to believe that as long as you do something with honest intentions and you're not lying to people, then what you're doing is right. Like we said, we haven't got a message for people.

Is that a message in itself?

Barney: Well, we said that in Joy Division in our first interview. I suppose we have really because of just the way we do things. Through experience, now I can see that by the way we do things, we're not actually writing down a message in interviews and not telling people the way that we do things. And that is the message itself.

Do you think it's as simple as that?

Barney: No, that's just the most physical manifestation of the message. (laughs)

Why is that?

Barney: What we're doing is probably so simple that if you put it into words, it would be seen as being insignificant. But it's so simple that people can't grasp it. It's so down to earth and simple and straight that people can't see the wood for the trees. There's a deep meaning, but there's really a simple solution.

What is your purpose within music?

Barney: Well, what I think about what we're doing is firstly; having a good time with what you're doing, because if you don't enjoy what you're doing, there's no point in doing it. Secondly, don't get involved with business, because business is a mutation of society. People accept that as a way of life, and it's not, it's a mutation of that. Because life isn't making money, it's about being happy. And lastly, if you write a piece of music, make sure that you mean it or at least feel something within it emotionally. That's what I think about what we're doing...

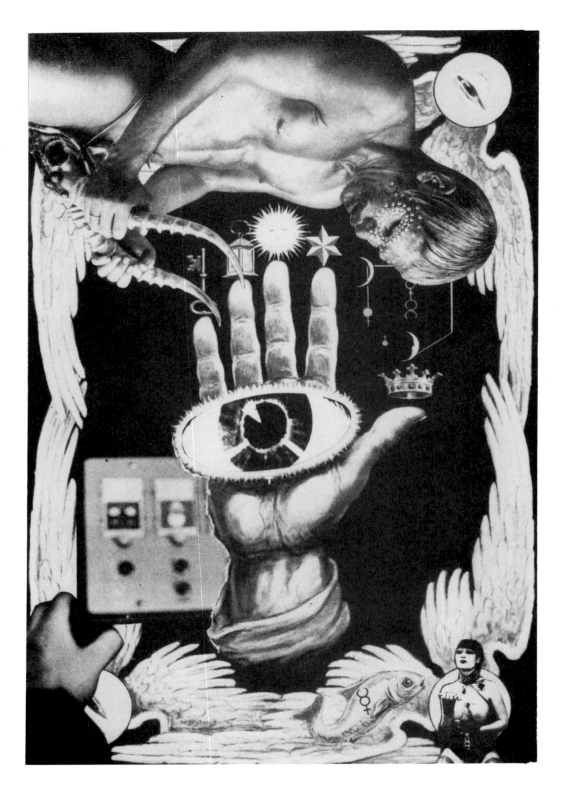

THEE KEY
THEE DOOR
THEE ROOM
THEE PERSON
THEE IDEA

MONTAGES BY

GENESIS P-ORRIDGE

1987

**PHOTOGRAPHIC
ACKNOWLEDGEMENTS**

Peggy Amison 177
Tom Bessoir 113, 146
Neville Brody 9
Bleddyn Butcher 73, 85, 89, 143, 197
Panni Charrington 1, 15
Andrew Catlin 51, 57(right), 127, 168, 169, 241, 248
Mick Clarke 151
Jon Crossland 180
Monica Dee 39, 45, 93, 178
Jörg Hillebrand 17
Tomaz Hostnik 224
Andy Johnson 129
Lee Renaldo 141
Richard 60
Jon Savage 212
Temple archive 34
Test Department 159, 167
Lawrence Watson 115, 122
Wolfgang Wesener 57(left)
Jon Wozencroft 191

Photographs not credited were unknown at the
time of publication. Those concerned can
contact the Publisher and a credit will be
included in any further editions.

 PO Box 151,
Harrow, Middx. HA3 0DH
SAF (Publishing) Ltd.